2-in-1 Book Series

Lee's
EXCELLENT
ENGLISH

BEGINNER COURSE
+
The Bible of Phrasal Verbs

Ukrainian Edition

Lee's Books

No unauthorized photocopying

All rights reserved. No part of this publication may be reproduced, stored in a retrieval system, or transmitted, in any form or by any means, without the prior permission in writing of Teacher King's Books.

This book is sold subject to the condition that it shall not, by the way of trade or otherwise, be lent, resold, hired out, or otherwise circulated without the publisher's prior consent in any form of binding or cover than that in which it is published and without a similar condition including this condition being imposed on the subsequent purchaser.

Beginner Course   **Page 3**

The Bible of Phrasal Verbs   **Page 311**

Copyright © 2022 Lee's Books
All rights reserved.

ISBN: 9798836953065

Lee's EXCELLENT ENGLISH

BEGINNER COURSE

Ukrainian Edition

Contents

Lesson 1: My pencil case мій пенал — Page 6

Lesson 2: In the classroom в класі — Page 12

Lesson 3: Colors кольори — Page 18

Lesson 4: My family моя родина — Page 24

Lesson 5: Shapes фігури — Page 30

Lesson 6: At the zoo в зоопарку — Page 36

Lesson 7: Jobs професії — Page 42

Lesson 8: At the fruit market на фруктовому ринку — Page 48

Lesson 9: The body тіло — Page 54

Lesson 10: Sports спорт — Page 60

Lesson 11: Places місця — Page 66

Lesson 12: Clothes хатня робота — Page 72

Lesson 13: School subjects шкільні предмети — Page 78

Lesson 14: Vegetables овочі — Page 84

Lesson 15: At the toy shop у магазині іграшок — Page 90

Lesson 16: In the kitchen на кухні — Page 96

Lesson 17: Feelings почуття — Page 102

Lesson 18: At the ice cream shop в кафе-морозиві — Page 108

Lesson 19: The weather погода — Page 114

Lesson 20: In the living room в вітальні — Page 120

Lesson 21: Chores хатня робота — Page 126

Lesson 22: Pets домашні тварини — Page 132

Lesson 23: Skills навички — Page 138

Lesson 24: Meats м'ясо — Page 144

Lesson 25: Countries країни — Page 150

Lesson 26: Languages мови　　　　　　　　　　　　　Page 156

Lesson 27: In the refrigerator в холодильнику　　　　Page 162

Lesson 28: Desserts десерти　　　　　　　　　　　　Page 168

Lesson 29: At school в школі　　　　　　　　　　　　Page 174

Lesson 30: Transportation транспорт　　　　　　　　Page 180

Lesson 31: Fast food фастфуд　　　　　　　　　　　Page 186

Lesson 32: Landscapes пейзажі　　　　　　　　　　　Page 192

Lesson 33: Homework домашнє завдання　　　　　　Page 198

Lesson 34: The calendar календар　　　　　　　　　Page 204

Lesson 35: Camping кемпінг　　　　　　　　　　　　Page 210

Lesson 36: Daily life повсякденне життя　　　　　　Page 216

Lesson 37: On the street на вулиці　　　　　　　　　Page 222

Lesson 38: Hobbies хобі　　　　　　　　　　　　　　Page 228

Lesson 39: In the bedroom в спальні　　　　　　　　Page 234

Lesson 40: More places додаткові місця　　　　　　Page 240

Lesson 41: The face обличчя　　　　　　　　　　　Page 246

Lesson 42: Personalities риси характеру　　　　　　Page 252

Lesson 43: Music музика　　　　　　　　　　　　　Page 258

Lesson 44: Activities діяльность　　　　　　　　　　Page 264

Lesson 45: Outdoor activities заходи на свіжому повітрі　Page 270

Lesson 46: Ocean life життя в океані　　　　　　　Page 276

Lesson 47: In the bathroom у ванні　　　　　　　　Page 282

Lesson 48: Capital cities столиці　　　　　　　　　Page 288

Lesson 49: In the toolbox в ящику для інструментів　Page 294

Lesson 50: At the cinema в кінотеатрі　　　　　　　Page 300

Answers　　　　　　　　　　　　　　　　　　　　　Page 306

Lesson 1

- Learn the words
- Learn the sentences
- Learn the phonics
- Test yourself!

My pencil case

мій пенал

Learn the words

1. **a pencil** — олівець
2. **an eraser** — гумка
3. **some glue** — клей
4. **a pencil sharpener** — точилка
5. **some whiteout** — коректор
6. **a pen** — ручка
7. **a ruler** — лінійка
8. **some tape** — сантиметр
9. **a marker** — маркер
10. **a crayon** — кольоровий олівець

Write the missing letters!

1. p_ _c_ _
2. e_a_e_
3. g_ _ _
4. pe_c_l sh_r_ _n_ _
5. w_i_ _o_t
6. p_ _
7. r_ _ _r
8. t_ _ _
9. m_r_e_
10. c_a_o_

Have fun with the words!

Word Search

```
c e z c a p n g y j c t x m e m h k
z l y r r e m s d r d m a r k e r q
h u n a h n h h f i k i f v x u l j
u n w y p e n c i l e a j s n d o y
x q d o g c e r a s e r x b x a i o
f b h n w t n g w h i t e o u t h e
u o c v g t a k h c s r x v a h q y
f v u x l p c p v i g u u x m u q g
r c s c u a w f e b e l j d r o c x
z e p b e o j p k d p e b a z r h e
t c b y h a l k d k v r f z o a f l
w a p e n c i l s h a r p e n e r v
```

Words are hidden → ↓ and ↘ .

pencil sharpener   **pen**

marker   **whiteout**

crayon   **ruler**

tape   **glue**

pencil   **eraser**

Learn the sentences

What is this?

It is <u>a pencil</u>.

It is not <u>an eraser</u>.

What is that?

It is <u>a crayon</u>.

It is not <u>a marker</u>.

Write the missing words!

What _____ this?

It is a _____ sharpener.

It is _____ a _____ .

What _____ _____ ?

_____ is an _____ .

It _____ a _____ .

What _____ this?

It _____ a _____ .

_____ is _____ _____ .

_____?

_____.

_____.

Learn the sentences

Is this a <u>marker</u>?   Is that <u>whiteout</u>?

Yes, it is.   Yes, it is.

No, it is not.   No, it is not.

Write the missing words!

Is this a _____?

Yes, it _____.

No, _____ is _____.

Is this _____ _____?

_____, it _____.

_____, it is _____.

Is _____ a _____?

Yes, _____ _____.

No, _____ _____.

_____?
_____.
_____.

Learn the phonics

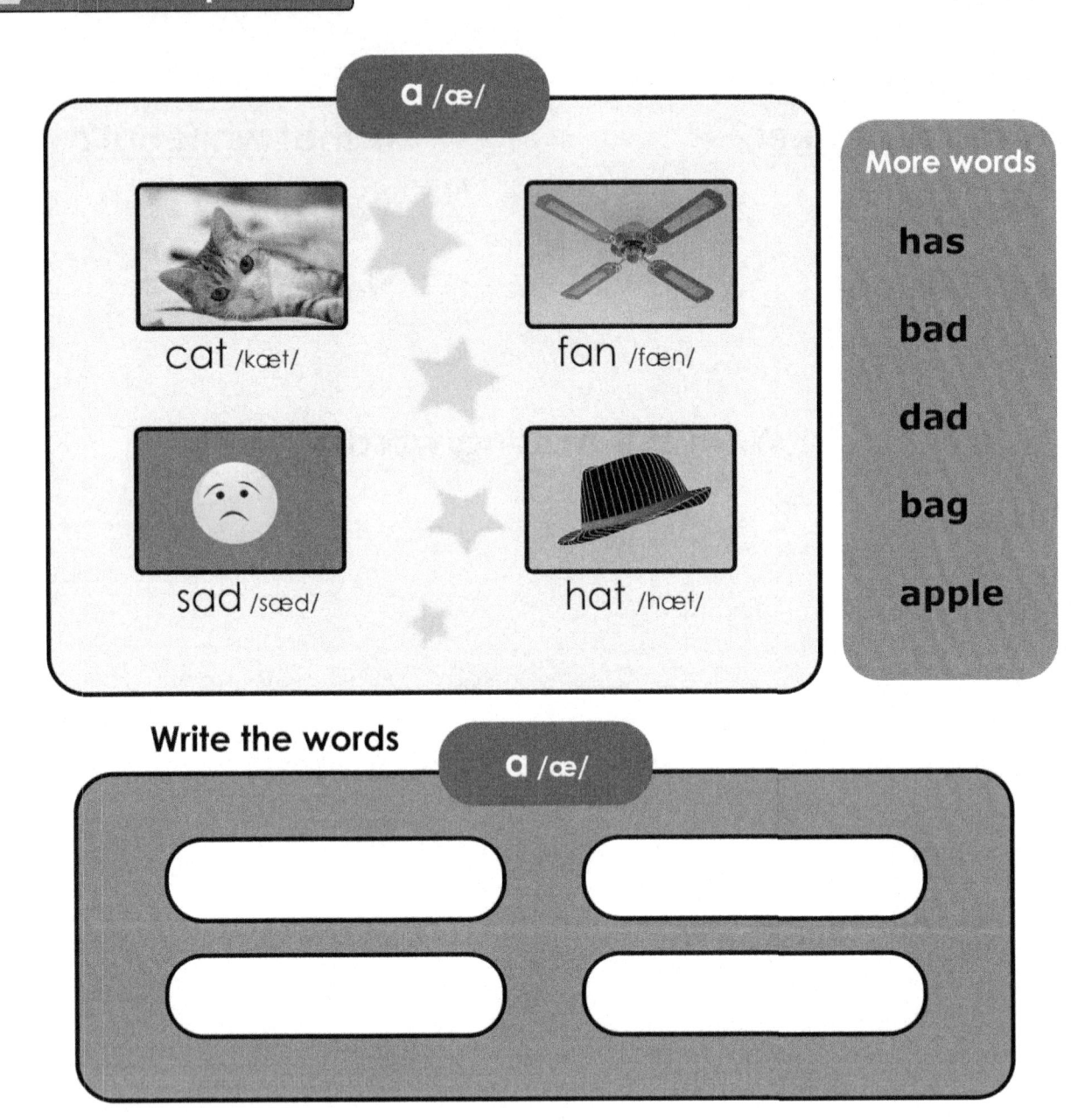

a /æ/

cat /kæt/

fan /fæn/

sad /sæd/

hat /hæt/

More words

has

bad

dad

bag

apple

Write the words

a /æ/

Write the letters & Read the sentences!

My d_d h_s a s_d c_t.

This h_t is b_d.

The _pple is in the b_g.

Test

Complete the words

1. p_____l   3. m_____r   5. c_____n

2. t_____e   4. e_____r   6. w_____t

Write the answer next to the letter "A"

A: ___ 7. ___ is ___ eraser.

a. This, a
b. they, an
c. It, an

A: ___ 8. It ___ not a ___.

a. is, eraser
b. is, pencil sharpener
c. are, marker

A: ___ 9. What is this? It is ___ tape.

a. a
b. an
c. x

A: ___ 10. Is this ___? No, it ___.

a. pencil, is not
b. tape, is not
c. whiteout, not

Answers on Page 306

Lesson 2 — In the classroom

- Learn the words
- Learn the sentences
- Learn the phonics
- Test yourself!

в класі

Learn the words

1. **chair** — стілець
2. **desk** — стіл
3. **blackboard** — класна дошка
4. **whiteboard** — біла дошка
5. **computer** — комп'ютер
6. **globe** — глобус
7. **clock** — годинник
8. **book** — книга
9. **bookshelf** — книжкова полиця
10. **poster** — плакат

Write the missing letters!

1. c_ _ _r
2. d_ _ _
3. bl_c_b_a_ _
4. w_it_b_a_d
5. _o_p_t_r
6. g_ _ _e
7. cl_c_
8. b_ _k
9. b_o_sh_l_
10. p_s_e_

Have fun with the words!

1. desk
2. blackboard
3. computer
4. bookshelf
5. clock
6. whiteboard
7. poster
8. book
9. globe
10. chair

Learn the sentences

What are these?   What are those?

They are <u>chair</u>s.   They are <u>whiteboard</u>s.

They are not <u>desk</u>s.   They are not <u>blackboard</u>s.

Write the missing words!

What _____ these?

They are _____ .

They _____ bookshelves.

What _____ those?

They _____ .

They are _____ .

What _____ _____ ?

_____ are _____ .

_____ _____ not _____ .

_____?
_____.
_____.

Learn the sentences

Are these <u>globes</u>?　　Are those <u>computers</u>?

Yes, they are.　　　　　Yes, they are.

No, they are not.　　　No, they are not.

Write the missing words!

Are these _____ ?

Yes, they _____ .

No, _____ are _____ .

Are those _____ ?

_____ , they _____ .

_____ , they are _____ .

_____ these _____ ?

Yes, _____ _____ .

No, _____ _____ .

_____ ?
_____ .
_____ .

Learn the phonics

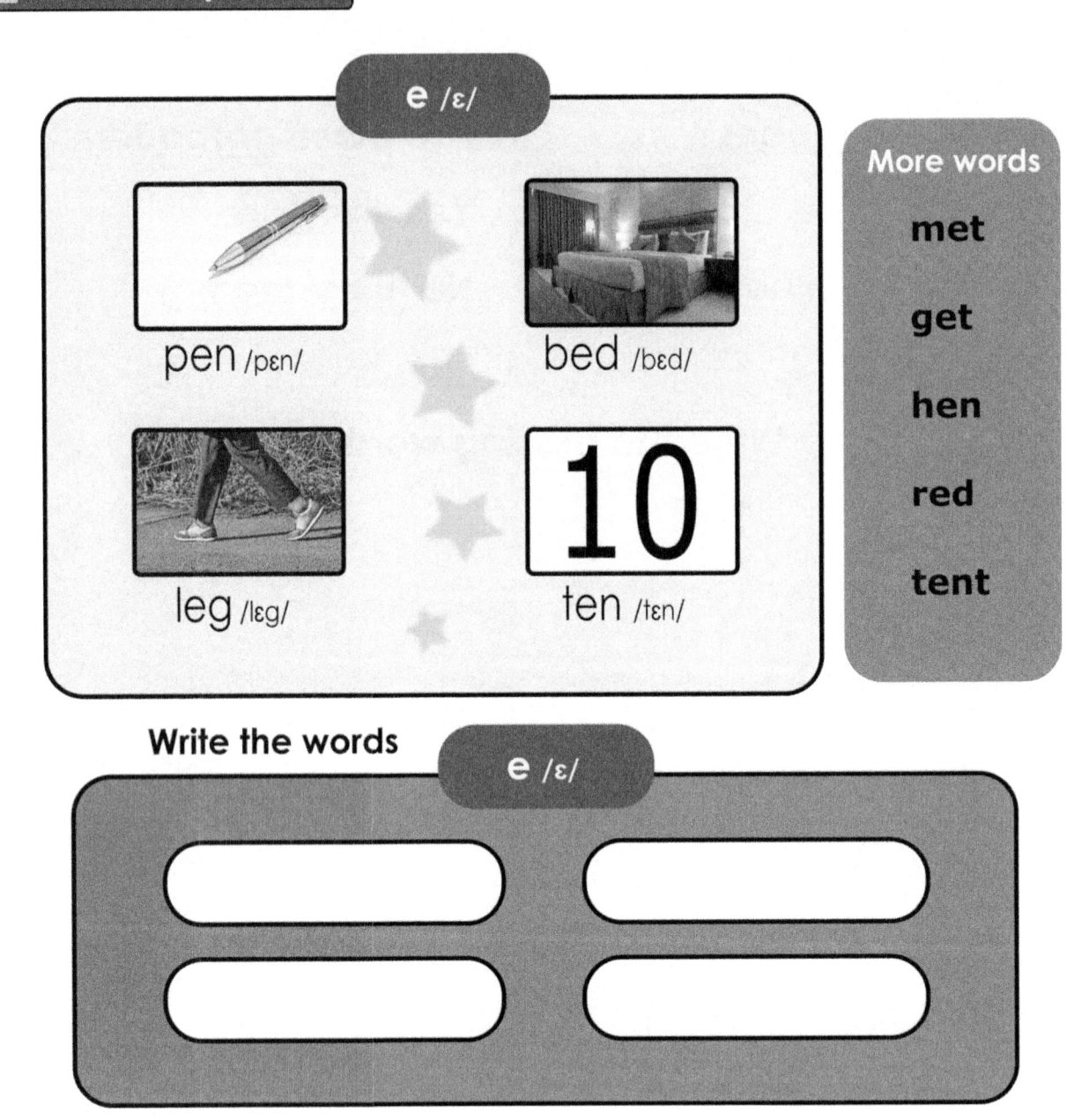

e /ɛ/

pen /pɛn/

bed /bɛd/

leg /lɛg/

ten /tɛn/

More words

met

get

hen

red

tent

Write the words

e /ɛ/

Write the letters & Read the sentences!

I will g_t a r_d p_n.

I see t_n h_ns in the t_nt.

T_d m_t K_n and Fr_d.

Test

Complete the words

1. c_____r   3. p_____r   5. w_____d

2. g_____e   4. b_____f   6. d_____k

Write the answer next to the letter "A"

A: ___ **7.** They ___.

a. are bookshelves
b. is bookshelves
c. are bookshelfs

A: ___ **8.** What are these?

a. They are whiteboard.
b. They are whiteboards.
c. It is a whiteboard.

A: ___ **9.** Are these posters?

a. Yes, they is.
b. No, they are.
c. Yes, they are.

A: ___ **10.** Are those ___? Yes, they are.

a. books
b. blackboard
c. bookshelf

Answers on Page 306

Lesson 3

- Learn the words
- Learn the sentences
- Learn the phonics
- Test yourself!

Colors

кольори

Learn the words

1. **red**
   червоний
2. **yellow**
   жовтий
3. **green**
   зелений
4. **blue**
   синій
5. **purple**
   фіолетовий

6. **orange**
   помаранчевий
7. **brown**
   коричневий
8. **pink**
   рожевий
9. **black**
   чорний
10. **white**
    білий

Write the missing letters!

1. r_ _
2. y_ _l_w
3. g_e_n
4. b_u_
5. p_ _p_e

6. o_a_ _e
7. b_o_ _
8. p_ _ _
9. b_a_ _
10. w_i_ _

Have fun with the words!

Write the 3 missing words

1. _____
2. _____
3. _____

green
red
blue
yellow
pink
black
orange

1. _____
2. _____
3. _____

black
purple
yellow
white
brown
pink
blue

1. _____
2. _____
3. _____

white
purple
orange
brown
red
black
green

1. _____
2. _____
3. _____

orange
purple
white
green
pink
yellow
blue

1. _____
2. _____
3. _____

purple
black
brown
green
orange
red
white

1. _____
2. _____
3. _____

black
blue
brown
pink
yellow
red
green

Learn the sentences

What color is this?　　　　What color is that?

It is <u>yellow</u>.　　　　　　It is <u>purple</u>.

It isn't <u>green</u>.　　　　　　It isn't <u>blue</u>.

Write the missing words!

What _____ is this?

It is _____ .

It _____ _____ .

What _____ _____ that?

It _____ _____ .

_____ isn't _____ .

_____ _____ this?

_____ is _____ .

_____ white.

_____ ?

_____ .

_____ .

Learn the sentences

Is this <u>pen</u> <u>red</u>?

Yes, it is.

No, it isn't. It is <u>brown</u>.

Is that <u>crayon</u> <u>pink</u>?

Yes, it is.

No, it isn't. It is <u>orange</u>.

Write the missing words!

Is this apple _____?

Yes, it _____.

No, it _____. It's _____.

Is _____ chair _____?

Yes, _____ is.

_____, it _____. It is _____.

_____ this _____?

Yes, _____ _____.

No, _____ _____. It _____ _____.

_____?

_____.

_____.

Learn the phonics

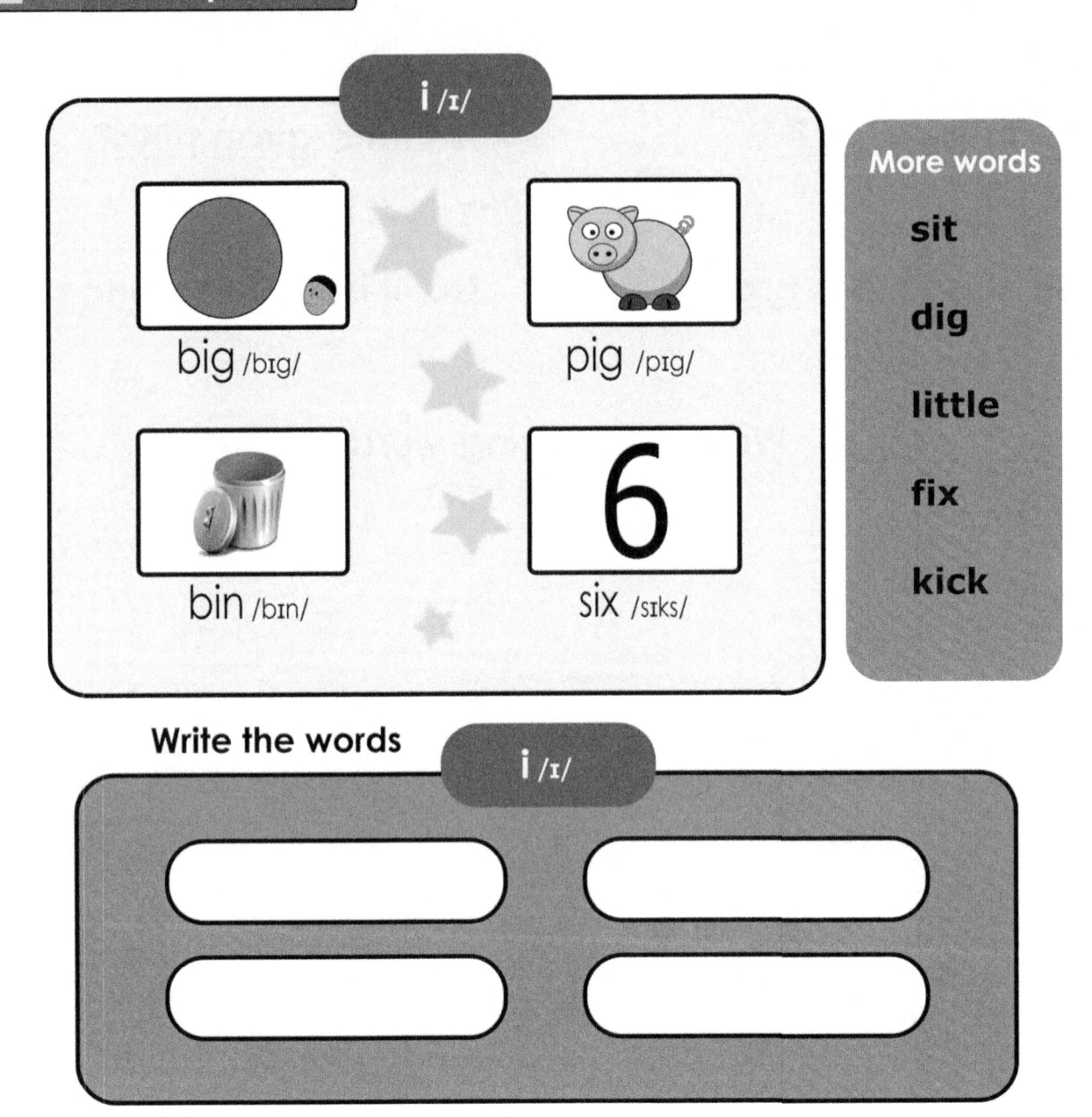

i /ɪ/

big /bɪg/

pig /pɪg/

bin /bɪn/

six /sɪks/

More words

sit

dig

little

fix

kick

Write the words

i /ɪ/

Write the letters & Read the sentences!

Th_s p_g _s b_g.

I f_x s_x b_ns.

I s_t on the l_ttle bench w_th h_m.

Test

Complete the words

1. y_____w
2. b_____n
3. o_____e
4. g_____n
5. b_____k
6. p_____e

Write the answer next to the letter "A"

A: ___ **7.** What color ___?

a. is these
b. is this
c. are that

A: ___ **8.** What color is that?

a. It is a green.
b. Its purple.
c. It is blue.

A: ___ **9.** Is this pen blue?

a. Yes, it is.
b. Yes it is.
c. No, it is. It's red.

A: ___ **10.** Is that ___?

a. brown desk
b. desk brown
c. desks brown

Answers on Page 306

Lesson 4

- Learn the words
- Learn the sentences
- Learn the phonics
- Test yourself!

My family

моя родина

Learn the words

1. **grandmother**
бабуся

2. **grandfather**
дідусь

3. **baby sister**
молодша сестра

4. **baby brother**
молодший брат

5. **aunt**
тітка

6. **uncle**
дядько

7. **sister**
сестра

8. **brother**
брат

9. **mother**
мати

10. **father**
батько

Write the missing letters!

1. g_a_ _m_t_e_

2. g_a_df_ _h_ _

3. b_ _y s_s_ _r

4. b_b_ b_o_h_ _

5. a_n_

6. _n_ _e

7. s_ _ _e_

8. b_o_h_ _

9. m_t_ _ _

10. f_ _h_ _

Have fun with the words!

Circle the family words!

1. pencil   (mother)   chair   purple   oval

2. heart   whiteboard   father   eraser   red

3. ruler   sister   poster   square   black

4. pink   computer   uncle   whiteout   chair

5. clock   glue   triangle   white   aunt

6. pen   blue   grandmother   star   globe

7. brother   marker   blackboard   circle   white

8. yellow   grandfather   desk   book   tape

Write the 8 words

1.
2.
3.
4.
5.
6.
7.
8.

Learn the sentences

Who is she?　　　　　　　　　Who is he?

She is my <u>mother</u>.　　　　　He is my <u>uncle</u>.

She isn't my <u>aunt</u>.　　　　　He isn't my <u>father</u>.

Write the missing words!

Who _____ he?

He is my _____.

He _____ my _____.

Who _____ _____?

She is _____ _____.

_____ isn't _____.

_____ _____ he?

_____ is _____ _____.

He _____ my _____.

_____?

_____.

_____.

Learn the sentences

Is she your <u>sister</u>? Is he your <u>brother</u>?
Yes, she is. Yes, he is.
No, she isn't. No, he isn't.

Write the missing words!

Is he your _____ _____?

Yes, he _____.

No, he _____.

Is _____ your _____ sister?

Yes, _____ is.

_____, she _____.

_____ he _____ _____?

Yes, _____ _____.

No, _____ _____.

_____?
_____.
_____.

Learn the phonics

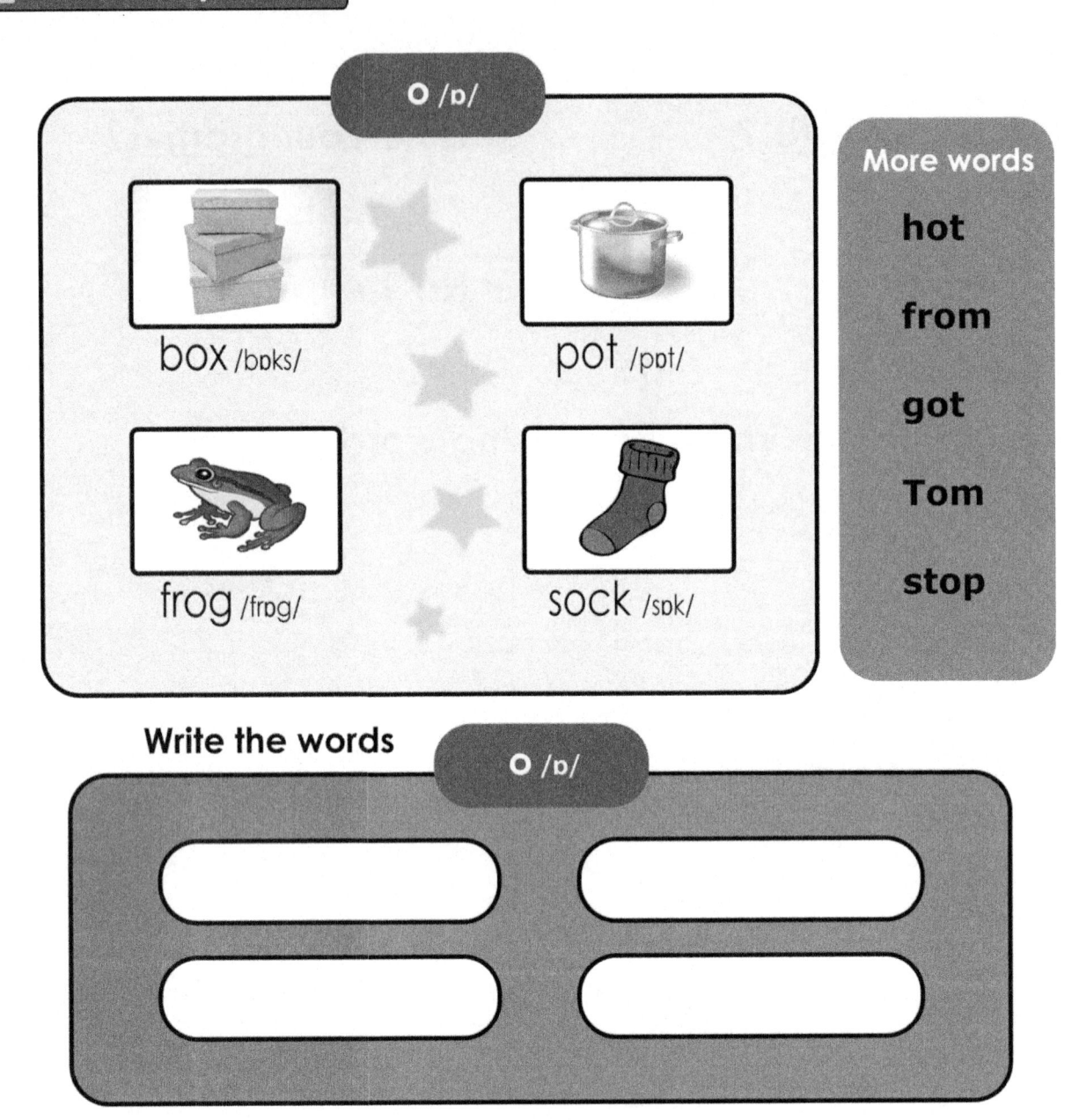

O /ɒ/

box /bɒks/
pot /pɒt/
frog /frɒg/
sock /sɒk/

More words

hot
from
got
Tom
stop

Write the words

O /ɒ/

Write the letters & Read the sentences!

The p_t is n_t h_t.

A s_ck is _n t_p _f the b_x.

T_m g_t a fr_g fr_m the sh_p.

Test

Complete the words

1. b _____ r
2. s _____ r
3. u _____ e
4. a _____ t
5. f _____ r
6. m _____ r

Write the answer next to the letter "A"

A: ___ 7. ___ is she?

a. What
b. Who
c. Whose

A: ___ 8. ___ is my uncle.

a. She's
b. She
c. He

A: ___ 9. Is she your sister?

a. Yes, it is.
b. Yes, she is.
c. No, she is.

A: ___ 10. Is he ___?

a. your father
b. your aunt
c. you're brother

Answers on Page 306

Lesson 5

- Learn the words
- Learn the sentences
- Learn the phonics
- Test yourself!

Shapes

фігури

Learn the words

1. **square**
   квадрат
2. **circle**
   коло
3. **triangle**
   трикутник
4. **oval**
   овал
5. **diamond**
   ромб
6. **star**
   зірка
7. **rectangle**
   прямокутник
8. **octagon**
   восьмикутник
9. **heart**
   серце
10. **pentagon**
    п'ятикутник

Write the missing letters!

1. s_ _a_e
2. c_rcl_
3. tr_a_g_e
4. o_ _ _
5. d_a_o_ _
6. _t_ _
7. r_ _t_n_le
8. oc_a_o_
9. h_ _r_
10. p_n_ _ _o_

Have fun with the words!

Find the 8 shapes!

eraser   whiteboard   pentagon
oval
         crayon   clock   sister
apple   uncle
book   triangle   yellow
       green   whiteout
chair   square
          pink   grandfather
pencil   star
                   desk   heart
   computer   blue   marker
       diamond   mother
brother   circle
            bookshelf   father

Write the 8 shapes

1. _____   3. _____   5. _____   7. _____

2. _____   4. _____   6. _____   8. _____

Learn the sentences

What is this shape?   What are these shapes?

It's a <u>square</u>.   They're <u>octagons</u>.

It isn't a <u>rectangle</u>.   They aren't <u>pentagons</u>.

Write the missing words!

What _____ this _____?

_____ a star.

It _____ a _____.

What _____ these shapes?

_____ diamonds.

They aren't _____.

What _____ this _____?

_____ a _____.

_____ an _____.

_____?
_____.
_____.

Learn the sentences

Is this a <u>triangle</u>? Are these <u>stars</u>?

Yes, it is. Yes, they are.

No, it isn't. No, they aren't.

Write the missing words!

Is this an _____?

Yes, _____ is.

No, it _____ .

_____ these _____?

Yes, _____ are.

No, _____ .

_____ this _____?

_____ , _____ is.

No, _____ .

_____ ?
_____ .
_____ .

Learn the phonics

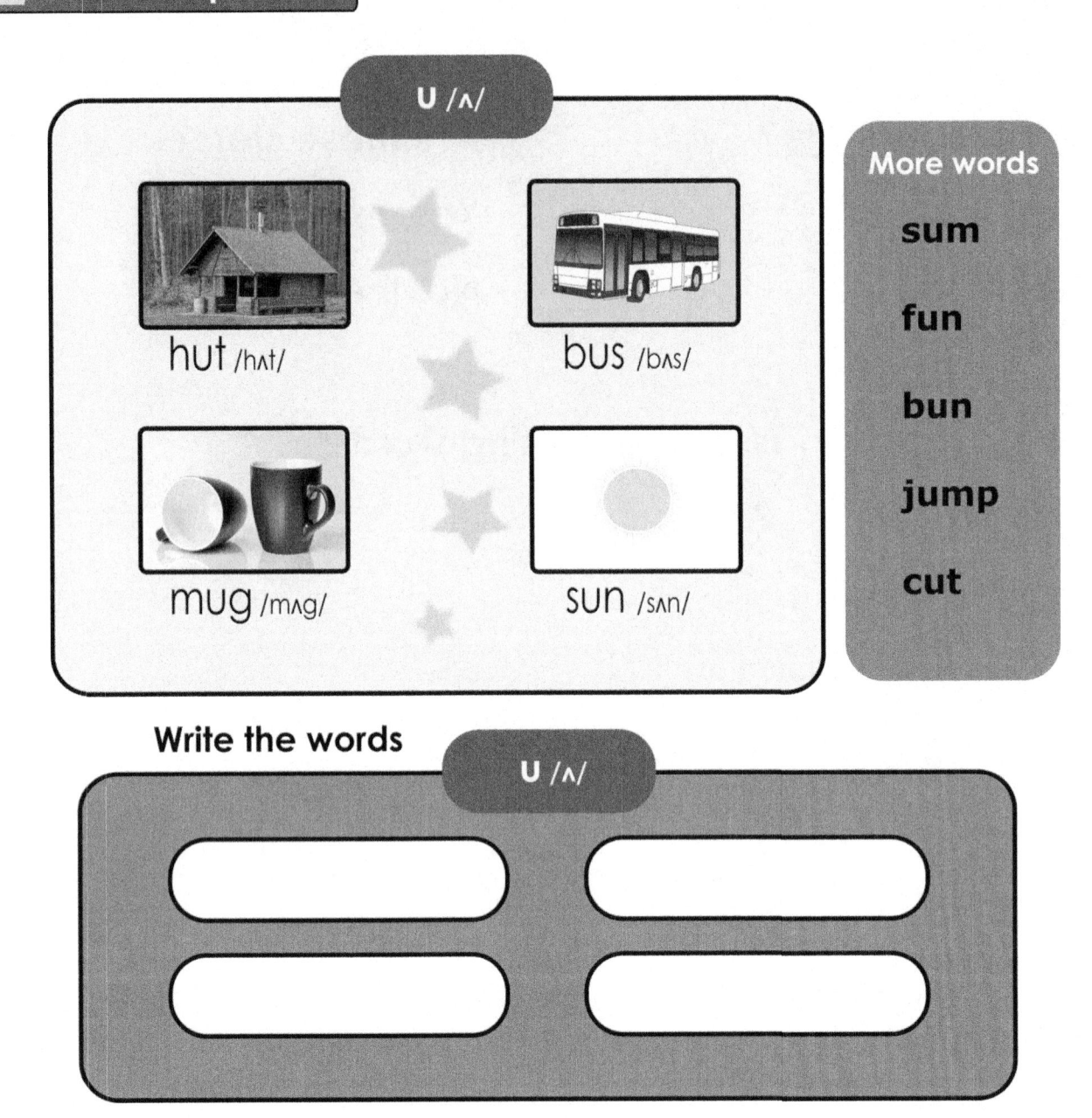

U /ʌ/

hut /hʌt/

bus /bʌs/

mug /mʌg/

sun /sʌn/

More words

sum

fun

bun

jump

cut

Write the words

U /ʌ/

Write the letters & Read the sentences!

Have f_n in the s_n.

My m_g is on the b_s.

R_n and j_mp to the h_t.

Test

Complete the words

1. s_____r
2. t_____e
3. o_____n
4. r_____e
5. h_____t
6. d_____d

Write the answer next to the letter "A"

A: ___ 7. What ___ shape?

a. are these
b. is this
c. is it

A: ___ 8. ___ aren't ___.

a. It, heart
b. They're, hearts
c. They, hearts

A: ___ 9. Is this a pentagon?

a. Yes, it is.
b. No, they aren't.
c. Yes, they are.

A: ___ 10. ___ these ___ circles?

a. Are, shape
b. Is, a
c. Are, x

Answers on Page 306

Lesson 6

- Learn the words
- Learn the sentences
- Learn the phonics
- Test yourself!

At the zoo

в зоопарку

Learn the words

1. **monkey**
   мавпа
2. **lion**
   лев
3. **tiger**
   тигр
4. **bear**
   ведмідь
5. **rhino**
   носоріг

6. **penguin**
   пінгвін
7. **giraffe**
   жирафа
8. **elephant**
   слон
9. **crocodile**
   крокодил
10. **kangaroo**
    кенгуру

Write the missing letters!

1. m_n_ _y
2. l_ _ _
3. _ig_ _
4. _ _ a_
5. r_ _ _o

6. pe_g _ _n
7. gi_a_f_
8. el_ _h_n_
9. _ro_od_ _e
10. k_n_ _r_o

Have fun with the words!

Word Search

```
e d z q f d k o v o s d j v m d y y
l f z d s o x s u o m f f x l g l y
e m k a n g a r o o o y d x k i b h
p g a o p q t n i j n u c p l r o m
h t d w e v n p a r k g g z i a e n
a u b b h b i o l p e p j v o f r j
n r p e n g u i n b y r b m v f d r
t s g c r o c o d i l e h e z e p c
m o v f a z m n f d l e t i a c r m
u i y p p v m j n e r y n i n r i m
v f i p m t i g e r x z h e d o k d
t v s k u y p a r e f w e c p v x e
```

Words are hidden → ↓ and ↘.

kangaroo   **lion**

giraffe   **tiger**

elephant   **bear**

penguin   **crocodile**

rhino   **monkey**

Learn the sentences

What is that animal?   What are those animals?

That animal is a <u>tiger</u>.   Those animals are <u>tiger</u>s.

That animal isn't a <u>rhino</u>.   Those animals aren't <u>lion</u>s.

Write the missing words!

What _____ that _____?

_____ animal is a _____.

That animal _____ a _____.

_____ are _____ animals?

Those _____ _____ rhinos.

They aren't _____.

What _____ _____ animal?

That _____ _____ an _____.

_____ animal _____ a _____.

_____?
_____.
_____.

- 38 -

Learn the sentences

Is that animal a <u>giraffe</u>?   Are those <u>bears</u>?
Yes, that's a giraffe.   Yes, those are bears.
No, that isn't a giraffe.   No, those aren't bears.

Write the missing words!

Is _____ animal a _____?
Yes, _____ a penguin.
No, that _____ a _____.

_____ those tigers?
Yes, those _____ _____.
No, _____ _____ tigers.

_____ that _____ _____?
_____, _____ _____ rhino.
_____, that _____ a _____.

_____?
_____.
_____.

Learn the phonics

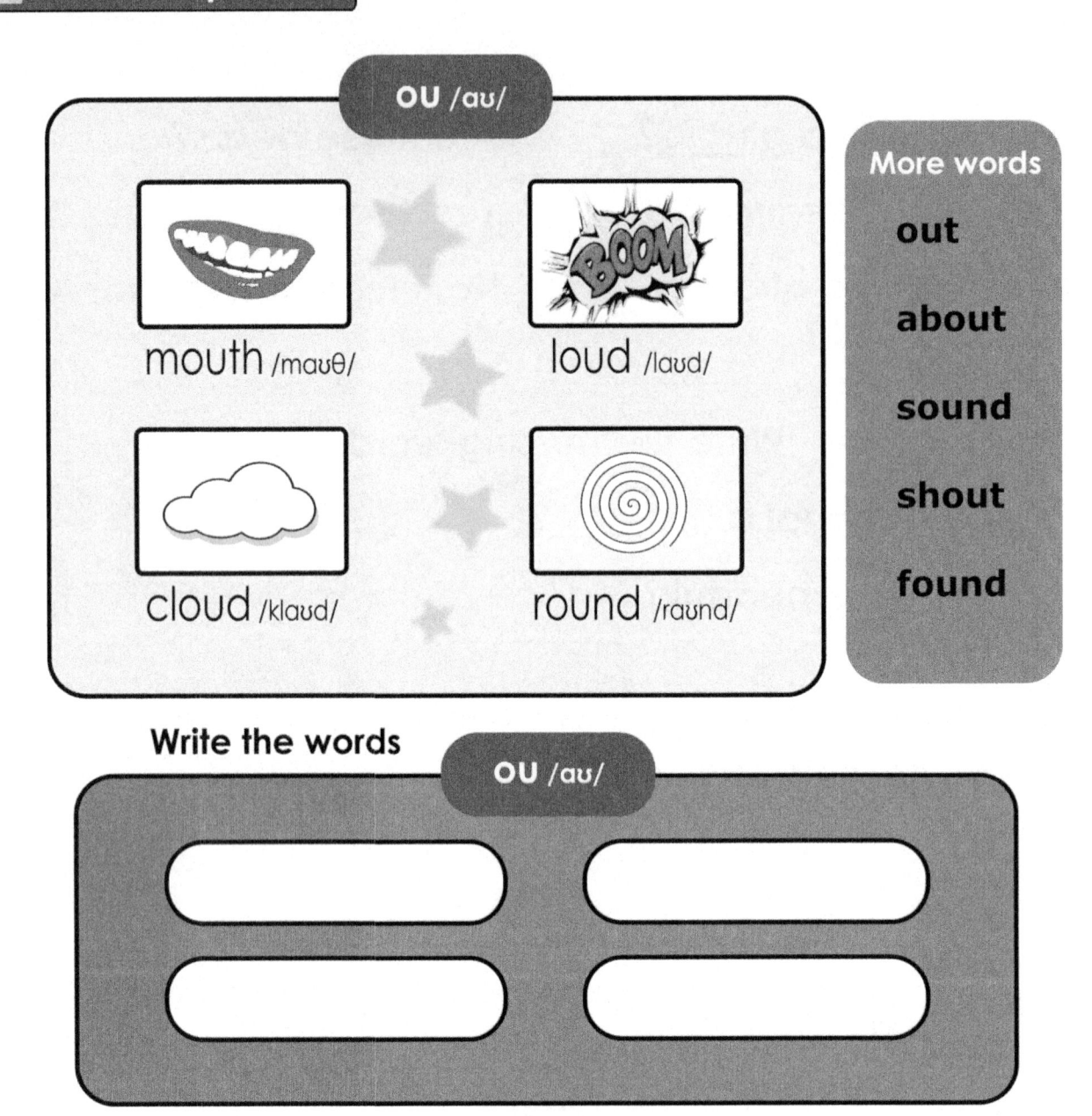

OU /aʊ/

mouth /maʊθ/
loud /laʊd/
cloud /klaʊd/
round /raʊnd/

More words
out
about
sound
shout
found

Write the words

OU /aʊ/

Write the letters & Read the sentences!

I f_ _nd a r_ _nd circle.

That is a big cl_ _d.

The lion has a l_ _d m_ _th.

- 40 -

Test

Complete the words

1. s____e
2. c____a
3. p____k
4. r____t
5. s____t
6. g____m

Write the answer next to the letter "A"

A: ___ **7.** What ___ animals?

a. are those
b. is that
c. is this

A: ___ **8.** That ___ is a ___.

a. animals, kangaroo
b. animal, bears
c. animal, crocodile

A: ___ **9.** Are those monkeys?

a. Yes, those are monkey.
b. No, those aren't monkeys.
c. Yes, that's a monkey.

A: ___ **10.** ___ that animal a ___?

a. Are, rhinos
b. Is, rhino
c. Are, rhino

Answers on Page 306

Lesson 7

- Learn the words
- Learn the sentences
- Learn the phonics
- Test yourself!

Jobs

професії

Learn the words

1. **doctor**
лікар
2. **chef**
повар
3. **nurse**
медсестра
4. **police officer**
поліцейський
5. **taxi driver**
таксист
6. **teacher**
вчитель
7. **farmer**
фермер
8. **salesclerk**
продавець
9. **firefighter**
пожежник
10. **builder**
будівельник

Write the missing letters!

1. d_ _to_
2. c_e_
3. n_rs_
4. p_ _i_e of_ic_ _
5. _a_i d_i_e_
6. te_c_ _r
7. fa_ _ _r
8. s_ _e_c_e_ _
9. f_r_ _i_h_er
10. b_i_d_ _

Have fun with the words!

f i r e f i g h t e r

salesclerk
farmer
police officer
doctor
teacher

chef
builder
nurse
firefighter
taxi driver

Learn the sentences

What's his job?

He's a <u>nurse</u>.

He's not a <u>builder</u>.

What's her job?

She's a <u>doctor</u>.

She's not a <u>chef</u>.

Write the missing words!

What's _____ _____?

He's a _____.

_____ _____ a salesclerk.

_____ her _____?

_____ a _____.

She's not _____ _____.

_____ his _____?

He's a _____ driver.

_____ _____ a _____.

_____?
_____.
_____.

Learn the sentences

Is he a <u>police officer</u>?   Is she a <u>salesclerk</u>?
Yes, he is.   Yes, she is.
No, he's a <u>firefighter</u>.   No, she's a <u>teacher</u>.

Write the missing words!

Is _____ a _____ officer?
Yes, he _____ .
No, _____ a _____ .

_____ she a _____ ?
Yes, _____ _____ .
No, she's _____ taxi _____ .

_____ he _____ _____ ?
_____ , _____ _____ .
_____ , _____ a _____ .

_____?
_____.
_____.

Learn the phonics

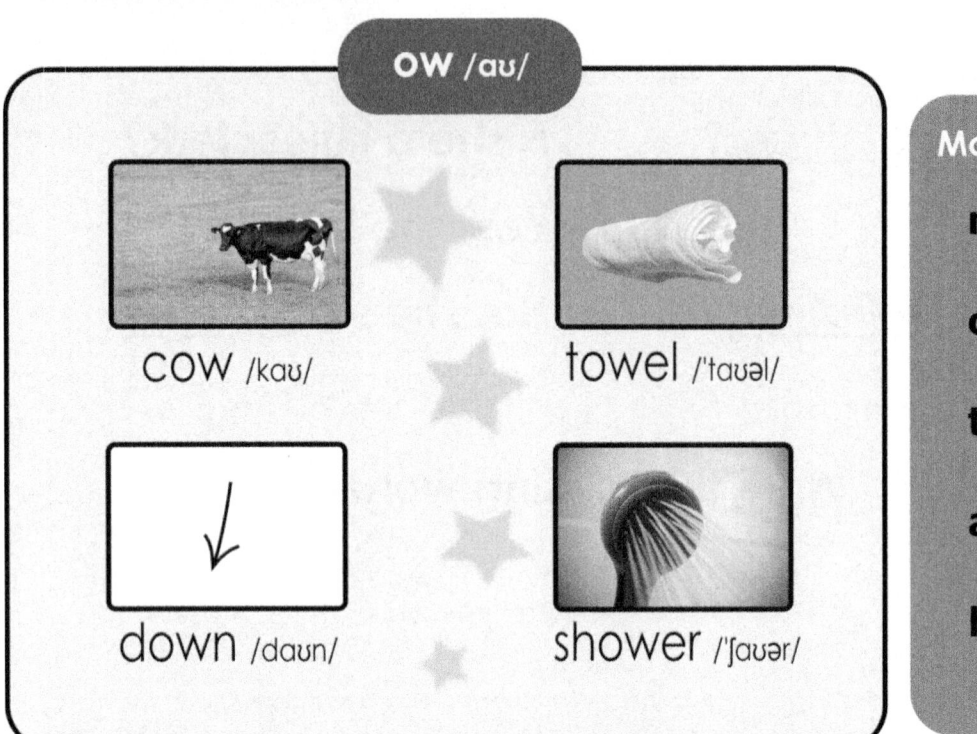

ow /aʊ/

cow /kaʊ/
towel /ˈtaʊəl/
down /daʊn/
shower /ˈʃaʊər/

More words

now
crowd
town
allow
how

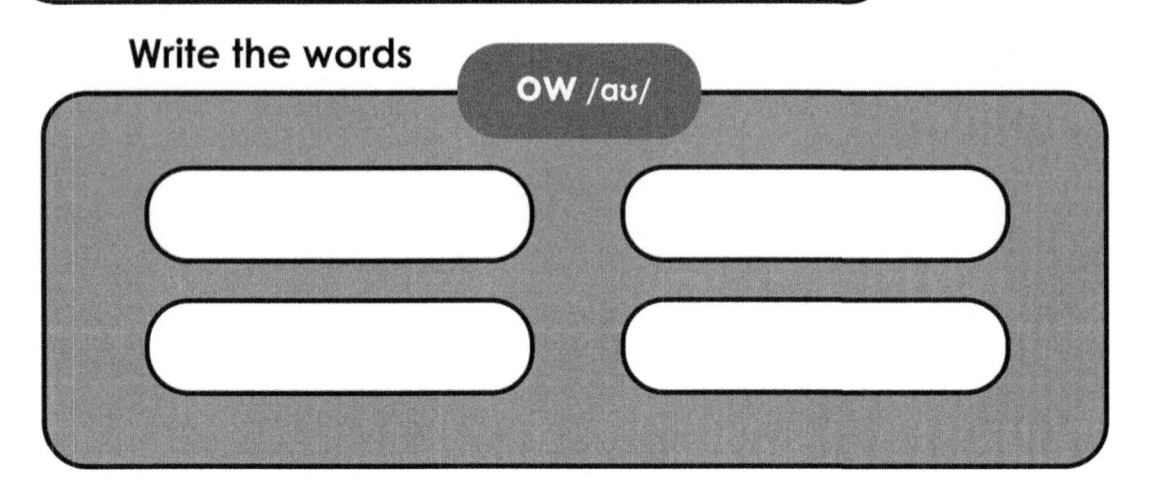

Write the words

ow /aʊ/

Write the letters & Read the sentences!

H_ _ is that c_ _ out?

W_ _! There is a big cr_ _d d_ _nt_ _n.

Take a sh_ _er n_ _.

Test

Complete the words

1. b_____r
2. n_____e
3. s_____k
4. d_____r
5. t_____r
6. c_____f

Write the answer next to the letter "A"

A: ___ 7. ___ his job?

a. Who's
b. What's
c. What

A: ___ 8. She's ___ a firefighter.

a. isn't
b. is
c. not

A: ___ 9. Is he a teacher?

a. No, she's a salesclerk.
b. No, he's a nurse.
c. No, he a doctor.

A: ___ 10. Is she ___?

a. a farmer
b. an nurse
c. police officer

Answers on Page 306

Lesson 8

- Learn the words
- Learn the sentences
- Learn the phonics
- Test yourself!

At the fruit market

на фруктовому ринку

Learn the words

1. **apple**
   яблуко
2. **orange**
   апельсин
3. **lemon**
   лимон
4. **banana**
   банан
5. **watermelon**
   кавун
6. **pineapple**
   ананас
7. **strawberry**
   полуниця
8. **grape**
   виноград
9. **cherry**
   вишня
10. **pear**
    груша

Write the missing letters!

1. _p_l_
2. o_ _ _g_
3. l_m_ _
4. ba_ _n_
5. w_t_ _m_ _o_
6. p_n_a_ _l_
7. s_ _a_ _er_ _
8. g_a_e
9. c_e_ _y
10. p_ _ _

Have fun with the words!

Write the 3 missing words

1._____
2._____
3._____

- apple
- lemon
- banana
- cherry
- strawberry
- watermelon
- pear

1._____
2._____
3._____

- cherry
- pineapple
- apple
- watermelon
- orange
- lemon
- grape

1._____
2._____
3._____

- pineapple
- strawberry
- orange
- banana
- grape
- pear
- cherry

1._____
2._____
3._____

- pear
- lemon
- grape
- apple
- watermelon
- banana
- pineapple

1._____
2._____
3._____

- pineapple
- strawberry
- orange
- cherry
- watermelon
- grape
- lemon

1._____
2._____
3._____

- strawberry
- apple
- pineapple
- banana
- lemon
- pear
- orange

Learn the sentences

Which fruit do you want?   Which fruit does he want?

I want a <u>strawberry</u>.   He wants an <u>apple</u>.

I don't want a <u>lemon</u>.   He doesn't want a <u>banana</u>.

Write the missing words!

Which _____ do you _____ ?

I want a _____ .

I _____ want a _____ .

_____ fruit _____ she want?

She _____ a _____ .

She _____ want an _____ .

_____ fruit _____ you _____ ?

I _____ _____ _____ .

_____ don't _____ a _____ .

_____ ?

_____ .

_____ .

Learn the sentences

Do you want a <u>grape</u>? Does she want an <u>orange</u>?

Yes, I do. Yes, she does.

No, I don't. No, she doesn't.

Write the missing words!

Do _____ want a _____ ?

Yes, I _____ .

No, _____ .

_____ he _____ a _____ ?

_____ , _____ does.

No, he _____ .

_____ you _____ an _____ ?

Yes, _____ _____ .

_____ , I _____ .

_____ ?
_____ .
_____ .

Learn the phonics

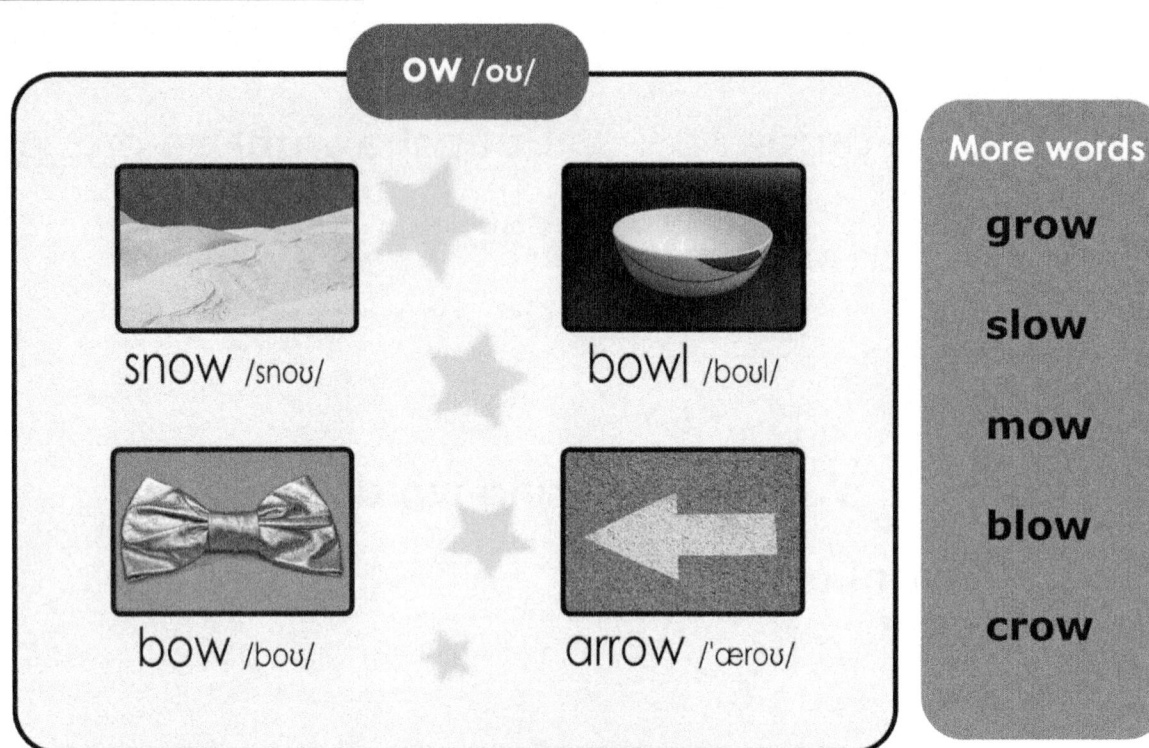

OW /ou/

snow /snou/

bowl /boul/

bow /bou/

arrow /'ærou/

More words

grow

slow

mow

blow

crow

Write the words

OW /ou/

Write the letters & Read the sentences!

Your yell_ _ b_ _ is in the b_ _l.

The grass gr_ _s sl_ _ly.

The black cr_ _ is in the sn_ _.

Test

Complete the words

1. s_____y 3. w_____n 5. b_____a

2. c_____y 4. p_____e 6. l_____n

Write the answer next to the letter "A"

A: ___ **7.** Which fruit ___ she ___?

a. do, want
b. does, want
c. does, wants

A: ___ **8.** I ___ pineapple.

a. want a
b. wants a
c. want an

A: ___ **9.** Do you want a watermelon?

a. Yes, I does.
b. No, I do.
c. No, I don't.

A: ___ **10.** Does ___ want ___ orange?

a. he, a
b. you, an
c. she, an

Answers on Page 306

Lesson 9

- Learn the words
- Learn the sentences
- Learn the phonics
- Test yourself!

The body

тіло

Learn the words

1. **arm**
   рука
2. **stomach**
   живіт
3. **shoulder**
   плече
4. **head**
   голова
5. **neck**
   шия

6. **toe**
   палець на нозі
7. **foot**
   ступня
8. **finger**
   палець
9. **hand**
   кисть руки
10. **leg**
    нога

Write the missing letters!

1. _ _m
2. s_o_ _c_
3. _h_ _ld_r
4. _e_ _
5. n_ _ _

6. t_ _
7. _ _ _t
8. f_n_e_
9. h_ _ _
10. l_ _

Have fun with the words!

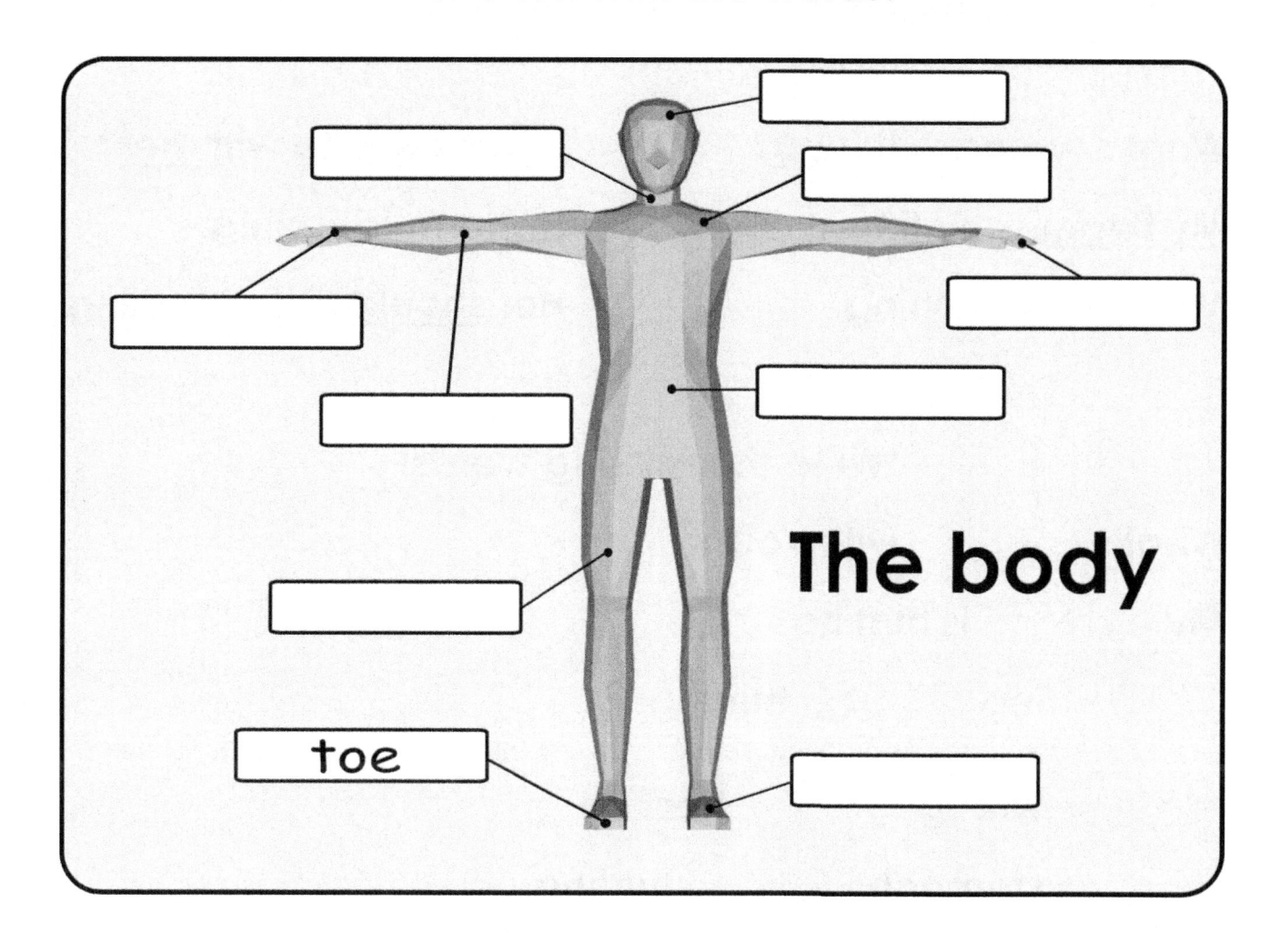

The body

toe

Unscramble the letters!

1. helosurd _____

2. nfgire _____

3. atohmcs _____

4. enkc _____

5. nhda _____

Learn the sentences

What's wrong with <u>you</u>?   What's wrong with <u>her</u>?

My <u>finger</u> is hurting.   Her <u>arm</u> is hurting.

My <u>toe</u> isn't hurting.   Her <u>shoulder</u> isn't hurting.

Write the missing words!

What's _____ with you?

My _____ is hurting.

_____ leg _____ hurting.

_____ wrong _____ her?

_____ stomach _____ hurting.

Her _____ isn't _____.

What's _____ _____ him?

His _____ _____ _____.

_____ toe _____ _____.

_____?

_____.

_____.

Learn the sentences

Is your <u>neck</u> hurting?   Is his <u>leg</u> hurting?
Yes, my neck is hurting.   Yes, her leg is hurting.
No, my neck isn't hurting.   No, her leg isn't hurting.

Write the missing words!

Is _____ arm _____ ?

Yes, _____ arm _____ hurting.

No, my _____ isn't _____ .

_____ his _____ _____ ?

_____ , his _____ is _____ .

No, _____ hand _____ _____ .

_____ her _____ _____ ?

Yes, _____ foot _____ _____ .

_____ , her _____ _____ .

_____?
_____.
_____.

Learn the phonics

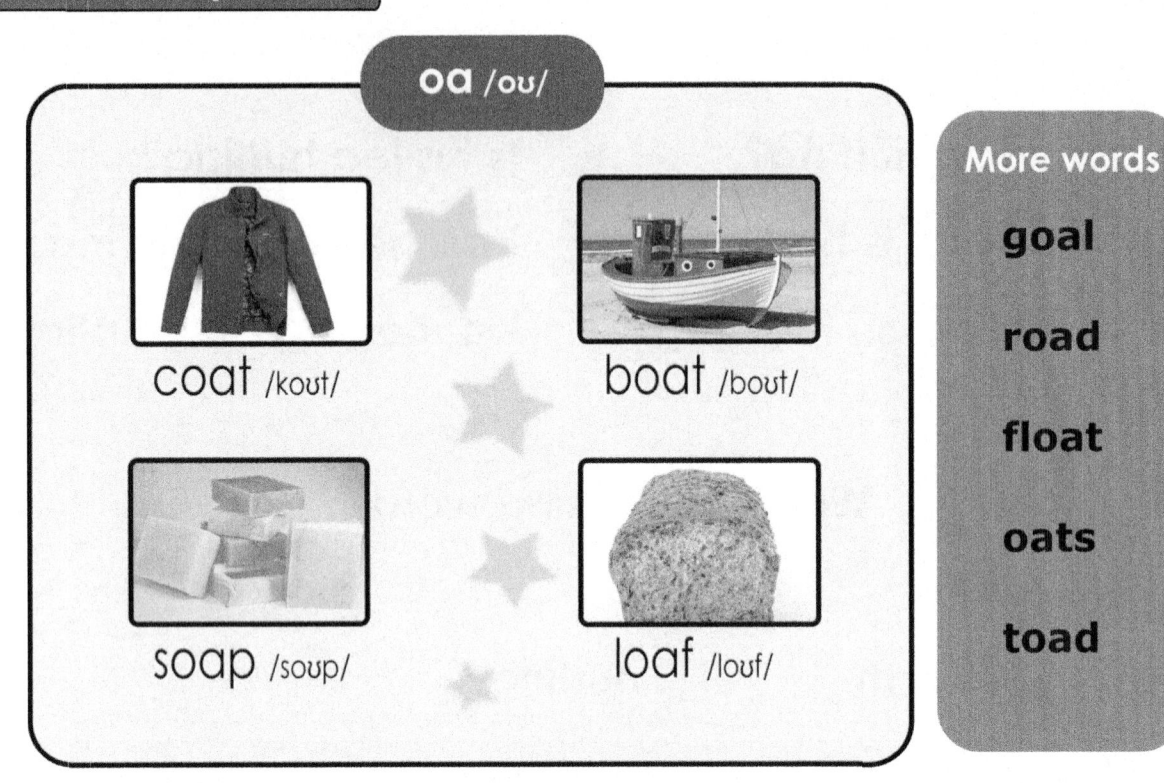

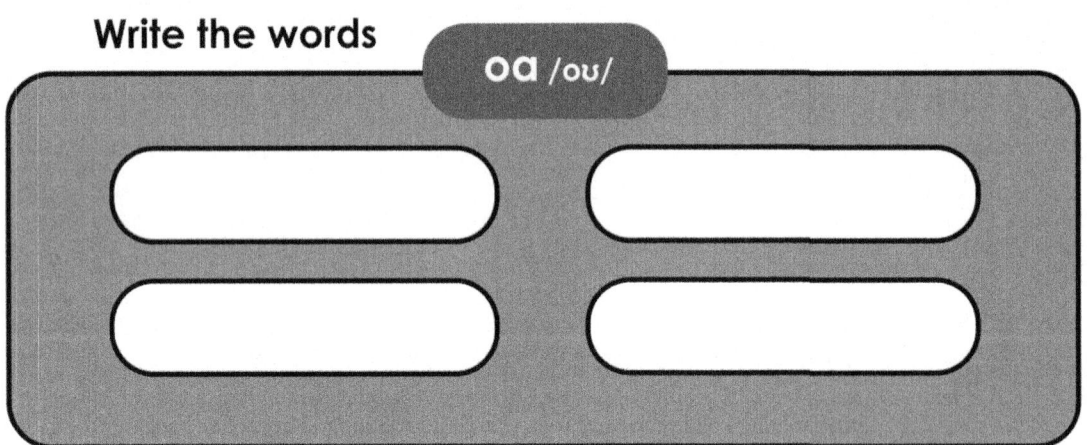

oa /ou/

coat /kout/

boat /bout/

soap /soup/

loaf /louf/

More words

goal

road

float

oats

toad

Write the words

oa /ou/

Write the letters & Read the sentences!

A t_ _d is on the r_ _d.

The s_ _p is on my c_ _t.

That b_ _t doesn't fl_ _t.

Test

Complete the words

1. s____h
2. h____d
3. f____t
4. f____r
5. s____r
6. n____k

Write the answer next to the letter "A"

A: ___ 7. What's wrong with you?

a. His toe is hurting.
b. Her toe is hurting.
c. My toe is hurting.

A: ___ 8. His shoulder ___.

a. are hurting
b. is hurting
c. is hurt

A: ___ 9. Is her neck hurting?

a. Yes, his neck is hurting.
b. No, her neck isn't hurting.
c. Yes, her nose is hurting.

A: ___ 10. Is ___ leg hurting? Yes, my leg is leg hurting.

a. your
b. his
c. her

Answers on Page 306

Lesson 10 — Sports

спорт

Learn the words

1. **basketball**
баскетбол
2. **badminton**
бадмінтон
3. **golf**
гольф
4. **hockey**
хокей
5. **soccer**
футбол
6. **cricket**
крикет
7. **baseball**
бейсбол
8. **volleyball**
волейбол
9. **football**
футбол
10. **tennis**
теніс

Write the missing letters!

1. b_s_e_b_ _l
2. b_d_ _n_o_
3. g_ _ _
4. h_c_e_
5. _o_ce_
6. c_i_k_t
7. _ _s_b_l_
8. v_l_e_b_ _l
9. _o_t_ _l
10. t_n_ _s

Have fun with the words!

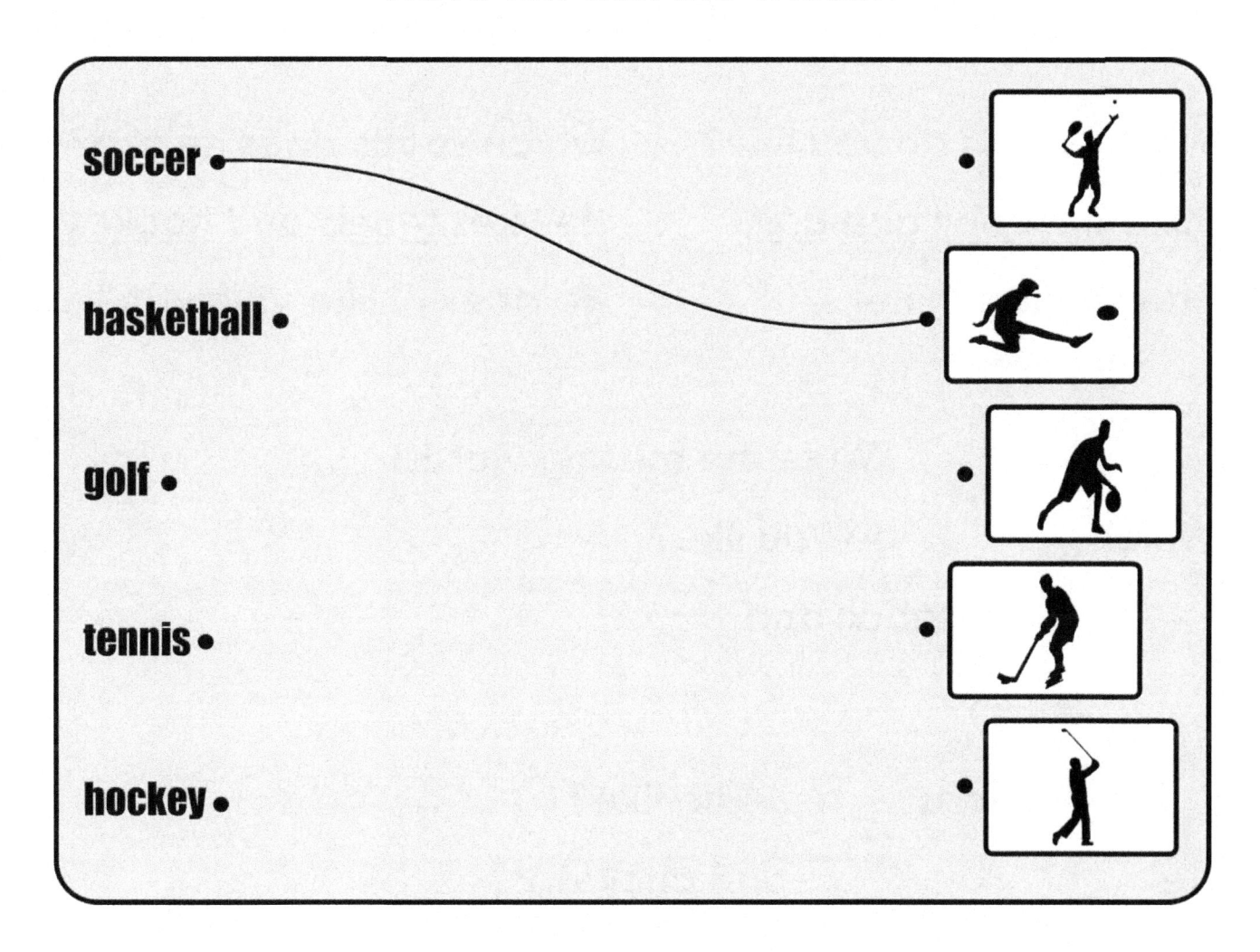

soccer

basketball

golf

tennis

hockey

Unscramble the letters!

1. bbsaalel _____

2. lolvleaybl _____

3. lfotbalo _____

4. rctkice _____

5. nbdmtinao _____

Learn the sentences

Which sports do you like? Which sports does he like?
I like <u>baseball</u> and <u>golf</u>. He likes <u>tennis</u> and <u>hockey</u>.
I don't like <u>cricket</u>. He doesn't like <u>volleyball</u>.

Write the missing words!

Which _____ do you like?
I _____ baseball and _____.
I _____ like _____.

_____ sports _____ he like?
He _____ _____ and cricket.
He _____ _____ _____.

Which _____ does _____ _____?
_____ likes football _____ _____.
She _____ _____ _____.

_____ ?
_____ .
_____ .

Learn the sentences

Do you like <u>badminton</u>?   Does she like <u>tennis</u>?
Yes, I do.   Yes, she does.
No, I don't.   No, she doesn't.

Write the missing words!

Do you _____ _____?
Yes, _____ _____.
No, _____ _____.

_____ he _____ _____?
_____, he _____.
No, _____ _____.

_____ she _____ _____?
Yes, _____ _____.
_____, _____ doesn't.

_____?
_____.
_____.

Learn the phonics

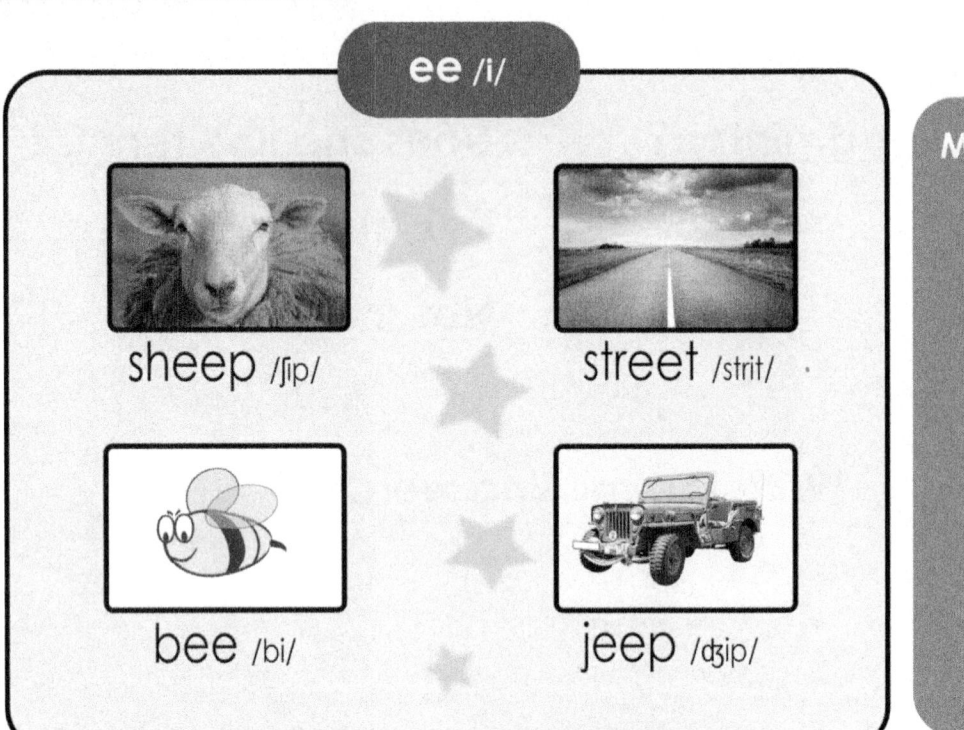

ee /i/

sheep /ʃip/

street /strit/

bee /bi/

jeep /dʒip/

More words

see

keep

knee

teeth

deep

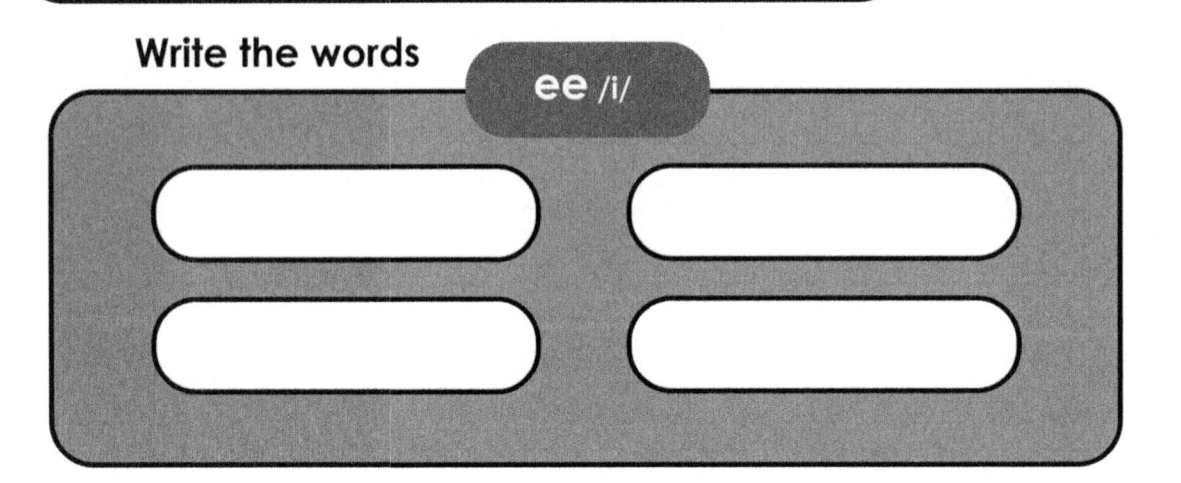

Write the words

ee /i/

Write the letters & Read the sentences!

I s_ _ a j_ _p on the str_ _t.

A b_ _ is on the sh_ _p's kn_ _.

She k_ _ps her t_ _th clean.

Test

Complete the words

1. t_____s 3. g_____f 5. b_____n

2. v_____l 4. c_____t 6. h_____y

Write the answer next to the letter "A"

A: ___ **7.** Which sports ___ you like?

a. do
b. does
c. is

A: ___ **8.** He ___ volleyball.

a. don't like
b. doesn't likes
c. doesn't like

A: ___ **9.** Does she like badminton?

a. Yes, she does.
b. No, he doesn't.
c. No, she does.

A: ___ **10.** ___ you like tennis?

a. Does
b. Do
c. Are

Answers on Page 306

Lesson 11

- Learn the words
- Learn the sentences
- Learn the phonics
- Test yourself!

Places

місця

Learn the words

1. **store**
   магазин
2. **swimming pool**
   басейн
3. **department store**
   універмаг
4. **supermarket**
   супермаркет
5. **night market**
   нічний ринок
6. **cinema**
   кінотеатр
7. **beach**
   пляж
8. **park**
   парк
9. **gym**
   спортзал
10. **restaurant**
    ресторан

Write the missing letters!

1. s_o_ _
2. sw_m_i_g p_ _l
3. d_p_ _t_e_t s_o_e
4. su_ _r_a_k_ _
5. n_ _ _t m_r_e_
6. c_n_ _ _
7. b_a_ _
8. p_ _ _
9. g_ _
10. r_s_a_r_ _t

Have fun with the words!

Word Search

```
k u w t n v a h l g d r w t y n n a
w u w d c s w i m m i n g p o o l g
n i g h t m a r k e t m r b k y z z
l s u p e r m a r k e t y p l r t m
l l n l i x o d w r u d y y a m n s
u g s b a o z b x a w c p a z r x h
a u f e d y q k m h l p z g y m k m
d e p a r t m e n t s t o r e t q d
s n t c z y c i n e m a g r a c p q
c z f h p o s t o r e v d n s i z i
v u p l u r o t y u c y e p w r b o
v v b a r e s t a u r a n t b e c c
```

Word directions: → ↘ ↓

- **beach**
- **cinema**
- **department store**
- **gym**
- **night market**

- **park**
- **restaurant**
- **store**
- **supermarket**
- **swimming pool**

Learn the sentences

Where do you want to go?
I want to go to the <u>beach</u>.
I don't want to go to the <u>gym</u>.

Where does he want to go?
He wants to go to the <u>store</u>.
He doesn't want to go to the <u>gym</u>.

Write the missing words!

Where _____ you want _____ go?

I want to _____ to the _____ .

I _____ want to go _____ the department _____ .

_____ does _____ want to _____ ?

He _____ to go _____ the _____ pool.

He _____ want _____ go to the _____ .

Where _____ you _____ to _____ ?

I _____ to _____ the _____ .

I _____ to _____ to the _____ .

_____?
_____.
_____.

Learn the sentences

Do you want to go to the <u>park</u>? Does she want to go to the <u>cinema</u>?
Yes, I do. Yes, she does.
No, I don't want to. No, she doesn't want to.

Write the missing words!

Do you _____ to _____ to the _____ pool?

Yes, _____ _____ .

No, I _____ _____ to.

_____ he _____ to go _____ the _____ ?

_____ , he _____ .

No, he _____ want _____ .

_____ you _____ to go to _____ _____ ?

Yes, _____ _____ .

_____ , I _____ _____ .

_____ ?
_____ .
_____ .

Learn the phonics

ea /i/

beach /bitʃ/

read /rid/

leaf /lif/

bean /bin/

More words

jeans

cheap

team

wheat

clean

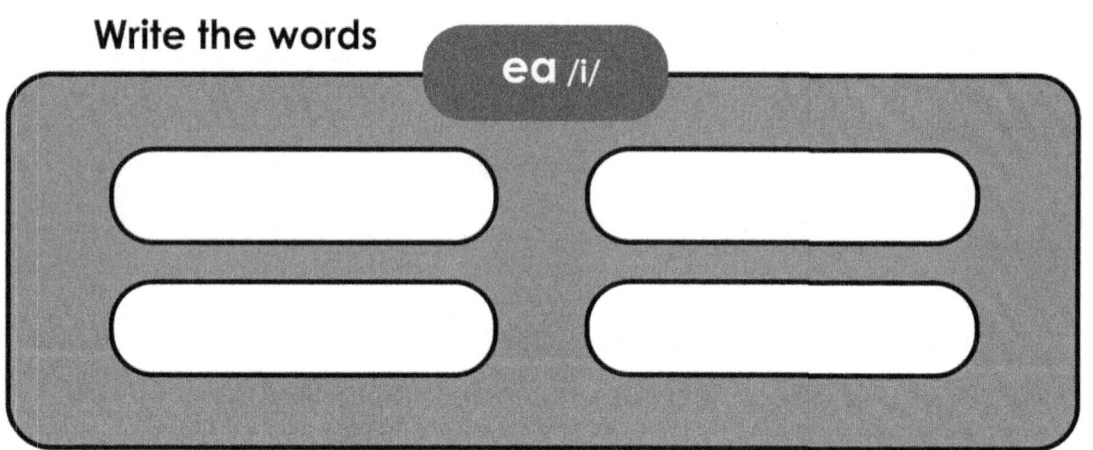

Write the words

ea /i/

Write the letters & Read the sentences!

These j_ _ns are r_ _lly ch_ _p.

A b_ _n is on the green l_ _f.

Pl_ _se cl_ _n the b_ _ch.

Test

Complete the words

1. s_____e
2. c_____a
3. p_____k
4. r_____t
5. s_____t
6. g_____m

Write the answer next to the letter "A"

A: ___ **7.** Where ___ he want to go?

a. do
b. does
c. is

A: ___ **8.** I ___ go to the night market.

a. want
b. want to
c. wants to

A: ___ **9.** Does she want to go to the park?

a. No, she don't want to.
b. No, she does.
c. No, she doesn't want to.

A: ___ **10.** Do you want to ___ the swimming pool?

a. go to
b. go
c. goes to

Answers on Page 306

Lesson 12

- Learn the words
- Learn the sentences
- Learn the phonics
- Test yourself!

Clothes

одяг

Learn the words

1. **T-shirt** — футболка
2. **blouse** — блузка
3. **dress** — плаття
4. **coat** — пальто
5. **scarf** — шарф
6. **hat** — капелюх
7. **sweater** — светр
8. **necktie** — краватка
9. **skirt** — спідниця
10. **jacket** — куртка

Write the missing letters!

1. T-_ _ir_
2. b_o_s_
3. d_e_s_
4. c_ _t
5. s_ar_
6. h_ _
7. s_ea_e_
8. _e_kt_e
9. s_i_t
10. ja_k_t

Have fun with the words!

T-shirt
blouse
dress
coat
scarf

n e c k t i e

hat
sweater
necktie
skirt
jacket

Learn the sentences

What will you wear later?   What will he wear later?

I will wear a <u>dress</u>.   He will wear a <u>sweater</u>.

I won't wear a <u>skirt</u>.   He won't wear a <u>jacket</u>.

Write the missing words!

What _____ you _____ later?

I will _____ a _____ .

I _____ wear a _____ .

_____ will _____ wear _____ ?

He _____ wear _____ _____ .

He _____ _____ a _____ .

What _____ you _____ ?

_____ will _____ a skirt.

I _____ _____ a _____ .

_____ ?
_____ .
_____ .

- 74 -

Learn the sentences

Will you wear a <u>necktie</u> later? Will she wear a <u>T-shirt</u> later?
Yes, I will.   Yes, she will.
No, I won't.   No, she won't.

Write the missing words!

Will you _____ a _____ later?

Yes, I _____ .

No, _____ .

_____ he _____ a _____ ?

_____ , he _____ .

No, _____ .

_____ you _____ _____ _____ _____ ?

_____ , _____ will.

_____ , _____ .

_____ ?
_____ .
_____ .

Learn the phonics

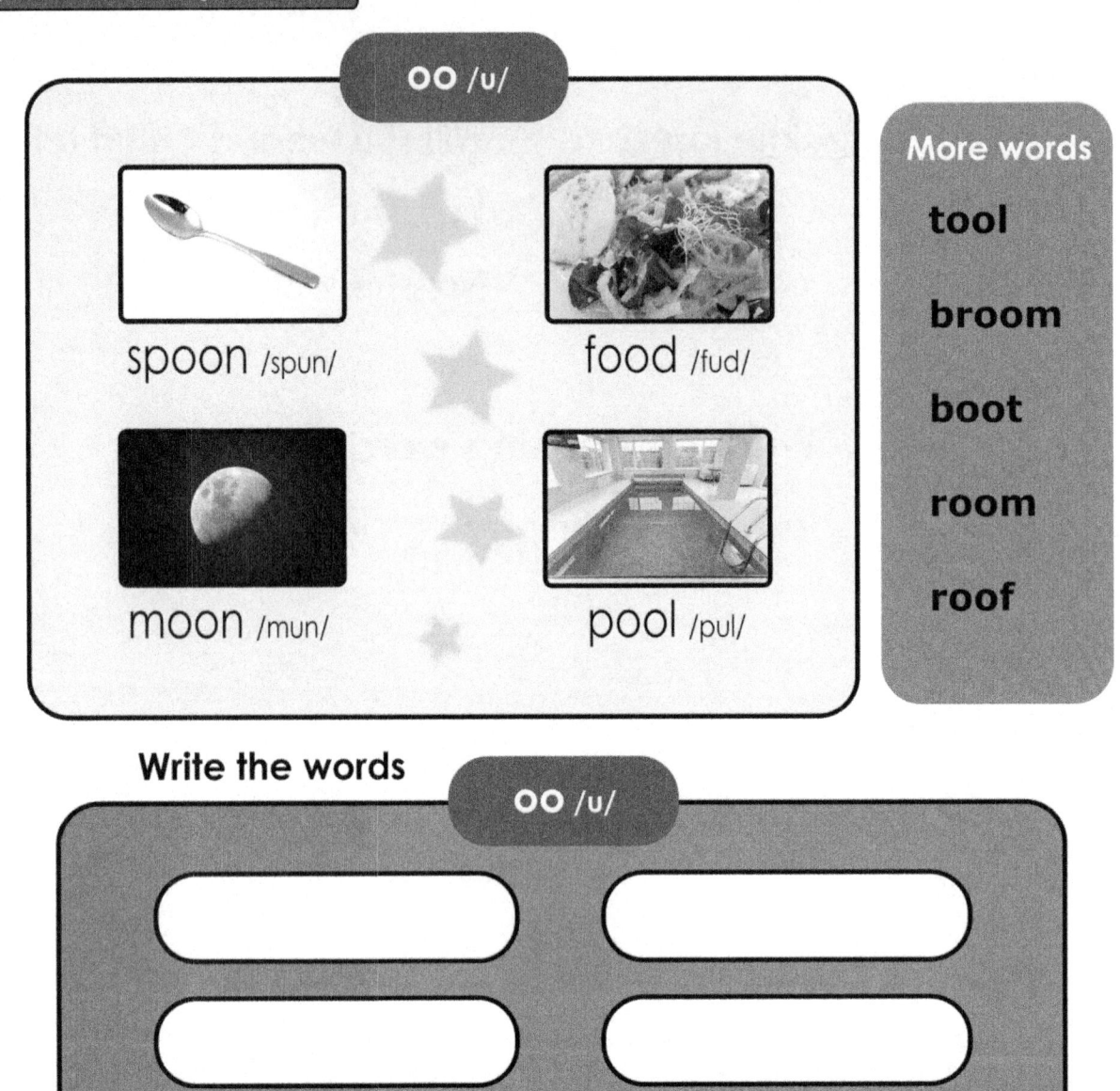

oo /u/

spoon /spun/

food /fud/

moon /mun/

pool /pul/

More words

tool

broom

boot

room

roof

Write the words

oo /u/

Write the letters & Read the sentences!

Eat your f_ _d with a sp_ _n.

There's a p_ _l in that r_ _m.

Use these t_ _ls to fix the r_ _f.

Test

Complete the words

1. b_____e   3. n_____e   5. s_____f

2. s_____r   4. j_____t   6. d_____s

Write the answer next to the letter "A"

A: ___ **7.** What ___ he wear later?

a. do
b. will
c. does

A: ___ **8.** He ___ a coat.

a. won't wears
b. won't wear
c. will wears

A: ___ **9.** Will she wear a skirt later?

a. No, she won't.
b. No, she willn't.
c. No, she will.

A: ___ **10.** Will you wear ___ later?

a. a necktie
b. dress
c. hats

Answers on Page 306

Lesson 13

- Learn the words
- Learn the sentences
- Learn the phonics
- Test yourself!

School subjects

шкільні предмети

Learn the words

1. **English**
   англійська
2. **computer**
   інформатика
3. **social studies**
   соціологія
4. **geography**
   географія
5. **physical education (P.E.)**
   фізична культура
6. **art**
   образотворче мистецтво
7. **math**
   математика
8. **science**
   природничі науки
9. **history**
   історія
10. **music**
    музика

Write the missing letters!

1. E_g_i_h
2. c_m_ut_r
3. so_ _a_ s_ud_e_
4. g_o_r_p_y
5. p_y_i_al e_u_a_ _on
6. a_ _
7. m_ _ _
8. s_i_ _ce
9. hi_t_ _ _
10. _us_c

- 78 -

Have fun with the words!

Write the 3 missing words

1. _____
2. _____
3. _____

- math
- English
- science
- physical education
- history
- social studies
- computer

1. _____
2. _____
3. _____

- history
- music
- physical education
- art
- math
- geography
- science

1. _____
2. _____
3. _____

- English
- math
- social studies
- geography
- computer
- art
- music

1. _____
2. _____
3. _____

- math
- art
- physical education
- music
- science
- geography
- social studies

1. _____
2. _____
3. _____

- history
- social studies
- music
- art
- English
- computer
- math

1. _____
2. _____
3. _____

- science
- history
- physical education
- art
- computer
- English
- geography

Learn the sentences

What class do you have today?
Today, I have <u>geography</u> class.
I don't have <u>music</u> class.

What class does he have today?
Today, he has <u>English</u> class.
He doesn't have <u>math</u> class.

Write the missing words!

What _____ do you _____ today?

_____, I have _____ class.

I _____ have _____ education _____.

_____ class _____ she have _____?

Today, she _____ _____ class.

_____ _____ have _____ studies class.

What class _____ you _____ _____?

Today, _____ have _____ _____.

I _____ _____ math _____.

_____?
_____.
_____.

- 80 -

Learn the sentences

Do you have <u>history</u> class today?   Does she have <u>art</u> class today?
Yes, I do.   Yes, she does.
No, I don't.   No, she doesn't.

Write the missing words!

Do you _____ social _____ class _____?

Yes, I _____.

No, _____.

_____ he _____ _____ class _____?

_____, he _____.

No, _____ _____.

_____ you _____ physical _____ _____ today?

_____, _____ do.

_____, I _____.

_____?
_____.
_____.

Learn the phonics

ai /eɪ/

rain /reɪn/

chain /tʃeɪn/

mail /meɪl/

train /keɪv/

More words

aim

wait

pain

rail

tail

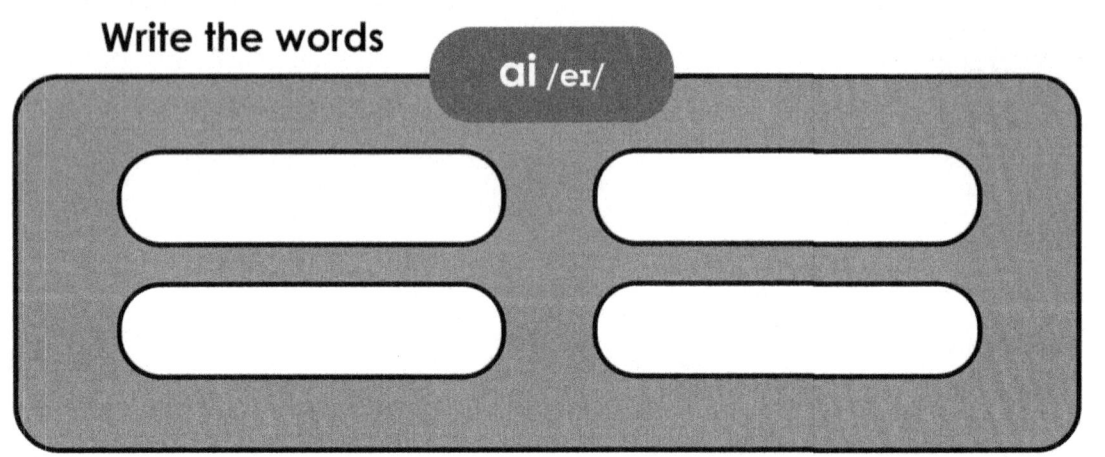

Write the words

ai /eɪ/

Write the letters & Read the sentences!

The sn_ _l is in the r_ _n ag_ _n.

I w_ _t for the tr_ _n.

There is b_ _t by the s_ _l.

Test

Complete the words

1. g_____y 3. h_____y 5. E_____h

2. c_____r 4. m_____c 6. s_____e

Write the answer next to the letter "A"

A: ___ **7.** What class ___ today?

a. does she have
b. does you have
c. does he has

A: ___ **8.** Today, he ___ social studies class.

a. have
b. has
c. haves

A: ___ **9.** Do you have physical education class today?

a. Yes, I have.
b. Yes, I do.
c. Yes, I does.

A: ___ **10.** ___ she ___ math class today?

a. Does, has
b. Do, have
c. Does, have

Answers on Page 306

Lesson 14 — Vegetables

- Learn the words
- Learn the sentences
- Learn the phonics
- Test yourself!

овочі

Learn the words

1. **potato** — картопля
2. **carrot** — морква
3. **pumpkin** — гарбуз
4. **broccoli** — брокколі
5. **asparagus** — спаржа
6. **cabbage** — капуста
7. **spinach** — шпинат
8. **corn** — кукурудза
9. **onion** — цибуля
10. **mushroom** — гриб

Write the missing letters!

1. p_t_t_
2. c_ _r_ _
3. _u_p_ _n
4. b_o_ _ol_
5. _s_a_ _g_s
6. c_b_a_e
7. s_i_a_ _
8. _o_ _
9. _n_o_
10. m_s_ _o_ _

Have fun with the words!

Circle the vegetable words!

1. golf — (carrot) — art — park — stomach
2. beach — asparagus — neck — eraser — lemon
3. history — tennis — pumpkin — leg — gym
4. grape — computer — onion — hockey — music
5. spinach — hat — apple — store — foot
6. pen — head — badminton — skirt — corn
7. blouse — potato — arm — circle — pear
8. orange — jacket — desk — cabbage — finger

Write the 8 words

1.
2.
3.
4.
5.
6.
7.
8.

Learn the sentences

What did you eat for dinner?   What did they eat for dinner?

We ate <u>corn</u> for dinner.   They ate <u>broccoli</u> for dinner.

We didn't eat <u>mushroom</u>.   They didn't eat <u>asparagus</u>.

Write the missing words!

What _____ you _____ for dinner?

We _____ spinach for _____.

We _____ eat _____.

What _____ they _____ for _____?

They _____ _____ for _____.

_____ didn't _____ _____.

What _____ you _____ _____ _____?

I _____ _____ _____ _____.

_____ _____ eat _____ for _____.

_____?

_____.

_____.

Learn the sentences

Did you eat <u>broccoli</u> for dinner?   Did they eat <u>potato</u> for dinner?

Yes, we did.   Yes, they did.

No, we didn't. We ate <u>cabbage</u>.   No, they didn't. They ate <u>onion</u>.

Write the missing words!

Did you _____ asparagus _____ dinner?

Yes, we _____ .

No, _____ didn't. We _____ _____ .

_____ they eat _____ for _____ ?

_____ , they _____ .

No, _____ _____ . They ate _____ .

Did you _____ _____ _____ dinner?

Yes, _____ _____ .

_____ , we _____ . We _____ _____ .

_____?

_____.

_____.

Learn the phonics

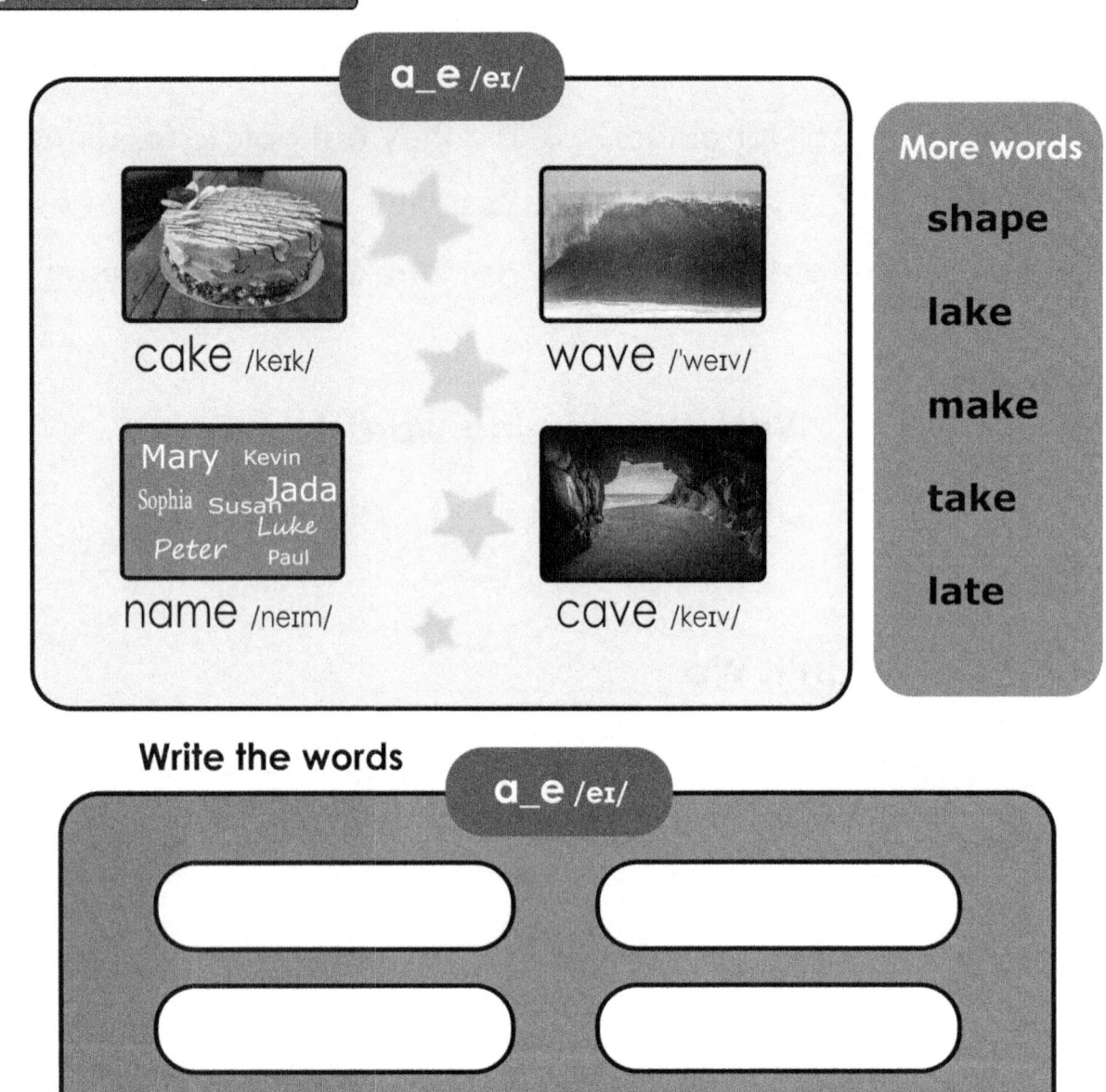

a_e /eɪ/

cake /keɪk/

wave /'weɪv/

name /neɪm/

cave /keɪv/

More words

shape

lake

make

take

late

Write the words

a_e /eɪ/

Write the letters & Read the sentences!

His n_m_ is the s_m_ as mine.

There is a c_v_ near the l_k_.

You can t_k_ the c_k_ home.

Test

Complete the words

1. c_____t   3. b_____i   5. m_____m

2. p_____o   4. s_____h   6. o_____n

Write the answer next to the letter "A"

A: ___ **7.** What did you eat ___ dinner?

a. of
b. for
c. on

A: ___ **8.** They ___ pumpkin.

a. didn't ate
b. didn't eaten
c. didn't eat

A: ___ **9.** Did you eat spinach for dinner?

a. No, we didn't. We ate potato.
b. No, we didn't. We eat cabbage.
c. No, we did. We ate corn.

A: ___ **10.** Did they ___ mushroom for dinner?

a. ate
b. eats
c. eat

Answers on Page 306

Lesson 15

- Learn the words
- Learn the sentences
- Learn the phonics
- Test yourself!

At the toy shop

у магазині іграшок

Learn the words

1. **car**
   машинка
2. **airplane**
   літак
3. **dinosaur**
   динозавр
4. **doll**
   лялька
5. **teddy bear**
   плюшевий ведмедик
6. **jump rope**
   скакалка
7. **board game**
   настільна гра
8. **toy block**
   конструктор
9. **robot**
   робот
10. **ball**
    м'яч

Write the missing letters!

1. c_ _
2. a_r_la_e
3. d_n_sa_r
4. do_ _
5. t_d_y b_a_
6. ju_p r_p_
7. b_a_d ga_e
8. t_y b_oc_s
9. r_bo_
10. _al_

Have fun with the words!

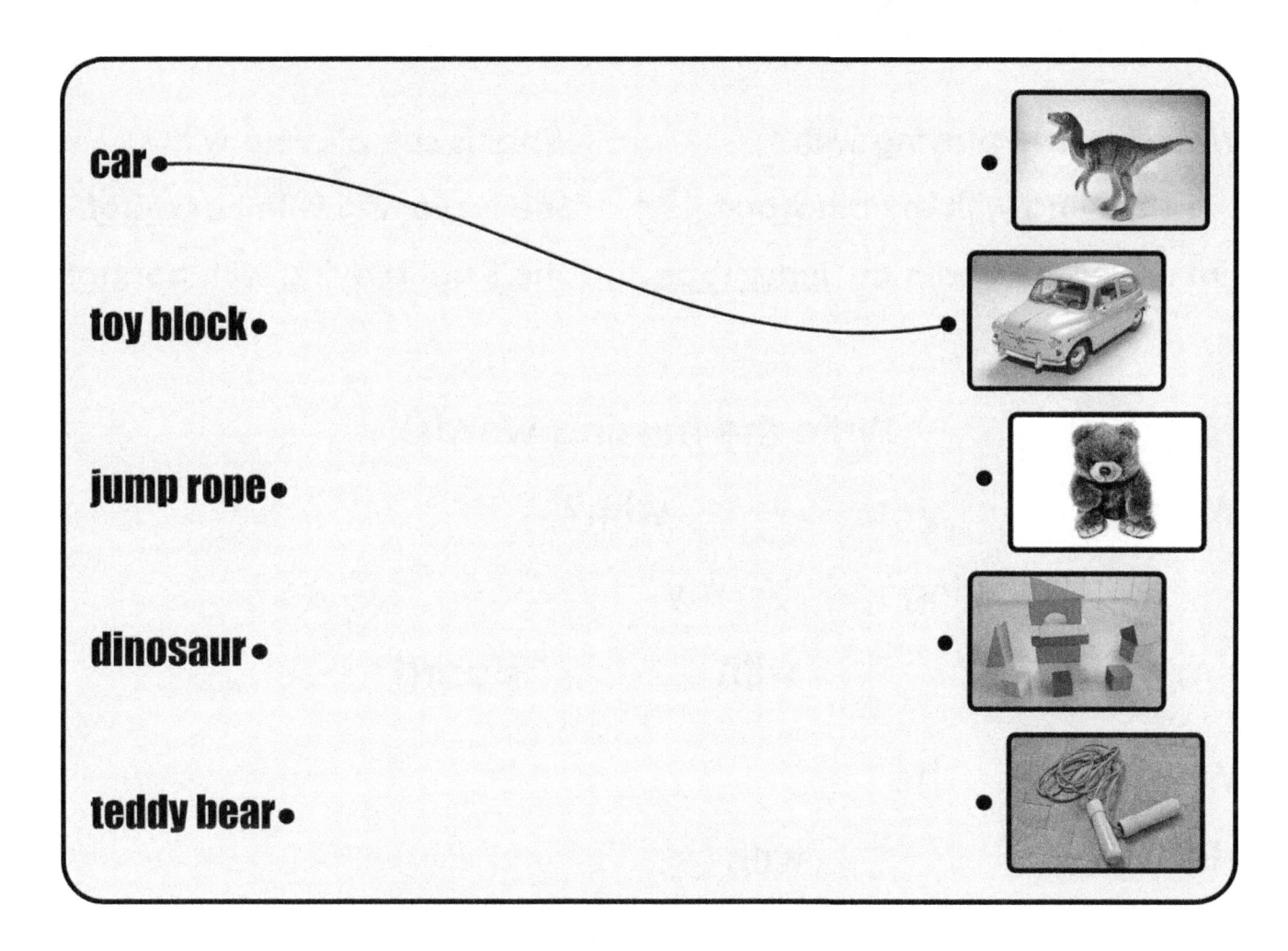

car

toy block

jump rope

dinosaur

teddy bear

Unscramble the letters!

1. analirpe

2. oldl

3. robad agem

4. albl

5. broto

Learn the sentences

What are you playing with?   What is she playing with?

I am playing with my <u>dinosaur</u>.   She is playing with her <u>robot</u>.

I'm not playing with my <u>jump rope</u>.   She's not playing with her <u>doll</u>.

Write the missing words!

What _____ you _____ with?

I _____ playing _____ my _____ .

I'm _____ _____ with _____ board _____ .

What _____ he _____ _____ ?

He _____ _____ with _____ _____ .

_____ not _____ _____ his _____ .

_____ is _____ playing _____ ?

She _____ with _____ _____ jump _____ .

_____ _____ playing _____ her _____ .

_____ ?

_____ .

_____ .

Learn the sentences

Are you playing with your <u>car</u>?
Yes, I am.
No, I'm playing with my <u>doll</u>.

Is he playing with his <u>ball</u>?
Yes, he is.
No, he's playing with his <u>robot</u>.

Write the missing words!

Are you _____ with _____ _____?

Yes, I _____.

No, _____ playing _____ my _____.

_____ she _____ _____ her _____ blocks?

_____, _____ is.

No, _____ _____ with _____ _____ bear.

Is _____ _____ with _____ _____?

_____, he _____.

_____, _____ _____ _____ his _____.

_____?
_____.
_____.

Learn the phonics

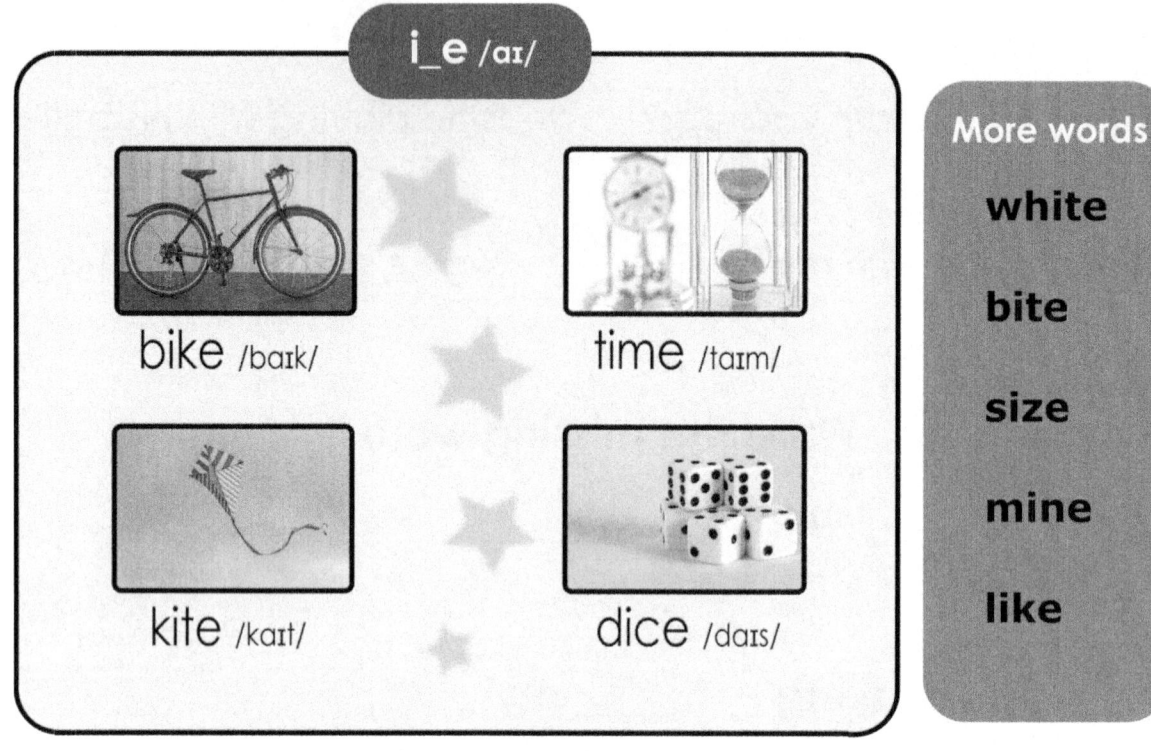

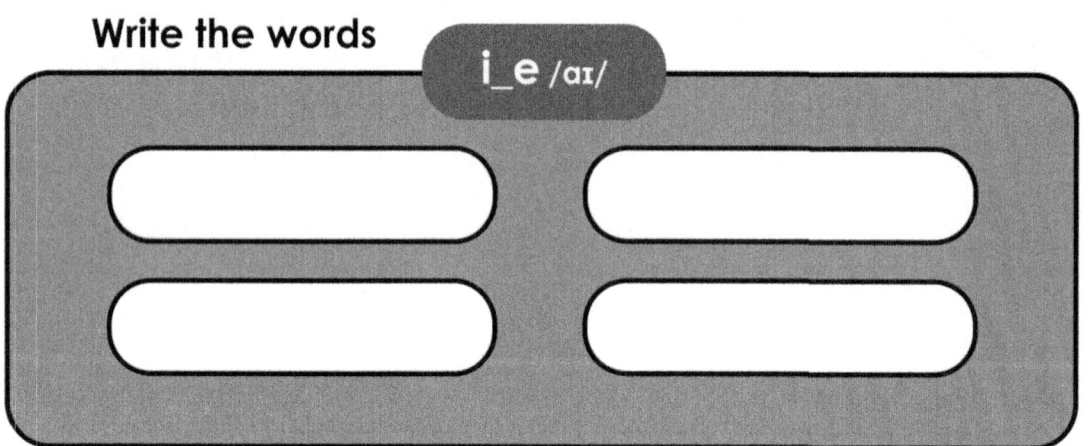

i_e /aɪ/

bike /baɪk/

time /taɪm/

kite /kaɪt/

dice /daɪs/

More words

white

bite

size

mine

like

Write the words

i_e /aɪ/

Write the letters & Read the sentences!

The wh_t_ b_k_ is m_n_.

I l_k_ this k_t_.

The small s_z_ is f_n_.

Test

Complete the words

1. a_____e 3. r_____t 5. b_____l

2. d_____r 4. t_____r 6. d_____l

Write the answer next to the letter "A"

A: ___ 7. What ___ she playing ___?

a. are, with
b. is, of
c. is, with

A: ___ 8. He is ___ teddy bear.

a. play with his
b. playing with his
c. playing with her

A: ___ 9. Are you playing with your jump rope?

a. No, I'm playing with my dinosaur.
b. No, I playing with my toy blocks.
c. Yes, I are.

A: ___ 10. ___ playing with ___ doll?

a. Is you, your
b. Is she, her
c. Are she, her

Answers on Page 306

Lesson 16 — In the kitchen

- Learn the words
- Learn the sentences
- Learn the phonics
- Test yourself!

на кухні а

Learn the words

1. **refrigerator** — холодильник
2. **cupboard** — шафа
3. **microwave oven** — мікрохвильова піч
4. **dish rack** — стійка для посуду
5. **coffee maker** — кавоварка
6. **toaster** — тостер
7. **stove** — піч
8. **pan** — tava
9. **rice cooker** — рисоварка
10. **blender** — блендер

Write the missing letters!

1. _ef_i_era_or
2. c_p_o_ _d
3. m_c_ow_ _e o_ _n
4. d_s_ ra_ _
5. _o_f_e m_c_ _ne
6. to_s_e_
7. _to_ _
8. p_ _
9. r_c_ c_ok_ _
10. _l_nd_r

- 96 -

Have fun with the words!

Find the 8 kitchen items!

banana   hockey   crocodile
doctor
           foot   teacher
ball   refrigerator
              tennis
       yellow   pan   robot
lion   head   elephant
giraffe   math   blender   pencil
                     baseball
monkey   arm   eraser
cupboard   computer   stove
    square   star   rice cooker
                         circle
dish rack   toaster   father

Write the 8 shapes

| 1. | 3. | 5. | 7. |
| 2. | 4. | 6. | 8. |

Learn the sentences

What does your kitchen need?
Our kitchen needs a new <u>stove</u>.
It doesn't need a <u>rice cooker</u>.

Write the missing words!

What _____ your _____ need?
_____ kitchen _____ a _____ _____ .
It _____ _____ a _____ rack.

What _____ _____ kitchen _____ ?
Their _____ needs _____ _____ _____ .
_____ doesn't _____ a microwave _____ .

_____ does _____ _____ _____ ?
Our _____ _____ _____ new _____ .
_____ need _____ _____ .

_____?
_____.
_____.

Learn the sentences

Does their kitchen need a new <u>refrigerator</u>?

Yes, their kitchen does.

No, it doesn't need a new one.

Write the missing words!

Does _____ kitchen _____ a new _____?

_____, our _____ does.

No, _____ need a _____ _____.

Does their _____ need a _____ _____ machine?

Yes, _____ kitchen _____.

_____, it doesn't _____ one.

_____ your _____ _____ a _____ _____?

_____, _____ _____ does.

No, _____ _____ new _____.

_____?
_____.
_____.

Learn the phonics

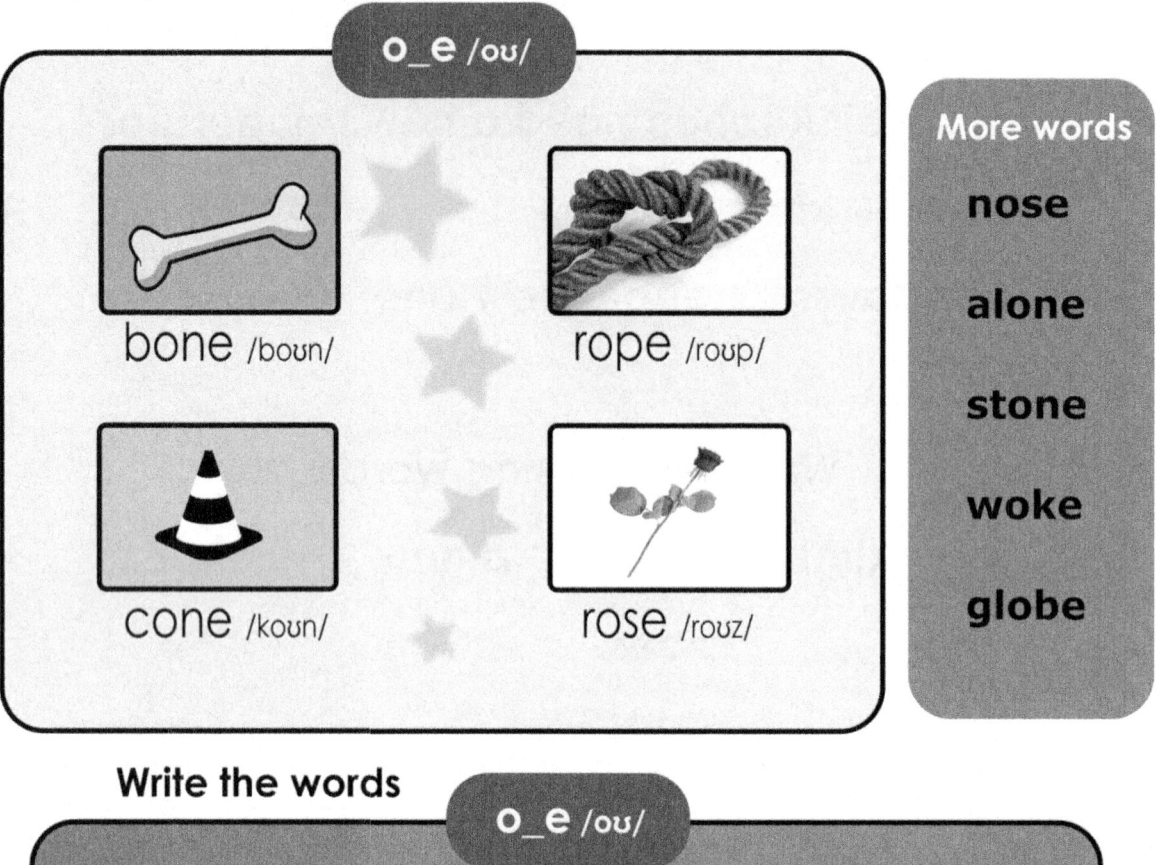

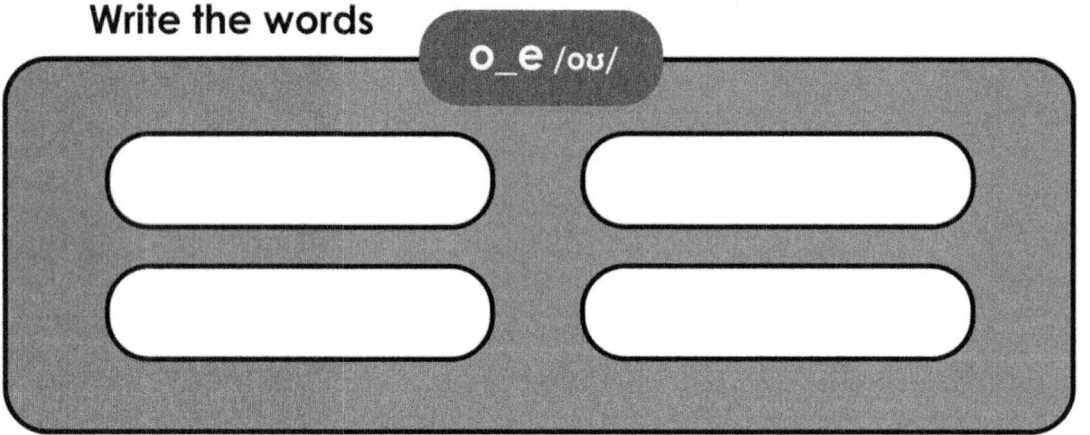

o_e /oʊ/

bone /boʊn/

rope /roʊp/

cone /koʊn/

rose /roʊz/

More words

nose

alone

stone

woke

globe

Write the words

o_e /oʊ/

Write the letters & Read the sentences!

A r_s_ is on the st_n_.

The dog smells the b_n_ with its n_s_.

He r_d_ his bike al_n_.

Test

Complete the words

1. b_____r
2. s_____e
3. p_____n
4. t_____r
5. c_____d
6. r_____r

Write the answer next to the letter "A"

A: ___ **7.** What ___ your kitchen ___?

a. does, need
b. does, needs
c. do, need

A: ___ **8.** It ___ need a microwave oven.

a. does'nt
b. doesn't
c. don't

A: ___ **9.** Does your kitchen need a new dish rack?

a. Yes, our kitchen does.
b. No, it does need a new one.
c. Yes, their kitchen does.

A: ___ **10.** ___ kitchen need a new stove?

a. Does they're
b. Does there
c. Does their

Answers on Page 306

Lesson 17

- Learn the words
- Learn the sentences
- Learn the phonics
- Test yourself!

Feelings

почуття

Learn the words

1. **fine**
в порядку
2. **sad**
сумний
3. **bored**
знуджений
4. **energetic**
енергійний
5. **tired**
втомлений
6. **angry**
сердитий
7. **happy**
щасливий
8. **excited**
збуджений
9. **frustrated**
розчарований
10. **sick**
хворий

Write the missing letters!

1. _in_

2. _a_

3. _o_ _d

4. e_er_et_ _

5. t_r_ _

6. a_g_ _

7. _a_ _y

8. _xci_e_

9. f_u_t_a_ _d

10. s_c_

Have fun with the words!

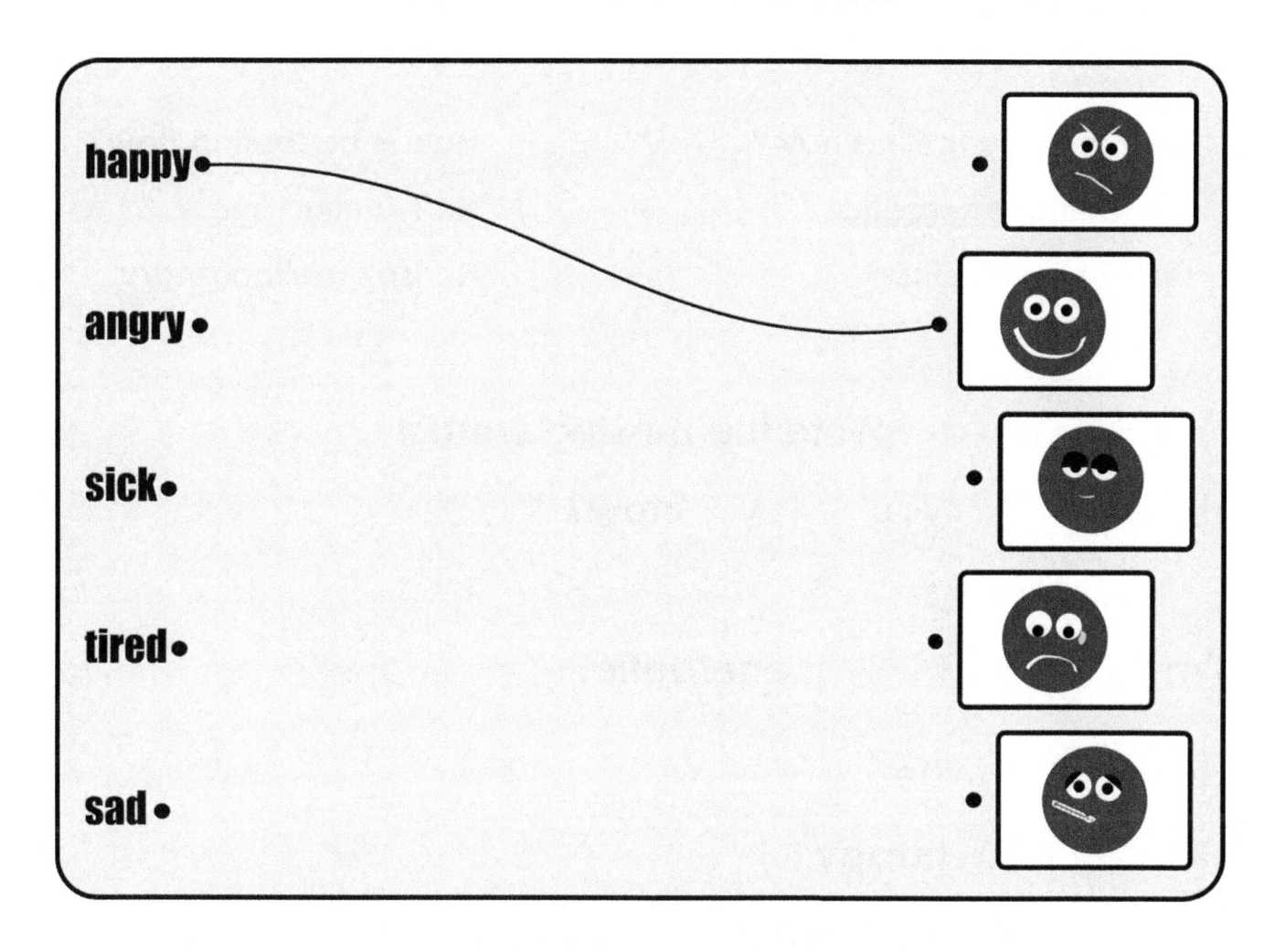

happy
angry
sick
tired
sad

Unscramble the letters!

1. nregetiec _____

2. rdufsrtaet _____

3. dbreo _____

4. xectdei _____

5. inef _____

Learn the sentences

How are you feeling now?   How is he feeling now?
I'm feeling <u>energetic</u>.   He's feeling <u>fine</u>.
I'm not feeling <u>tired</u>.   He isn't feeling <u>angry</u>.

Write the missing words!

How _____ you _____ now?

_____ feeling _____ .

I'm _____ _____ energetic.

How _____ he _____ _____ ?

He's _____ happy.

_____ _____ feeling _____ .

_____ are _____ feeling _____ ?

I'm _____ _____ .

_____ _____ _____ frustrated.

_____ ?
_____ .
_____ .

Learn the sentences

Are you feeling <u>frustrated</u> now?   Is she feeling <u>bored</u> now?

Yes, I am.   Yes, she is.

No, I'm feeling <u>happy</u>.   No, she's feeling <u>excited</u>.

Write the missing words!

Are _____ feeling _____ now?

Yes, I _____ .

No, _____ feeling _____ .

_____ she _____ tired _____ ?

_____ , she _____ .

No, she's _____ _____ .

_____ you _____ _____ _____ ?

Yes, _____ _____ .

_____ , I'm _____ _____ .

_____ ?
_____ .
_____ .

Learn the phonics

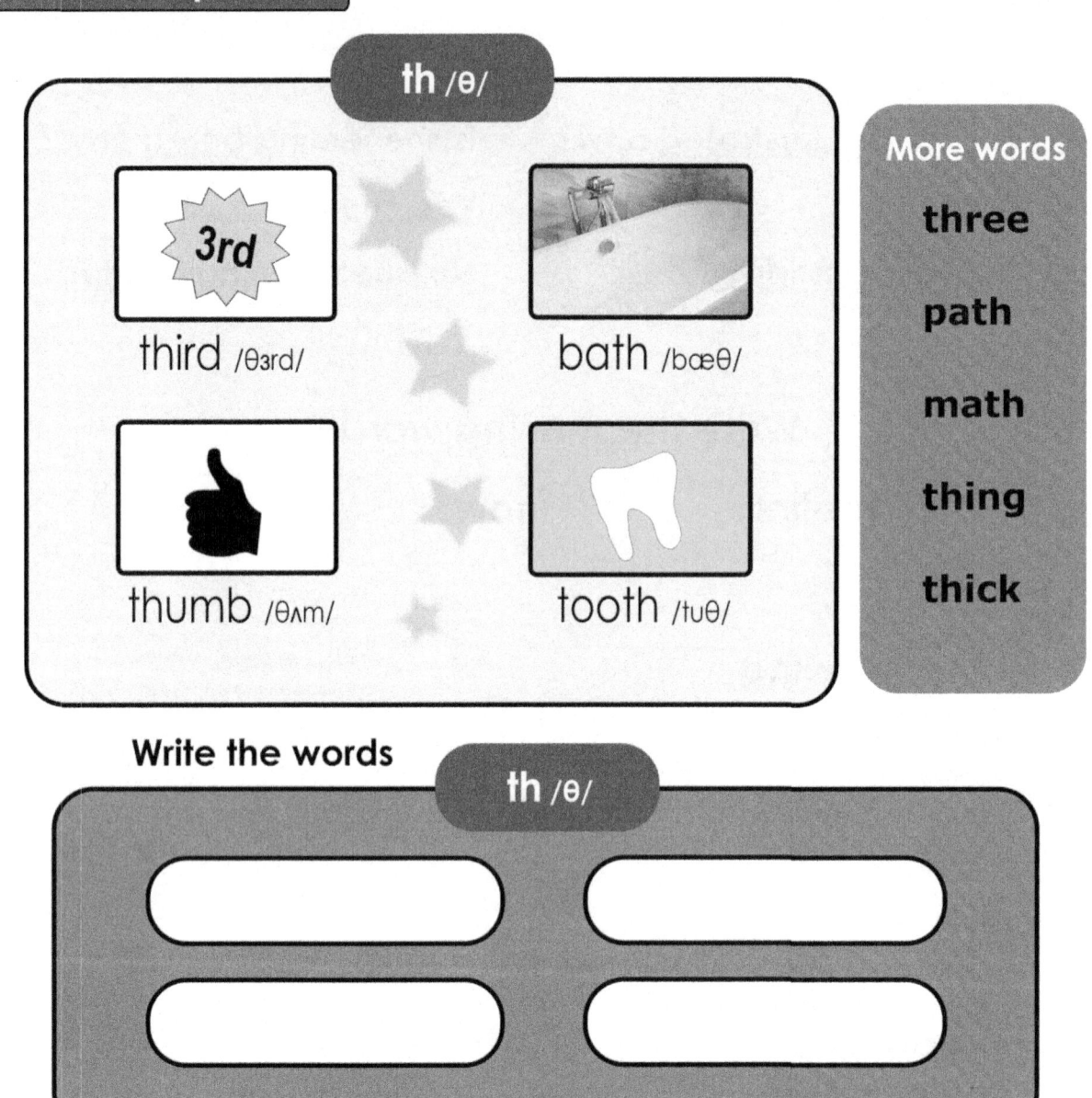

th /θ/

third /θɜrd/
bath /bæθ/
thumb /θʌm/
tooth /tuθ/

More words
three
path
math
thing
thick

Write the words

th /θ/

Write the letters & Read the sentences!

He put his _ _umb in the ba_ _.

He has _ _ree _ _ick ma_ _ books.

The _ _ird pa_ _ is wide.

Test

Complete the words

1. a_____y
2. s_____d
3. b_____d
4. t_____d
5. e_____c
6. f_____d

Write the answer next to the letter "A"

A: ___ **7.** How is he ___?

a. feeling
b. feels
c. felt

A: ___ **8.** How ___ you feeling?

a. is
b. am
c. are

A: ___ **9.** He ___ feeling frustrated.

a. isn't
b. aren't
c. not

A: ___ **10.** Are you feeling tired?

a. Yes, I'm not.
b. Yes, I am.
c. No, I isn't.

Answers on Page 306

Lesson 18

- Learn the words
- Learn the sentences
- Learn the phonics
- Test yourself!

At the ice cream shop

в кафе-морозиві

Learn the words

1. **mint**
м'ята
2. **cherry**
вишня
3. **strawberry**
полуниця
4. **chocolate**
шоколад
5. **raspberry**
малина
6. **almond**
мигдаль
7. **coconut**
кокос
8. **coffee**
кава
9. **vanilla**
ваніль
10. **caramel**
карамель

Write the missing letters!

1. m_ _ _
2. _h_ _r_
3. st_a_b_ _r_
4. c_o_o_ _t_
5. r_ _p_ _r_y
6. a_ _o_ _
7. c_ _o_u_
8. _o_ _e_
9. v_ _i_ _a
10. ca_ _m_ _

- 108 -

Have fun with the words!

Word Search

z	c	s	w	q	p	n	r	v	c	h	e	r	r	y	w	g	n
r	o	w	c	s	c	z	q	a	g	z	e	y	m	u	e	a	w
c	f	x	n	h	t	a	j	l	s	s	j	q	u	i	l	d	s
f	f	c	f	d	o	r	r	d	f	p	a	n	q	p	n	w	m
r	e	o	v	w	z	c	a	a	w	a	b	m	h	y	m	t	d
k	e	c	s	a	c	i	o	w	m	q	l	e	q	r	m	x	u
k	u	o	p	a	n	t	r	l	b	e	r	m	r	x	y	p	y
r	b	n	q	t	h	i	x	y	a	e	l	d	o	r	b	r	e
f	g	u	e	n	h	p	l	w	y	t	r	d	m	n	y	g	y
l	i	t	z	n	k	c	f	l	l	u	e	r	h	a	d	y	w
l	v	u	s	d	k	q	d	j	a	o	r	r	y	s	w	d	l
g	h	m	n	v	b	m	l	m	j	q	u	d	q	y	u	m	n

Word directions: → ↘ ↓

mint   **almond**

cherry   **coconut**

strawberry   **coffee**

chocolate   **vanilla**

raspberry   **caramel**

Learn the sentences

What's your favorite ice cream flavor?

My favorite ice cream flavor is <u>chocolate</u>.

My favorite ice cream flavor isn't <u>strawberry</u>.

Write the missing words!

What's _____ favorite _____ cream flavor?

My _____ ice _____ flavor is _____ .

_____ favorite ice cream _____ _____ vanilla.

_____ his _____ ice cream _____ ?

His _____ ice _____ flavor _____ .

_____ favorite _____ cream _____ isn't _____ .

_____ _____ favorite _____ cream _____ ?

Her _____ ice _____ _____ _____ .

_____ favorite _____ _____ flavor isn't _____ .

_____?

_____.

_____.

- 110 -

Learn the sentences

Do you like <u>mint</u> flavor?   Does he like <u>cherry</u> flavor?
Yes, mint flavor is my favorite.   Yes, cherry flavor is my favorite.
No, I don't like mint flavor.   No, he doesn't like cherry flavor.

Write the missing words!

Do you _____ raspberry _____?
Yes, _____ flavor is my _____.
_____, I _____ like raspberry _____.

_____ she like _____ flavor?
_____, almond flavor is _____ favorite.
No, she _____ like _____ flavor.

Does he like coffee flavor?
_____, coffee _____ is _____ favorite.
No, _____ doesn't _____ _____ flavor.

_____?
_____.
_____.

Learn the phonics

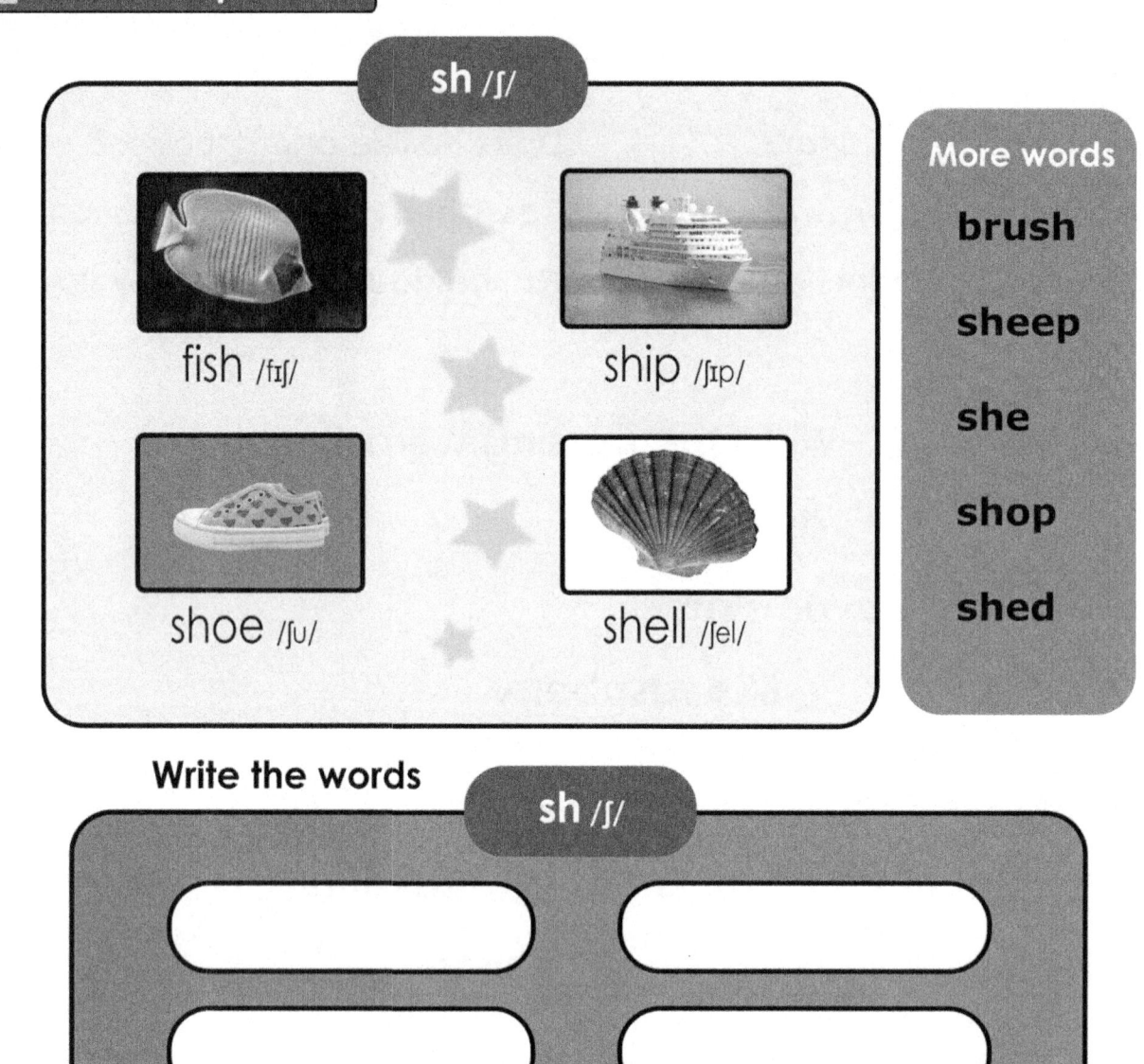

sh /ʃ/

fish /fɪʃ/

ship /ʃɪp/

shoe /ʃu/

shell /ʃel/

More words

brush

sheep

she

shop

shed

Write the words

sh /ʃ/

Write the letters & Read the sentences!

_ _e is bru_ _ing her teeth.

That _ _op has cheap _ _oes.

The _ _eep is in the _ _ed.

Test

Complete the words

1. s_____y 3. c_____e 5. c_____y

2. r_____y 4. v_____a 6. a_____d

Write the answer next to the letter "A"

A: ___ **7.** What's your favorite ice cream flavor?

a. My favorite ice cream is chocolate.
b. His favorite ice cream flavor is mint.
c. My favorite ice cream flavor is cherry.

A: ___ **8.** My favorite ice cream flavor ___ caramel.

a. aren't
b. isn't
c. is'nt

A: ___ **9.** Does she like cherry flavor?

a. Yes, cherry flavor is his favorite.
b. No, she doesn't likes cherry flavor.
c. No, she doesn't like cherry flavor.

A: ___ **10.** Do you like mint flavor? Yes, mint flavor ___ favorite.

a. is my
b. is her
c. is his

Answers on Page 306

Lesson 19

- Learn the words
- Learn the sentences
- Learn the phonics
- Test yourself!

The weather

погода

Learn the words

1. **sunny** — сонячна
2. **rainy** — дощова
3. **snowy** — сніжна
4. **cloudy** — марна
5. **windy** — вітряна
6. **cold** — холодна
7. **warm** — тепла
8. **hot** — жарка
9. **freezing** — крижана, морозна
10. **cool** — прохолодна

Write the missing letters!

1. s_n_ _
2. _a_n_
3. s_ _ _y
4. c_o_d_
5. w_n_ _
6. c_ _d
7. w_ _ _
8. h_ _
9. f_e_ in_
10. _ _ o _

- 114 -

Have fun with the words!

sunny
rainy
snowy
cloudy
windy
cold
warm
hot
freezing
cool

f r e e z i n g

Write the missing word: _____

Learn the sentences

How's the weather going to be?

The weather is going to be <u>sunny</u>.

The weather isn't going to be <u>rainy</u>.

Write the missing words!

How's the _____ going _____ be?

The weather _____ _____ to _____ _____.

_____ weather _____ going _____ be _____.

_____ the _____ to _____?

_____ is _____ to be _____.

The _____ isn't _____.

_____ weather _____ be?

_____ _____ going to _____ _____.

The _____ _____ to _____ _____.

_____?
_____.
_____.

- 116 -

Learn the sentences

Is the weather going to be <u>hot</u>?

Yes, it's going to be hot.

No, it's not going to be hot.

Write the missing words!

Is _____ weather _____ to _____ _____?

Yes, _____ going _____ _____ cloudy.

_____, it's _____ to be _____.

_____ the _____ going _____ _____ cool?

Yes, _____ _____ _____ be _____.

No, _____ not _____ be _____.

Is _____ _____ going _____ be _____?

Yes, _____ _____ to _____ _____.

_____, it's _____ _____ _____ windy.

_____?

_____.

_____.

Learn the phonics

ch /tʃ/

cheese /tʃiz/

chess /tʃɛs/

chick /tʃɪk/

bench /bɛntʃ/

More words

check

chin

cheap

chat

choose

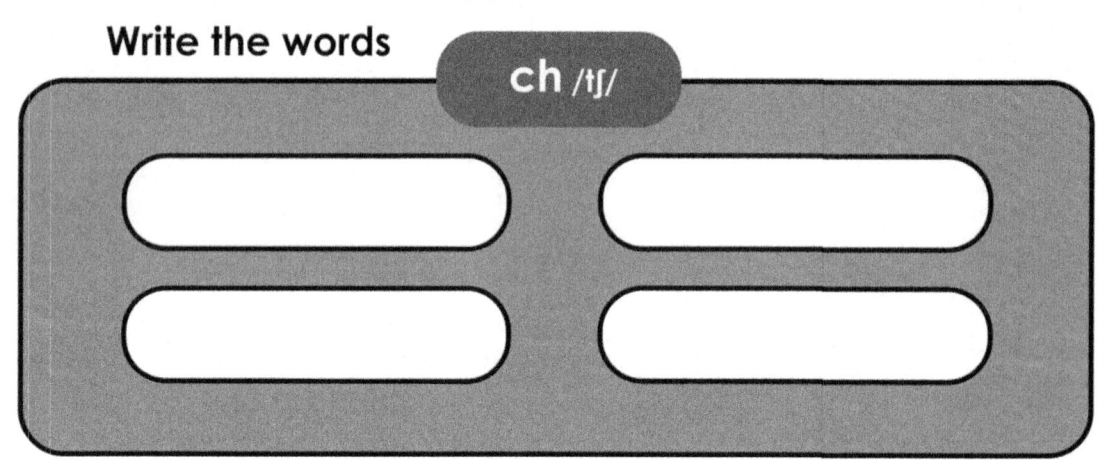

Write the words

ch /tʃ/

Write the letters & Read the sentences!

There is _ _eese on your _ _in.

We sit on the ben_ _ and _ _at.

I will _ _oose the _ _eap _ _air.

Test

Complete the words

1. c_____y
3. f_____g
5. w_____m
2. s_____y
4. r_____y
6. c_____d

Write the answer next to the letter "A"

A: ___ **7.** How's the weather going to be?

a. It's going be freezing.
b. It not going to be cold.
c. It's going to be warm.

A: ___ **8.** It's not ___ be windy.

a. going to
b. go to
c. going too

A: ___ **9.** Is the weather going to be cloudy?

a. No, it not going to be cloudy.
b. Yes, it's going be cloudy.
c. Yes, it's going to be cloudy.

A: ___ **10.** Is ___ going to be hot?

a. weather
b. this weather
c. the weather

Answers on Page 306

Lesson 20 — In the living room

- Learn the words
- Learn the sentences
- Learn the phonics
- Test yourself!

в вітальні

Learn the words

1. **coffee table** — журнальний столик
2. **armchair** — крісло
3. **clock** — годинник
4. **television** — телевізор
5. **bookcase** — книжкова шафа
6. **sofa** — диван
7. **vase** — ваза
8. **rug** — килим
9. **TV stand** — підставка під телевізор
10. **painting** — картина

Write the missing letters!

1. _of_ _e t_ _ l_
2. a_ _c_a_r
3. c_ _c_
4. te_e_ _si_n
5. b_ _k_a_e
6. s_ _ _
7. v_ _ _
8. _u_
9. T_ s_a_ _
10. _a_ _t_n_

Have fun with the words!

Unscramble the words

1. table / front / the / is / of / in / coffee

The sofa _____.

2. to / stand / TV / next / the / is

The vase _____.

3. next / the / painting / to / is

The clock _____.

4. the / in / of / sofa / front / isn't

The bookcase _____.

5. of / the / in / rug / front / isn't

The painting _____.

6. isn't / TV / the / stand / to / next

The armchair _____.

7. in / table / of / coffee / the / is / front

The television _____.

8. next / the / isn't / vase / to

The rug _____.

Learn the sentences

Where is the <u>coffee table</u>?

The coffee table is in front of the <u>TV stand</u>.

It isn't next to the <u>sofa</u>.

Write the missing words!

Where _____ the _____ stand?

The TV _____ is _____ to the _____.

It _____ in front _____ the _____.

_____ is _____ _____ table?

The coffee _____ is in _____ of the _____.

It _____ next _____ _____ _____.

Where _____ _____ _____?

The painting _____ _____ to _____ _____.

It _____ in _____ _____ the _____.

_____?
_____.
_____.

Learn the sentences

Is the <u>sofa</u> next to the <u>armchair</u>?

Yes, the sofa is.

No, the sofa isn't.

Write the missing words!

Is the _____ table _____ to _____ _____?

Yes, _____ coffee _____ _____.

_____, the _____ _____ isn't.

_____ the painting in _____ of the _____?

Yes, _____ _____ is.

No, _____ painting _____.

Is _____ TV _____ next _____ the _____?

Yes, _____ _____ stand _____.

_____, _____ TV _____ _____.

_____?

_____.

_____.

Learn the phonics

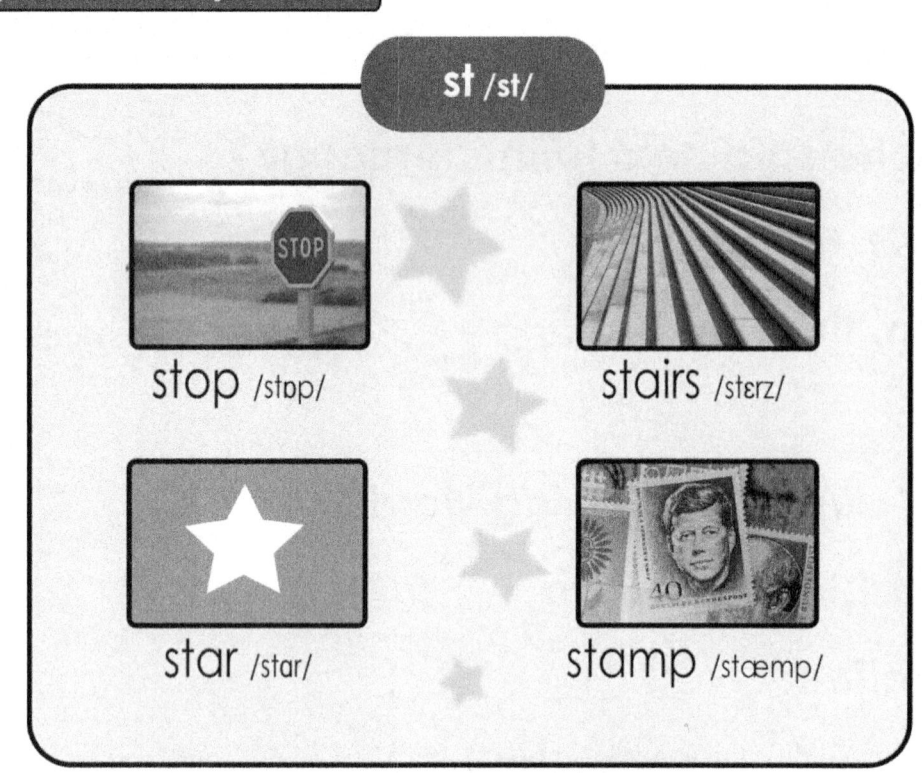

st /st/

stop /stɑp/

stairs /stɛrz/

star /stɑr/

stamp /stæmp/

More words

stool

store

storm

sting

stove

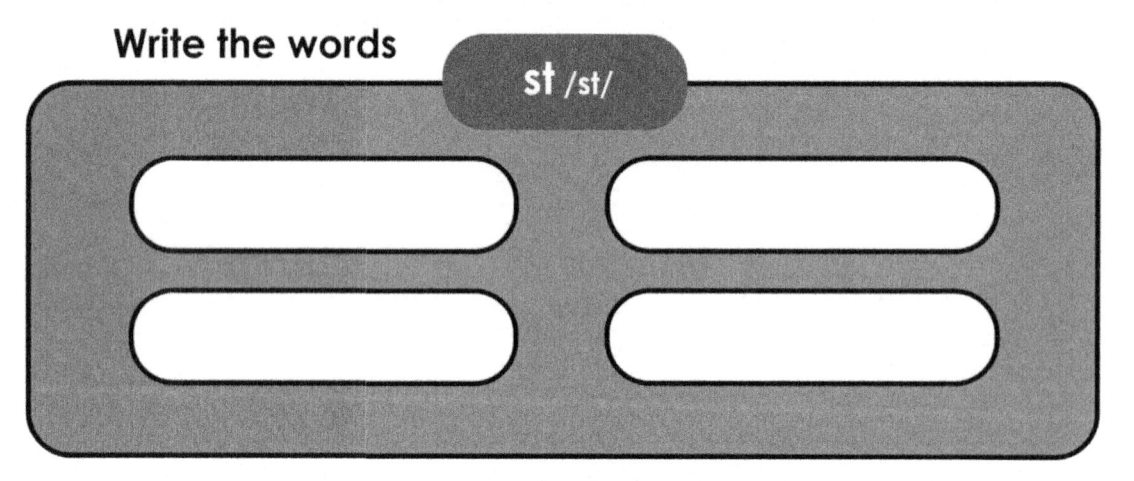

Write the words

st /st/

Write the letters & Read the sentences!

There is a _ _ar on this _ _amp.

_ _op at this _ _ore and buy a new _ _ove.

Put a _ _ool in front of the _ _airs.

- 124 -

Test

Complete the words

1. c_____k
2. a_____r
3. b_____e
4. s_____a
5. t_____n
6. p_____g

Write the answer next to the letter "A"

A: ___ 7. Where is the clock?

a. The clock is next of the bookcase.
b. The clock is next to the bookcase.
c. The clock is front of the bookcase.

A: ___ 8. The vase is in ___ the sofa.

a. front to
b. next to
c. front of

A: ___ 9. Is the television next to the coffee table?

a. Yes, the coffee table is.
b. Yes, television is.
c. No, the television isn't.

A: ___ 10. Is ___ in front of the rug?

a. the armchair
b. these armchair
c. armchair

Answers on Page 306

Lesson 21

- Learn the words
- Learn the sentences
- Learn the phonics
- Test yourself!

Chores

хатня робота

Learn the words

1. **take out the trash**
виносити сміття

2. **wash the dishes**
мити посуд

3. **feed the pets**
годувати домашніх тварин

4. **vacuum the carpet**
пилососити килим

5. **clean the bedroom**
прибирати в спальні

6. **iron the clothes**
прасувати одяг

7. **mop the floor**
мити підлогу

8. **cook dinner**
готувати обід

9. **do the laundry**
прати

10. **make the beds**
заправляти постіль

Write the missing letters!

1. ta_e o_t th_ t_a_h
2. w_ _h t_e di_h_s
3. _ _ed _he pe_ _
4. v_cu_m t_e c_r_e_
5. cl_ _n th_ b_ _r_om

6. i_o_ t_e c_ot_e_
7. m_p _he f_oo_
8. c_o_ d_n_e_
9. d_ t_e l_u_d_y
10. m_ _e _he b_ _s

Have fun with the words!

do • ———————————— • the beds

clean • ———————————— • the laundry

make • • the floor

iron • • the bedroom

mop • • dinner

cook • • the dishes

take out • • the clothes

wash • • the trash

Write the 2 missing chores!

1. _____

2. _____

Which chores do you have to do?

_____

Learn the sentences

Which chores do you have to do today?
Today, I have to <u>wash the dishes</u>.
I don't have to <u>clean the bedroom</u> today.

Write the missing words!

Which _____ do you _____ to _____ today?

Today, I have _____ take _____ the _____.

I _____ have to _____ the dishes _____.

Which chores _____ he have _____ do today?

_____, he has _____ feed the _____.

He doesn't _____ to _____ the clothes today.

_____ chores does _____ have _____ do _____?

Today, she _____ to do _____ _____.

She _____ have _____ _____ dinner _____.

_____?
_____.
_____.

Learn the sentences

Do you have to <u>mop the floor</u> today?

Yes, I have to mop the floor.

No, I have to <u>take out the trash</u>.

Write the missing words!

Do you _____ to _____ the carpet _____?

Yes, _____ have _____ vacuum the _____.

_____, I _____ to _____ _____ pets.

Does _____ have _____ clean the _____ today?

_____, she has to _____ _____ bedroom.

No, _____ _____ to _____ the clothes.

_____ he _____ to _____ the beds _____?

Yes, _____ has _____ make _____ _____.

_____, he _____ to _____ _____ dishes.

_____?

_____.

_____.

Learn the phonics

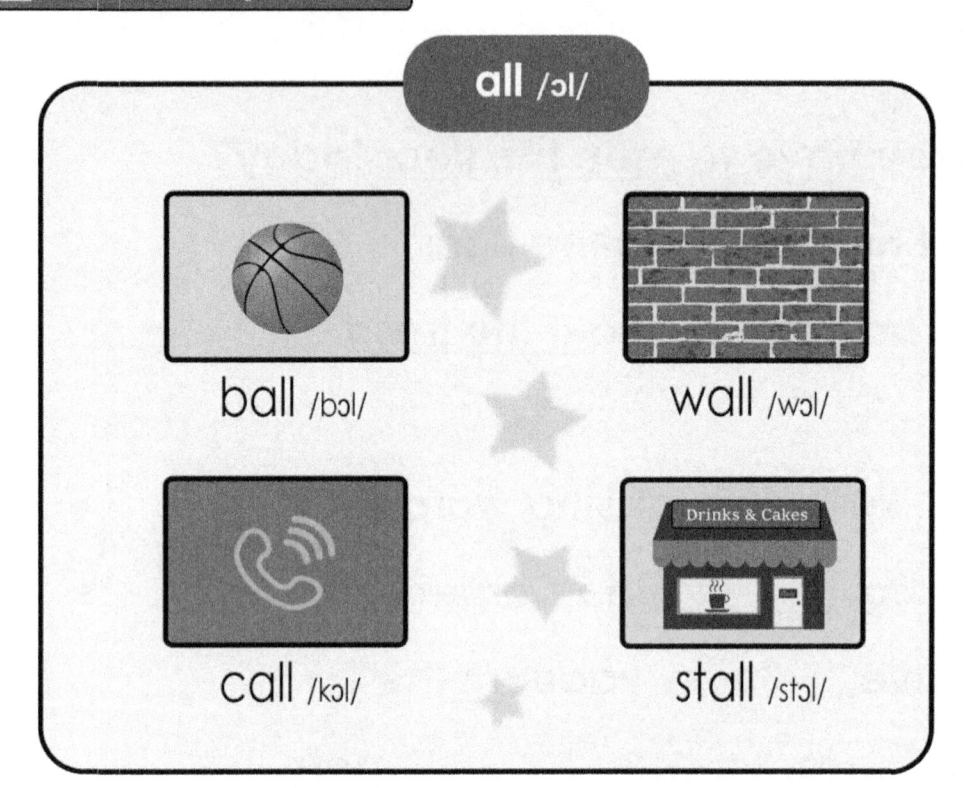

all /ɔl/

ball /bɔl/

wall /wɔl/

call /kɔl/

stall /stɔl/

More words

all

small

mall

tall

fall

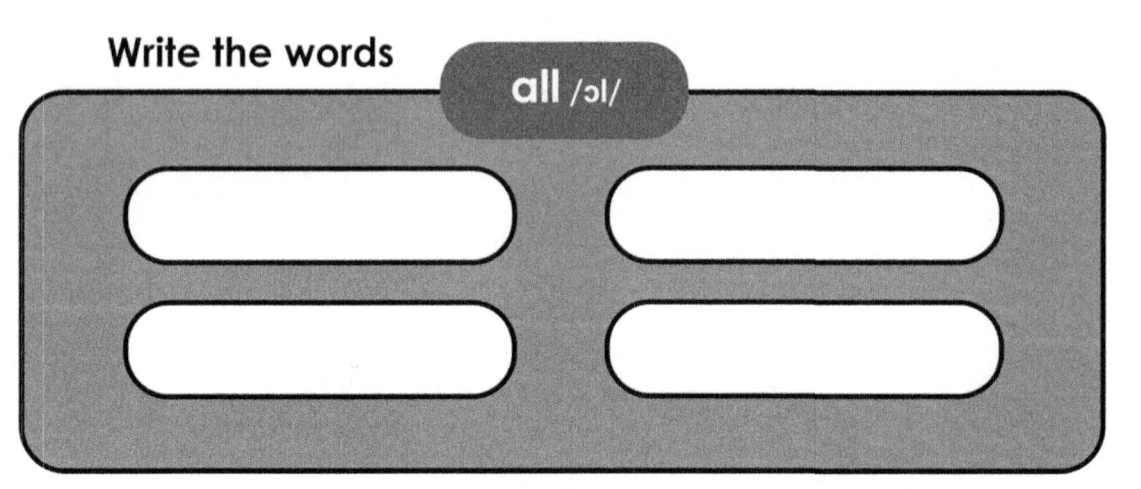

Write the words

all /ɔl/

Write the letters & Read the sentences!

This b_ _ _ is too sm_ _ _.

There is a st_ _ _ in the m_ _ _.

The t_ _ _ man will c_ _ _ you.

- 130 -

Test

Complete the words

1. l_____y 3. c_____s 5. b_____m

2. c_____t 4. f_____r 6. d_____r

Write the answer next to the letter "A"

A: ___ 7. Which chores ___ you have to ___ today?

a. do, do
b. does
c. is

A: ___ 8. She ___ make the beds. She ___ to mop the floor.

a. has to, doesn't has
b. have to, doesn't have
c. has to, doesn't have

A: ___ 9. Does he have to vacuum the carpet today?

a. Yes, he have to vacuum the carpet.
b. No, he has to vacuum the dishes.
c. No, he has to do the laundry.

A: ___ 10. Does ___ have to feed the pets today?

a. you
b. she
c. they

Answers on Page 306

Lesson 22

- Learn the words
- Learn the sentences
- Learn the phonics
- Test yourself!

Pets

домашні тварини

Learn the words

1. **rabbit** — кролик
2. **cat** — кіт
3. **dog** — собака
4. **guinea pig** — морська свинка
5. **bird** — пташка
6. **fish** — рибка
7. **turtle** — черепаха
8. **mouse** — мишка
9. **hamster** — хом'як
10. **snake** — змія

Write the missing letters!

1. r_ _b_t
2. _a_
3. d_ _
4. g_i_e_ p_ _
5. b_ _d
6. f_s_
7. t_r_l_
8. m_u_e
9. ha_s_ _r
10. s_ _ke

Have fun with the words!

r
a
b
b
i
t

hamster
snake
mouse
cat
guinea pig
dog
turtle
fish
rabbit
bird

Write the missing word:

Learn the sentences

Which pet would you like to get?

I would like to get a <u>hamster</u>.

I wouldn't like to get a <u>snake</u>.

Write the missing words!

Which _____ would you _____ to get?

I _____ like to _____ a _____ .

I wouldn't _____ _____ get _____ fish.

Which pet _____ she like _____ _____ ?

_____ would _____ to _____ a turtle.

She _____ like _____ a _____ .

_____ _____ would they _____ to _____ ?

They _____ like _____ get _____ _____ pig.

_____ wouldn't _____ to _____ a _____ .

_____ ?

_____ .

_____ .

Learn the sentences

Would you like to get a <u>dog</u>?

Yes, I would like to get a dog.

No, I would like to get a <u>cat</u>.

Write the missing words!

Would you _____ to get _____ fish?

Yes, I _____ like to get a _____ .

No, _____ would _____ to _____ a _____ .

Would they _____ to get a _____ ?

Yes, _____ would like _____ get _____ rabbit.

_____ , they _____ to get a _____ .

Would _____ like _____ get a _____ ?

_____ , he would like _____ _____ a _____ .

No, he _____ _____ _____ get _____ bird.

_____?

_____.

_____.

Learn the phonics

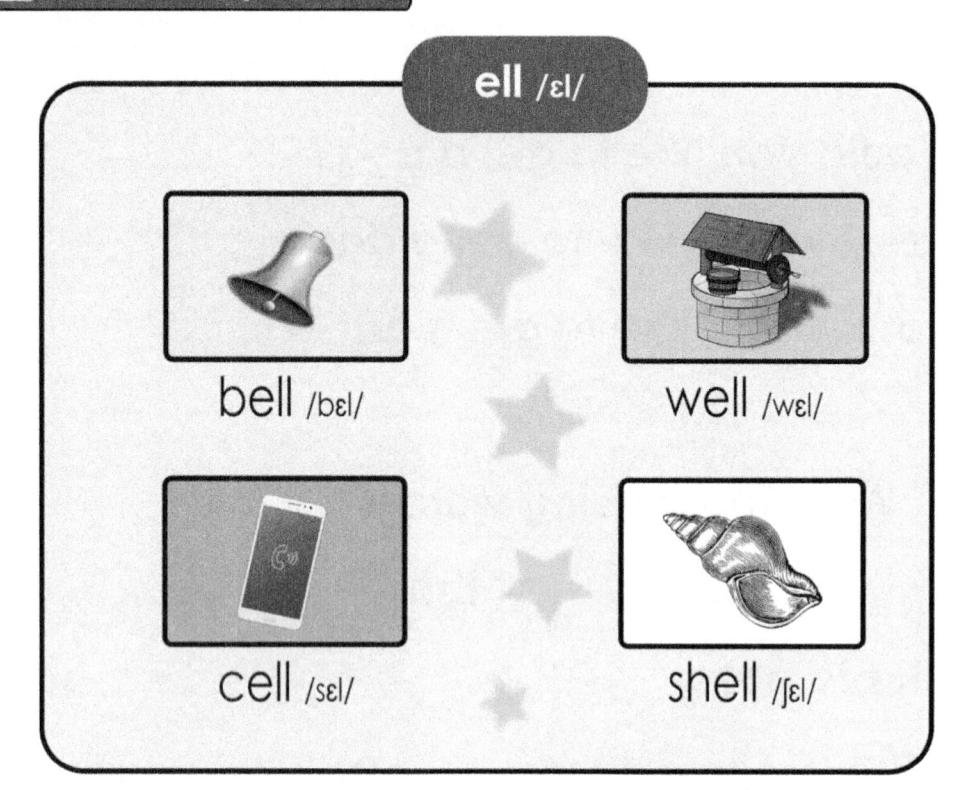

ell /ɛl/

bell /bɛl/

well /wɛl/

cell /sɛl/

shell /ʃɛl/

More words
tell
smell
fell
yell
sell

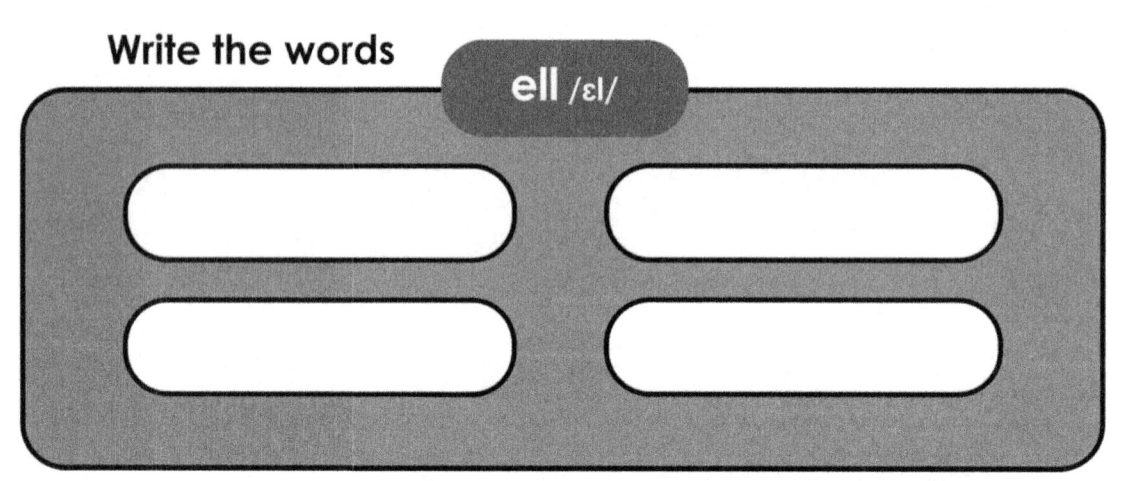

Write the words

ell /ɛl/

Write the letters & Read the sentences!

This sh_ _ _ sm_ _ _s like the beach.

T_ _ _ me why he is y_ _ _ing.

The b_ _ _ f_ _ _ down the w_ _ _.

Test

Complete the words

1. r_____t 3. s_____e 5. t_____e

2. h_____r 4. m_____e 6. b_____d

Write the answer next to the letter "A"

A: ___ **7.** Which pet would you like to get?

a. I would like to get a turtle.
b. I will like to get a hamster.
c. I will like a cat.

A: ___ **8.** She would like ___ a mouse. She ___ like to get a snake.

a. get, wouldnt'
b. to get, wouldn't
c. to get, would'nt

A: ___ **9.** Would he like to get a guinea pig?

a. No, he would like to get a guinea pig.
b. No, he wouldn't like to get a rabbit.
c. No, he would like to get a rabbit.

A: ___ **10.** Would she ___ a fish?

a. likes to get
b. like get to
c. like to get

Answers on Page 306

Lesson 23

- Learn the words
- Learn the sentences
- Learn the phonics
- Test yourself!

Skills

навички

Learn the words

1. **swim**
   плавати
2. **ski**
   кататися на лижах
3. **sing**
   співати
4. **draw**
   малювати
5. **read**
   читати
6. **cook**
   готувати
7. **surf**
   займатися серфінгом
8. **ride**
   їхати
9. **write**
   писати
10. **run**
    бігати

Write the missing letters!

1. s_i_
2. _k_
3. si_ _
4. d_ _w
5. r_ _d
6. _o_k
7. s_ _f
8. r_d_
9. _ri_e
10. r_ _

Have fun with the words!

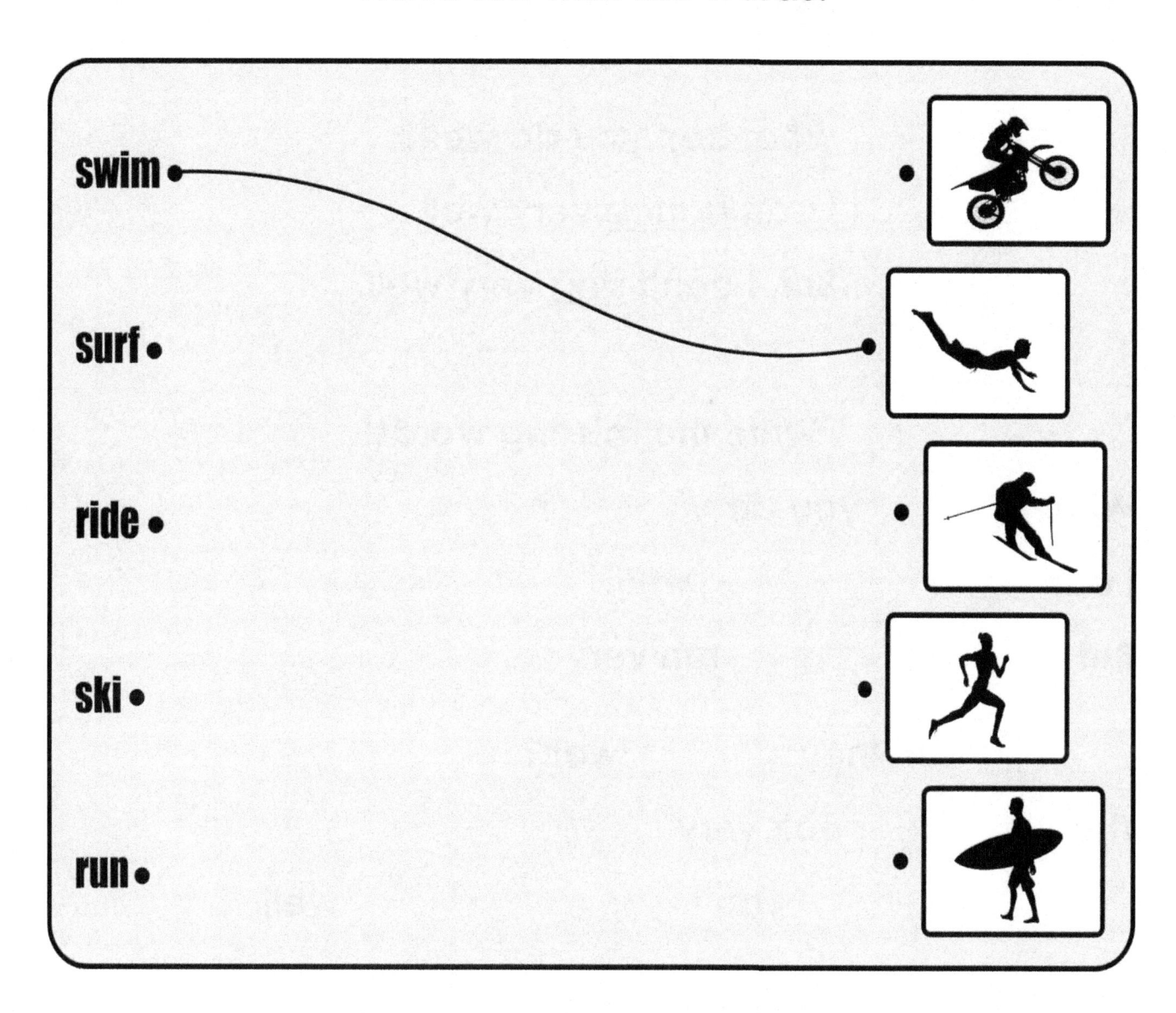

swim

surf

ride

ski

run

Write 4 more skills!

1. _____   3. _____

2. _____   4. _____

What can you do well?

_____

Learn the sentences

What can you do well?

I can <u>dance</u> very well.

But, I can't <u>sing</u> very well.

Write the missing words!

What _____ you do _____?

I can _____ _____ well.

But, _____ _____ run very _____.

_____ can they _____ well?

They _____ cook very _____.

_____, _____ can't _____ _____ well.

What _____ _____ do _____?

He _____ _____ _____ _____.

_____, he _____ _____ very _____.

_____?

_____.

_____.

Learn the sentences

Can you <u>surf</u> well?

Yes, I can surf very well.

No, but I can <u>ski</u> very well.

Write the missing words!

Can _____ write _____?

Yes, _____ can _____ very _____.

No, _____ I _____ read _____ well.

_____ she _____ well?

_____, she can draw _____ well.

No, _____ can _____ very _____.

_____ you _____ _____?

Yes, we _____ swim _____ well.

_____, but _____ can _____ very _____.

_____?
_____.
_____.

Learn the phonics

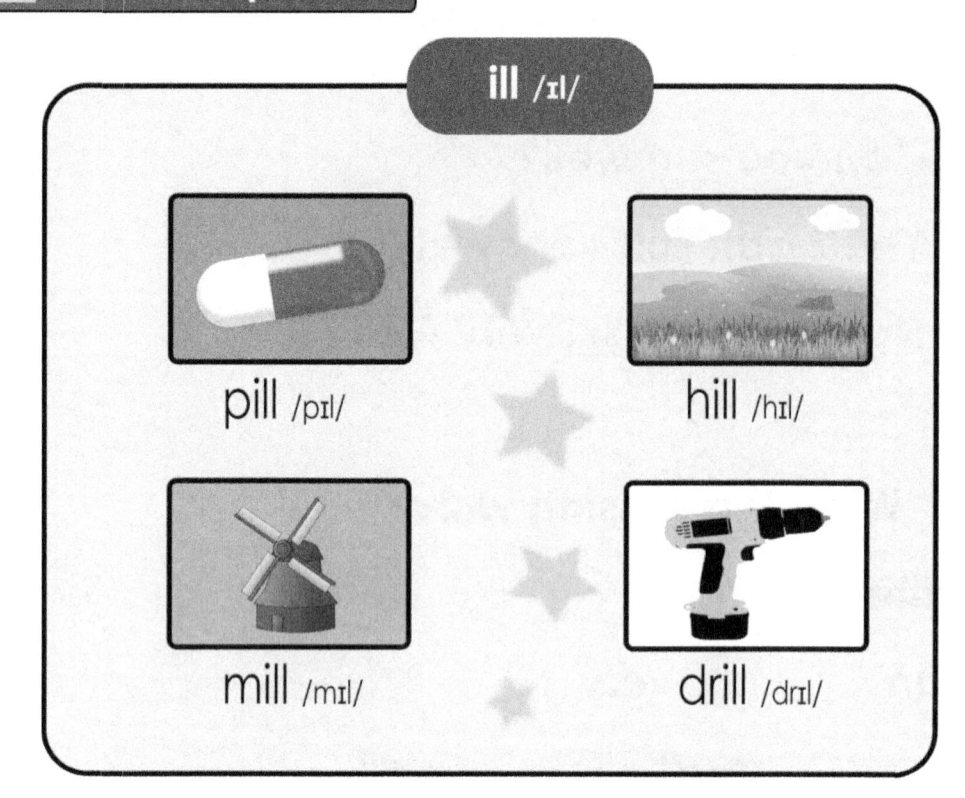

ill /ɪl/

pill /pɪl/

hill /hɪl/

mill /mɪl/

drill /drɪl/

More words

will

still

fill

grill

spill

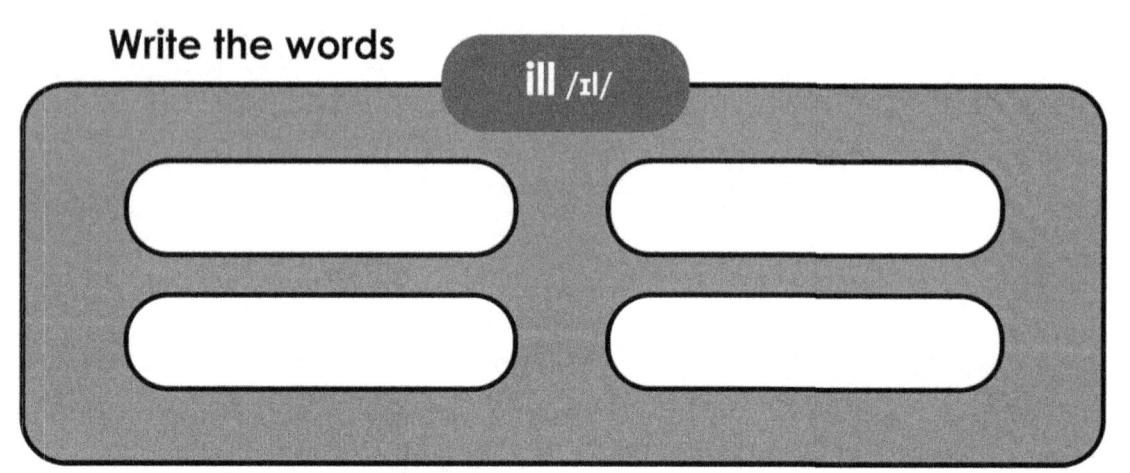

Write the words

ill /ɪl/

Write the letters & Read the sentences!

The beef is st_ _ _ on the gr_ _ _.

There is a m_ _ _ on the h_ _ _.

I w_ _ _ use my dr_ _ _ to fix the m_ _ _.

Test

Complete the words

1. s____m   3. r____d   5. w____e

2. s____g   4. c____k   6. d____w

Write the answer next to the letter "A"

A: ___ 7. What can you do ___?

a. goodly
b. good
c. well

A: ___ 8. He ___ very well. But, he ___ very well.

a. can swims, can't surfs
b. can swim, can't surf
c. can swim, can surf

A: ___ 9. Can she write well?

a. Yes, she can write very well.
b. Yes, she can writes very well.
c. No, but she can read very good.

A: ___ 10. Can he ___ well?

a. sings
b. draw
c. wrote

Answers on Page 306

Lesson 24

- Learn the words
- Learn the sentences
- Learn the phonics
- Test yourself!

Meats

м'ясо

Learn the words

1. **beef**
яловичина

2. **fish**
риба

3. **pork**
свинина

4. **salami**
салямі

5. **bacon**
бекон

6. **chicken**
курятина

7. **sausage**
ковбаса

8. **lamb**
баранина

9. **shrimp**
креветки

10. **ham**
шинка

Write the missing letters!

1. b_ _f

2. _i_h

3. _o_k

4. s_l_ _i

5. b_ _ _n

6. c_ _c_en

7. s_ _sa_e

8. l_m_

9. _h_i_p

10. h_ _

Have fun with the words!

Word Search

```
c d u y f t r r l p i f b a p s a e
x m z o r b t w q f u e w a q o x k
m e c h i c k e n a y r r o j x r s
b m b s s k u u i r l j o u s b c k
x a a l a x u s q h a r g r c i r q
x e c m u f x n a q m j z z s x p j
w b o t s p l v b l b j a y h a m y
o w n q a q n h y e a x d m r r n o
g g l l g c x g d n e m n d i k y z
p a e o e a v v v c c f i k m h y k
d x f h h h r f i s h b d p p p z o
l p h x q v y t n n p f f t x h p g
```

Word directions: → ↘ ↓

beef   **chicken**

fish   **sausage**

pork   **lamb**

salami   **shrimp**

bacon   **ham**

Learn the sentences

What will you be cooking for lunch?

I will be cooking <u>chicken</u> for lunch.

I won't be cooking <u>beef</u>.

Write the missing words!

What _____ you be _____ for _____?
I will _____ cooking pork _____ lunch.
_____ be cooking _____.

_____ will he _____ _____ for lunch?
He _____ be cooking _____ for _____.
_____ won't _____ bacon.

What will _____ _____ cooking _____ _____?
She _____ be _____ shrimp _____ lunch.
She _____ _____ cooking _____.

_____?
_____.
_____.

- 146 -

Learn the sentences

Will you be cooking <u>fish</u> for lunch?

Yes, I will be.

No, I won't be. I'll be cooking <u>sausage</u>.

Write the missing words!

Will you _____ cooking ham _____ lunch?

Yes, _____ will _____.

No, I _____ be. _____ be cooking _____.

_____ she be _____ _____ for _____?

Yes, she _____ _____.

No, _____ won't be. She'll _____ _____ salami.

Will _____ _____ cooking _____ _____ lunch?

_____, he _____ _____.

_____, he _____ be. _____ be _____.

_____?
_____.
_____.

Learn the phonics

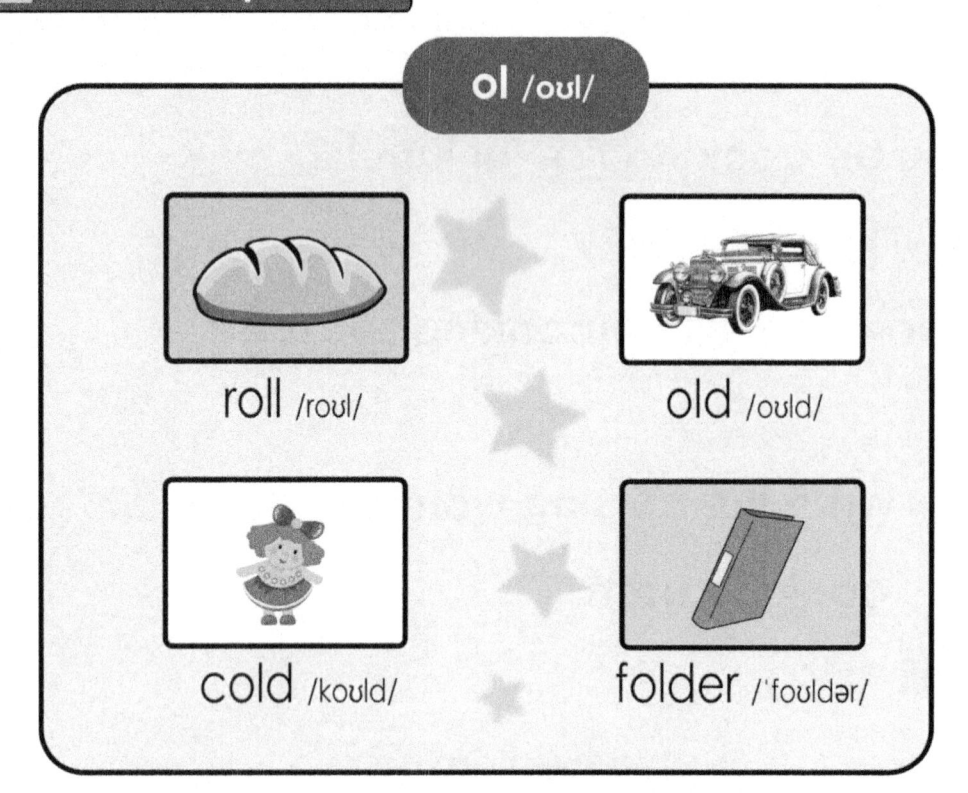

ol /oʊl/

roll /roʊl/

old /oʊld/

cold /koʊld/

folder /ˈfoʊldər/

More words

scroll

sold

told

mold

bold

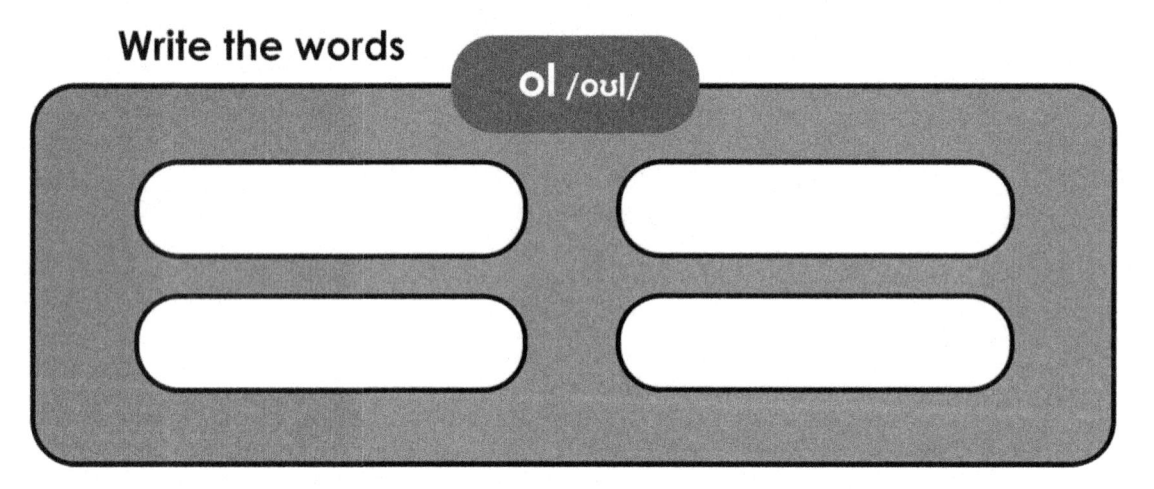

Write the words

ol /oʊl/

Write the letters & Read the sentences!

My father s_ _d the _ _d car.

There is m_ _d on the r_ _l.

I put the scr_ _l in the f_ _der.

- 148 -

Test

Complete the words

1. b_____f   3. s_____i   5. b_____n

2. c_____n   4. s_____p   6. s_____e

Write the answer next to the letter "A"

A: ___ 7. What will he be eating ___ lunch?

a. for
b. of
c. on

A: ___ 8. I ___ eating fish for lunch.

a. will been
b. will be
c. won't

A: ___ 9. Will she be eating beef for lunch?

a. No, she won't be. She'll be eat pork.
b. No, she won't. She'll be eating pork.
c. No, she won't be. She'll be eating pork.

A: ___ 10. Will they ___ ham for lunch?

a. be eat
b. eating
c. be eating

Answers on Page 306

Lesson 25

- Learn the words
- Learn the sentences
- Learn the phonics
- Test yourself!

Countries

країни

Learn the words

1. **Canada** — Канада
2. **Brazil** — Бразилія
3. **Japan** — Японія
4. **Australia** — Австралія
5. **South Africa** — Південна Африка
6. **Mexico** — Мексика
7. **Germany** — Німеччина
8. **China** — Китай
9. **Russia** — Росія
10. **England** — Англія

Write the missing letters!

1. C_ _a_a
2. B_a_ _l
3. _ap_n
4. A_st_a_ _a
5. S_u_h Af_i_ _

6. _ex_c_
7. G_r_a_y
8. C_i_ _
9. R_ _si_
10. _n_la_d

Have fun with the words!

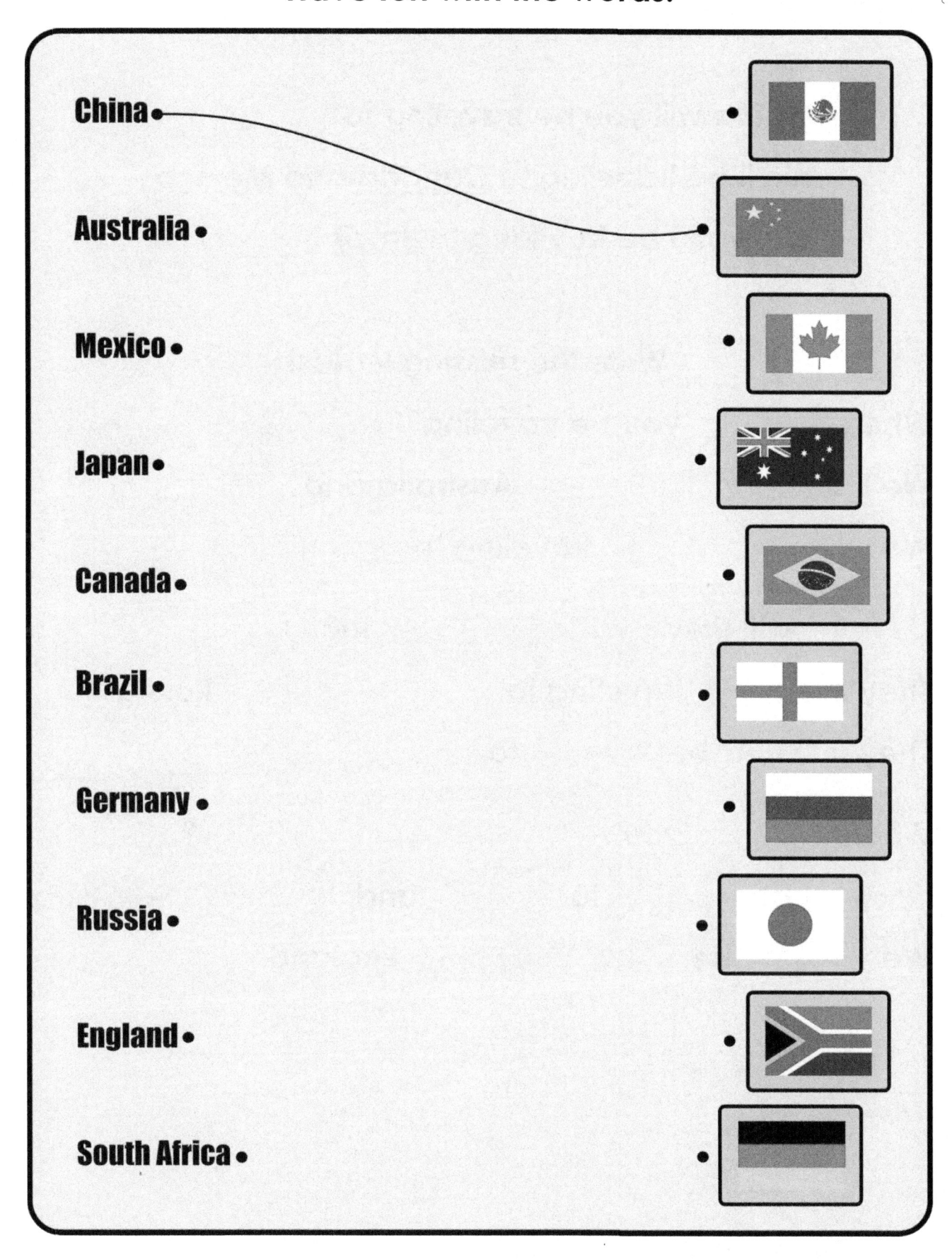

- China
- Australia
- Mexico
- Japan
- Canada
- Brazil
- Germany
- Russia
- England
- South Africa

Learn the sentences

Where will you be traveling to?
We'll be traveling to <u>Canada</u> and <u>Mexico</u>.
We won't be traveling to <u>Brazil</u>.

Write the missing words!

Where _____ you be traveling _____?

We'll be _____ _____ Australia and _____.

We _____ _____ traveling to _____.

_____ will they _____ _____ to?

They'll _____ traveling to _____ _____ Russia.

They _____ be _____ to _____.

Where _____ you _____ _____ _____?

_____ be _____ to _____ and _____.

We _____ be _____ _____ England.

_____?
_____.
_____.

- 152 -

Learn the sentences

Will they be traveling to <u>China</u>?

Yes, they will be.

No, they won't be. They'll be traveling to <u>Japan</u>.

Write the missing words!

Will they _____ traveling _____ South _____?

Yes, _____ will _____.

No, _____ won't be. They'll be _____ to _____.

_____ you be _____ to Russia?

Yes, we _____ _____.

No, _____ won't be. We'll _____ traveling to _____.

Will _____ be traveling to _____?

_____, they _____ _____.

No, they _____ be. _____ be _____ to _____.

_____?
_____.
_____.

Learn the phonics

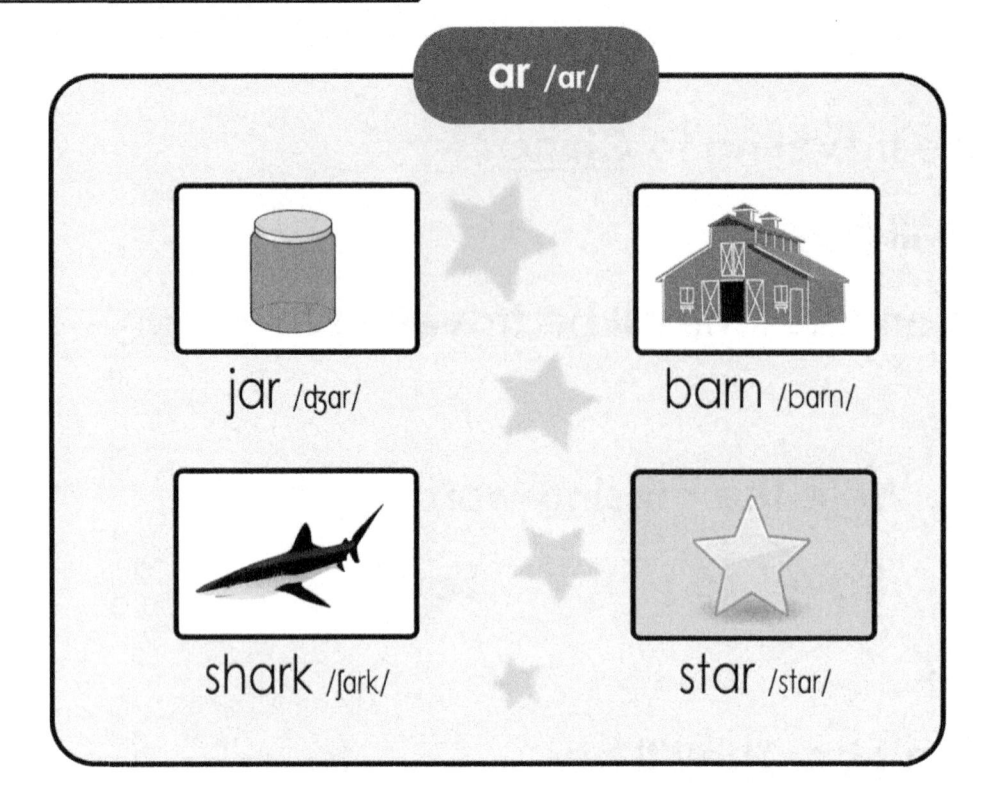

ar /ɑr/

jar /dʒɑr/
barn /bɑrn/
shark /ʃɑrk/
star /stɑr/

More words

dark
park
farm
car
arm

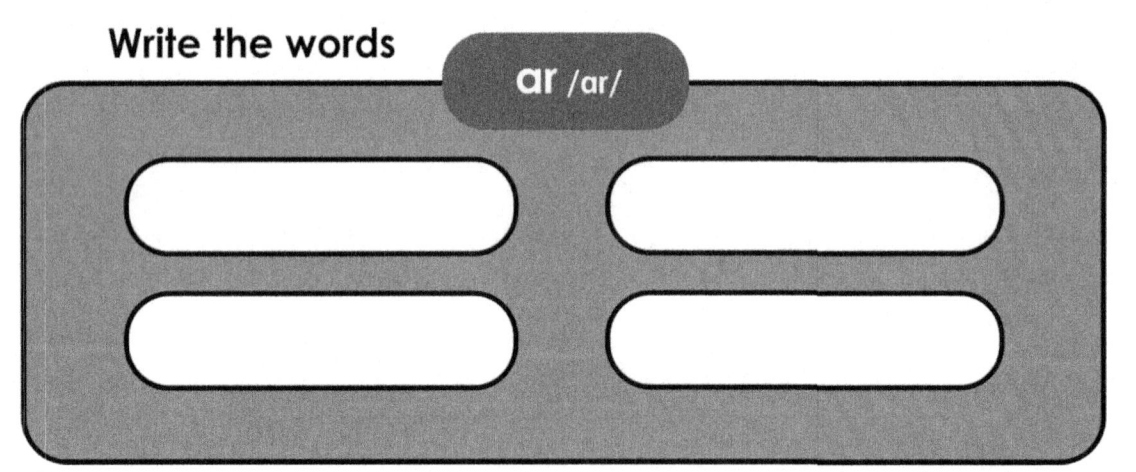

Write the words

ar /ɑr/

Write the letters & Read the sentences!

There is a b_ _n on the f_ _m.

That st_ _ is f_ _.

I hurt my _ _m at the p_ _k.

Test

Complete the words

1. A_____a   3. M_____o   5. J_____n

2. G_____y   4. E_____d   6. R_____a

Write the answer next to the letter "A"

A: ___ 7. Where will you ___ to?

a. be travel
b. be traveling
c. been traveling

A: ___ 8. ___ traveling to Mexico and Brazil.

a. They'll
b. They're be
c. They'll be

A: ___ 9. Will you be traveling to Canada?

a. No, we won't be. We'll be traveling to England.
b. No, we won't. We'll be travel to England.
c. No, we wont'. We'll be traveling to England.

A: ___ 10. Will they be ___ Japan?

a. traveling
b. traveling to
c. travel to

Answers on Page 306

Lesson 26

- Learn the words
- Learn the sentences
- Learn the phonics
- Test yourself!

Languages

мови

Learn the words

1. **English**
англійська
2. **German**
німецька
3. **Portuguese**
португальська
4. **Japanese**
японська
5. **Vietnamese**
в'єтнамська

6. **Spanish**
іспанська
7. **French**
французька
8. **Chinese**
китайська
9. **Hindi**
хінді
10. **Arabic**
арабська

Write the missing letters!

1. E_g_i_h
2. _er_a_
3. P_ _tu_u_se
4. _ap_n_se
5. Vi_t_ _me_e

6. S_a_i_h
7. F_en_ _
8. _h_ne_e
9. H_n_ _
10. A_a_i_

- 156 -

Have fun with the words!

➢ **Write the words in your language!**

Vietnamese	
German	
Japanese	
Spanish	
English	
Arabic	
Hindi	
Portuguese	
Chinese	
French	

Unscramble the letters!

1. HECNISE _____

2. HSASNIP _____

3. IATEVNEMES _____

4. EAPNEJAS _____

5. GORETUPUES _____

Learn the sentences

What language do people speak in <u>Germany</u>?

They speak German in Germany.

They don't speak <u>Spanish</u> in Germany.

Write the missing words!

What _____ do _____ speak _____ Vietnam?

They speak _____ in _____ .

They _____ speak _____ in Vietnam.

What language _____ people _____ _____ Mexico?

_____ speak Spanish _____ Mexico.

They don't _____ _____ in _____ .

_____ language _____ people _____ in _____ ?

_____ speak _____ _____ Japan.

They _____ speak _____ in _____ .

_____ ?

_____ .

_____ .

Learn the sentences

Do people speak <u>English</u> in <u>Australia</u>?

Yes, they do.

Nobody speaks <u>French</u> in Australia.

Write the missing words!

Do people _____ Portuguese _____ Brazil?

_____, they _____.

Nobody speaks _____ in _____.

Do _____ speak _____ in China?

Yes, _____ _____.

_____ Hindi _____ China.

_____ people speak _____ in _____?

_____, _____ do.

Nobody _____ _____ _____ England.

_____?
_____.
_____.

Learn the phonics

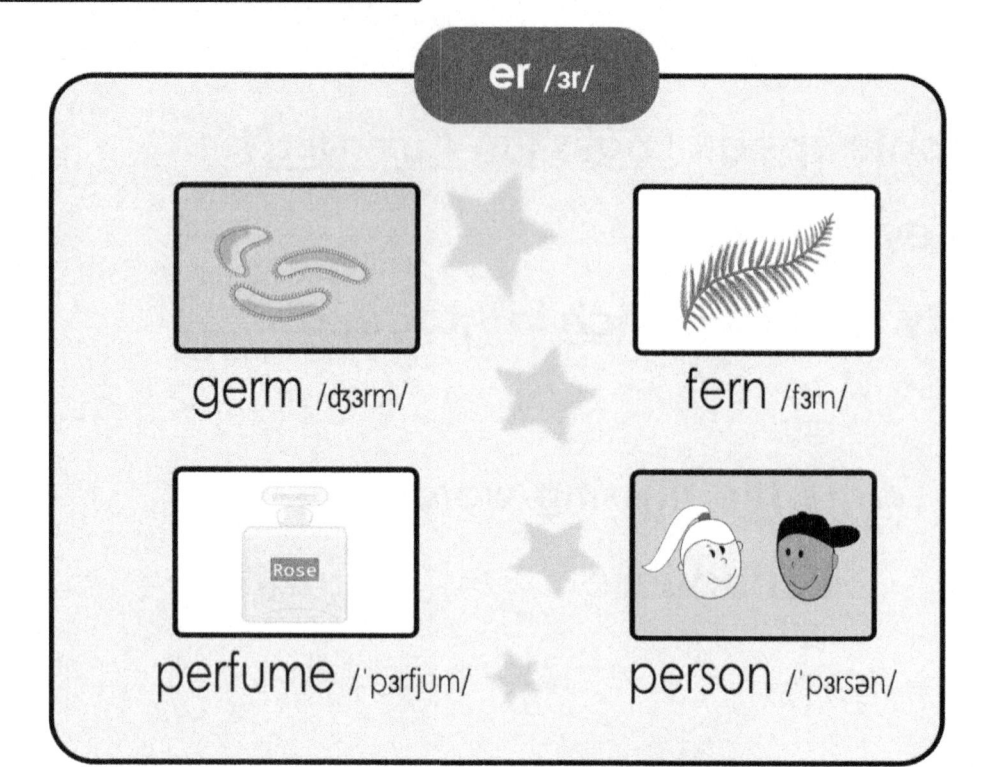

er /ɜr/

germ /dʒɜrm/

fern /fɜrn/

perfume /ˈpɜrfjum/

person /ˈpɜrsən/

More words

serve

mermaid

Germany

herb

her

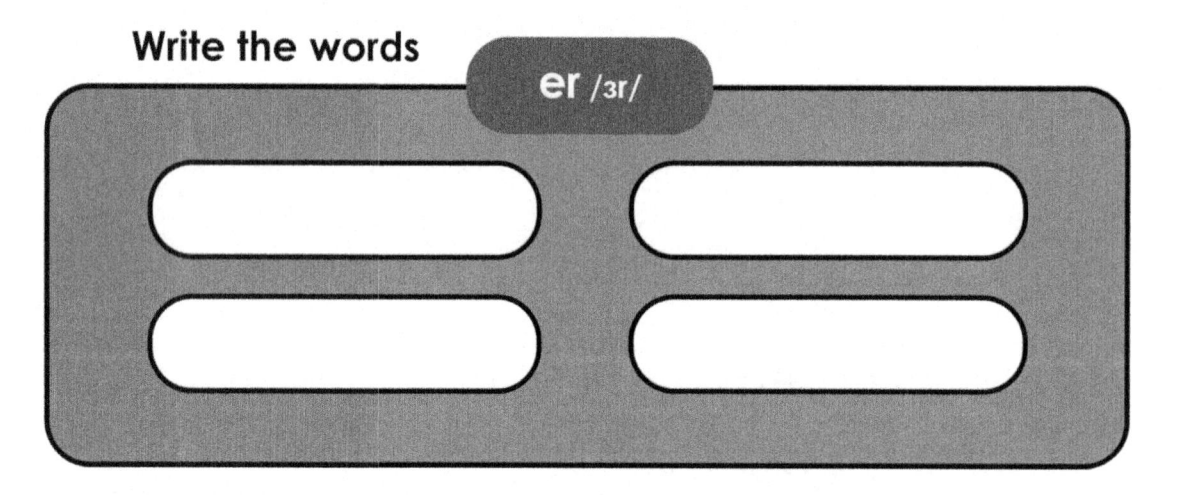

Write the words

er /ɜr/

Write the letters & Read the sentences!

This p_ _fume is h_ _s.

We saw some f_ _ns in G_ _many.

That p_ _son is buying some h_ _bs.

Test

Complete the words

1. P_____e 3. S_____h 5. A_____c

2. V_____e 4. H_____i 6. F_____h

Write the answer next to the letter "A"

A: ___ 7. What language ___ people speak in France?

a. does
b. do
c. is

A: ___ 8. They ___ Japanese in Japan. They ___ Arabic.

a. don't speak, speak
b. speak, dont' speak
c. speak, don't speak

A: ___ 9. Do people speak Portuguese in Brazil?

a. Yes, they did.
b. Yes, I do.
c. Yes, they do.

A: ___ 10. ___ German in Canada.

a. No body speaks
b. Nobody speaks
c. Nobody speak

Answers on Page 306

Lesson 27

- Learn the words
- Learn the sentences
- Learn the phonics
- Test yourself!

In the refrigerator

в холодильнику

Learn the words

1. **milk**
молоко

2. **meat**
м'ясо

3. **bread**
хліб

4. **ice**
лід

5. **water**
вода

6. **cola**
кола

7. **tea**
чай

8. **salad**
салат

9. **juice**
сік

10. **ice cream**
морозиво

Write the missing letters!

1. m_ _k
2. m_a_
3. b_e_ _
4. _c_
5. w_t_ _

6. c_l_
7. _e_
8. _al_d
9. j_ _ _e
10. i_e c_e_m

Have fun with the words!

Unscramble the words

1. need / I / bread / some / buy / to

_____.

2. to / milk / He / buy / any / doesn't / need

_____.

3. buy / this / week / to / Do / any / tea / you / need

_____?

4. ice / don't / to / need / cream / any / I / buy

_____.

5. doesn't / need / cola / any / She / buy / to

_____.

6. at / supermarket / to / need / he / buy / What / the / does

_____?

7. He / some / water / buy / needs / to

_____.

8. to / this / buy / Does / need / any / juice / she / week

_____?

Learn the sentences

What do you need to buy at the supermarket?

I need to buy some <u>milk</u>.

I don't need to buy any <u>cola</u>.

Write the missing words!

What _____ you _____ to buy at the supermarket?

I _____ to buy _____ bread.

I _____ need _____ buy any _____ .

What does he need _____ buy _____ the _____ ?

_____ needs to _____ some _____ .

He doesn't need _____ buy _____ pizza.

What _____ she _____ to _____ at the _____ ?

She _____ to _____ some _____ .

_____ _____ need _____ buy any _____ .

_____ ?

_____ .

_____ .

- 164 -

Learn the sentences

Do you need to buy any <u>salad</u> this week?

Yes, I need to buy some salad.

No, there's salad in the refrigerator.

Write the missing words!

Do you _____ to buy any ice _____ this week?

Yes, I _____ to _____ some _____ cream.

No, _____ ice cream in the _____.

Does she need _____ buy any _____ this _____?

_____, she needs to _____ some juice.

No, there's _____ in _____ refrigerator.

_____ he _____ to buy any _____ _____ week?

Yes, he _____ to buy _____ _____.

_____, _____ water _____ the _____.

_____?
_____.
_____.

Learn the phonics

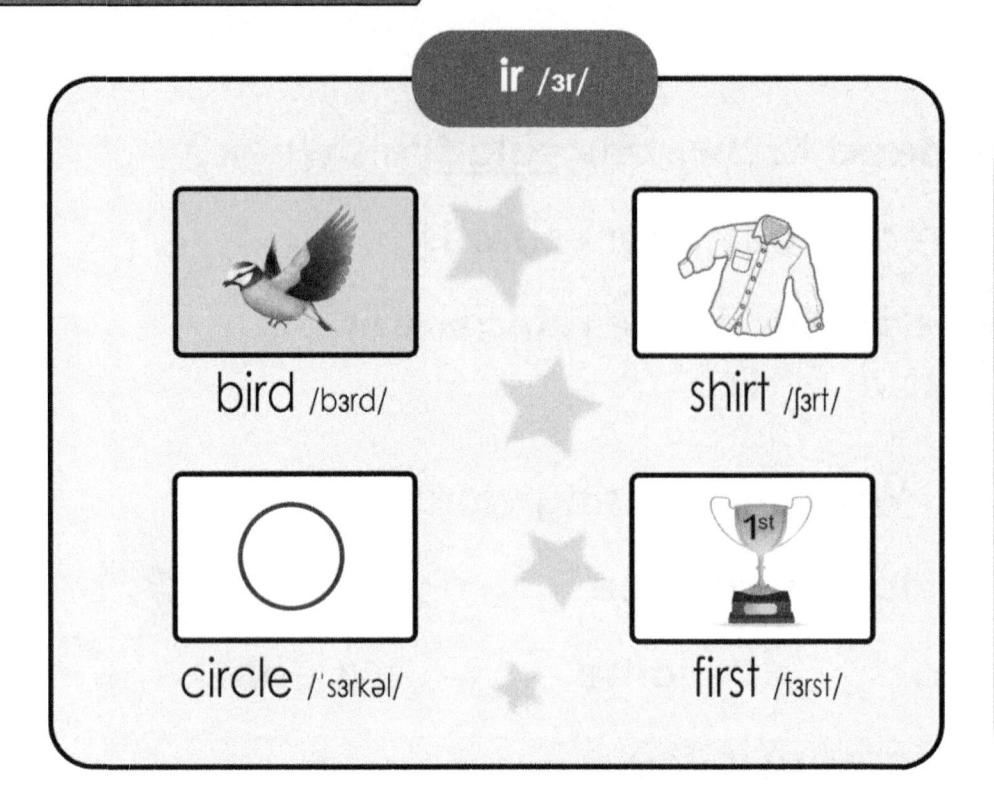

ir /ɜr/

bird /bɜrd/

shirt /ʃɜrt/

circle /'sɜrkəl/

first /fɜrst/

More words

girl

stir

firm

skirt

dirt

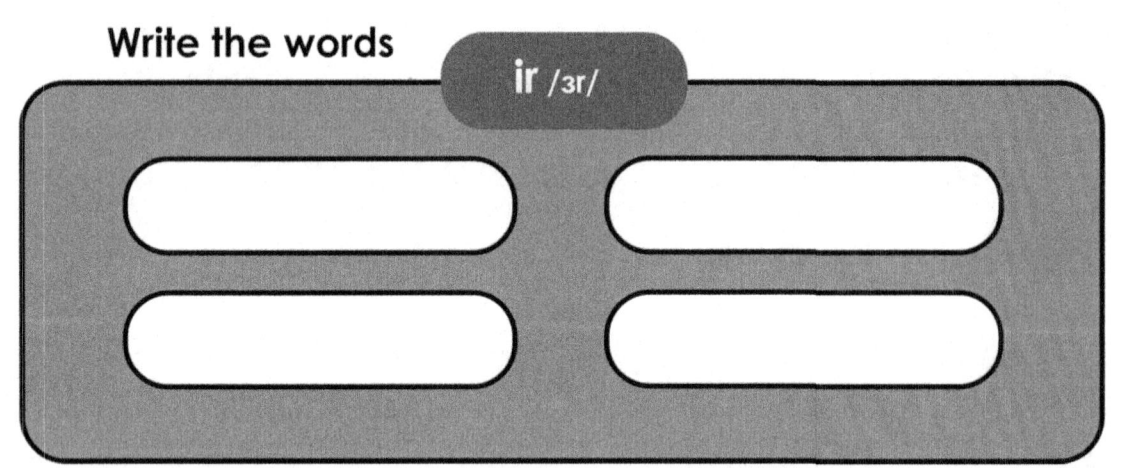

Write the words

ir /ɜr/

Write the letters & Read the sentences!

The g_ _l wore a pink sk_ _t.

There is some d_ _t on your sh_ _t.

We sat in a c_ _cle at my b_ _thday party.

■ Test

Complete the words

1. b_____d   3. s_____d   5. m_____t

2. w_____r   4. j_____e   6. c_____a

Write the answer next to the letter "A"

A: ___ 7. What ___ he ___ to buy at the supermarket?

a. does, needs
b. does, need
c. do, need

A: ___ 8. I ___ to buy any ice.

a. need
b. doesn't need
c. don't need

A: ___ 9. Do you need to buy any meat at the supermarket?

a. No, there's meat in the refrigerator.
b. No, theres meat in the refrigerator.
c. No, there's meat in refrigerator.

A: ___ 10. ___ she need to buy any milk at the supermarket?

a. Is
b. Does
c. Do

Answers on Page 306

Lesson 28

- Learn the words
- Learn the sentences
- Learn the phonics
- Test yourself!

Desserts

десерти

Learn the words

1. **ice cream** — морозиво
2. **apple pie** — яблучний пиріг
3. **cheesecake** — сирний пиріг
4. **pudding** — пудинг
5. **cake** — торт
6. **cupcakes** — кекси
7. **brownies** — шоколадні тістечка
8. **pastries** — тістечка
9. **waffles** — вафлі
10. **cookies** — печиво

Write the missing letters!

1. i_ _ c_e_m
2. _p_le p_ _
3. ch_ _se_a_e
4. p_d_i_g
5. c_k_
6. c_p_a_e_
7. b_o_n_es
8. p_s_ri_s
9. w_f_l_s
10. _o_k_es

Have fun with the words!

Find the 8 desserts!

sausage chicken bedroom Germany
carpet salad Chinese
Hindi cheesecake brownies
cupcakes shrimp floor juice
milk laundry
snake clothes pudding cookies
waffles turtle draw
bacon
run
Japan computer meat
pastries surf
salami cake England
mouse write hamster

Write the 8 shapes

1.
2.
3.
4.
5.
6.
7.
8.

Learn the sentences

What did you have for dessert last night?

We had <u>cheesecake</u> for dessert.

We didn't have <u>brownies</u> for dessert.

Write the missing words!

What did you _____ for dessert _____ night?

We _____ apple _____ for dessert.

_____ didn't _____ ice _____ for _____ .

What _____ he have _____ dessert last _____ ?

_____ had _____ for _____ .

He _____ have _____ dessert.

What _____ they _____ for _____ night?

They _____ _____ for _____ .

_____ didn't _____ waffles _____ _____ .

_____?

_____.

_____.

Learn the sentences

Did you have <u>pudding</u> for dessert last night?

Yes, I did.

No, I didn't. I had <u>cupcakes</u>.

Write the missing words!

Did you have _____ for _____ last _____?

Yes, _____ _____.

_____, I didn't. I _____ cake.

Did she _____ cheesecake for _____ _____ night?

_____, she _____.

No, she _____. _____ had _____.

_____ they have _____ for _____ last _____?

Yes, _____ _____.

No, _____ _____. They _____ ice _____.

_____?
_____.
_____.

Learn the phonics

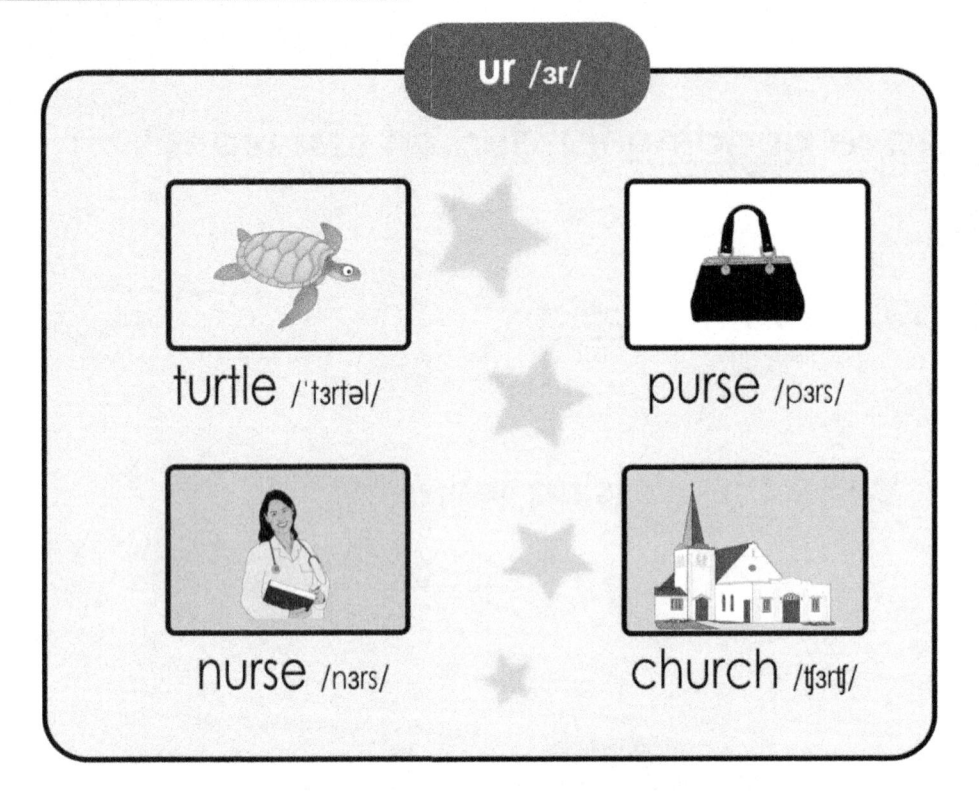

ur /ɜr/

turtle /ˈtɜrtəl/

purse /pɜrs/

nurse /nɜrs/

church /tʃɜrtʃ/

More words

turn

burn

surf

blur

hurt

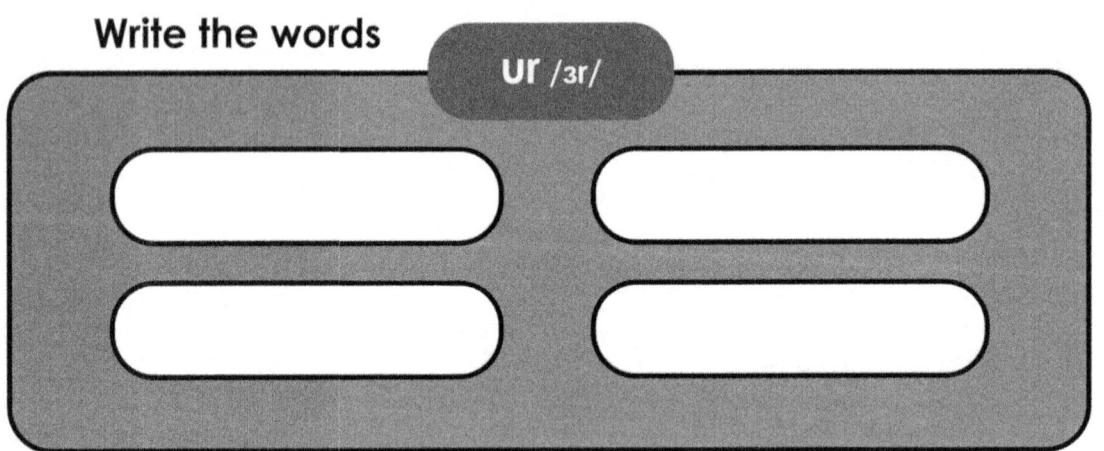

Write the words

ur /ɜr/

Write the letters & Read the sentences!

The n_ _se helped me after I h_ _t my leg.

She forgot her p_ _se at the ch_ _ch.

I saw a t_ _tle while s_ _fing.

Test

Complete the words

1. c_____s 3. a_____e 5. w_____s

2. p_____g 4. b_____s 6. p_____s

Write the answer next to the letter "A"

A: ___ **7.** What ___ you have ___ dessert last night?

a. did, of
b. do, for
c. did, for

A: ___ **8.** She didn't ___ cheesecake for dessert.

a. had
b. has
c. have

A: ___ **9.** Did they have pastries for dessert last night?

a. No, they didn't. They had cookies.
b. No, they did. They had cookies.
c. No, they didn't. They have cookies.

A: ___ **10.** Did they have pudding for dessert last night?

a. Yes, they do.
b. Yes, they did.
c. Yes they did.

Answers on Page 306

Lesson 29

- Learn the words
- Learn the sentences
- Learn the phonics
- Test yourself!

At school

в школі

Learn the words

1. **classroom**
   класна кімната
2. **nurse's office**
   кабінет медсестри
3. **hall**
   вестибюль
4. **gym**
   спортзал
5. **office**
   кабінет
6. **computer lab**
   комп'ютерний клас
7. **music room**
   музичний клас
8. **lunchroom**
   їдальня
9. **science lab**
   наукова лабораторія
10. **art room**
    художній зал

Write the missing letters!

1. c_a_sr_om
2. n_r_e's o_f_ce
3. h_l_
4. _y_
5. of_i_ _
6. c_m_ut_r la_
7. m_ _ic _o_m
8. l_n_hr_o_
9. s_ _en_e l_b
10. a_t r_ _m

- 174 -

Have fun with the words!

Write the 3 missing words

1._____
2._____
3._____

- classroom
- nurse's office
- science lab
- music room
- computer lab
- gym
- art room

1._____
2._____
3._____

- hall
- classroom
- art room
- science lab
- lunchroom
- office
- music room

1._____
2._____
3._____

- office
- hall
- computer lab
- gym
- classroom
- nurse's office
- lunchroom

1._____
2._____
3._____

- science lab
- art room
- gym
- music room
- hall
- lunchroom
- nurse's office

1._____
2._____
3._____

- office
- music room
- nurse's office
- classroom
- lunchroom
- computer lab
- gym

1._____
2._____
3._____

- computer lab
- office
- lunchroom
- hall
- science lab
- classroom
- art room

Learn the sentences

Where were you this morning?
I was in the <u>music room</u> this morning.
I wasn't in the <u>office</u>.

Write the missing words!

Where _____ you this _____ ?
I _____ in the _____ this _____ .
I wasn't in _____ gym.

_____ was she _____ morning?
She _____ _____ the art _____ _____ morning.
_____ wasn't in _____ science _____ .

Where _____ he _____ _____ ?
_____ was _____ the _____ room this _____ .
He _____ in _____ .

_____ ?
_____ .
_____ .

Learn the sentences

Were you in the <u>lunchroom</u> this morning?

Yes, I was.

No, I wasn't. I was in the <u>hall</u>.

Write the missing words!

Were _____ in the computer _____ this _____?

_____, I _____.

No, _____ wasn't. I was _____ the _____ lab.

Was he in _____ classroom _____ morning?

Yes, _____ _____.

_____, he wasn't. He was _____ gym.

_____ she in the _____ room this _____?

Yes, _____ _____.

No, she _____. She _____ in the _____ office.

_____?

_____.

_____.

Learn the phonics

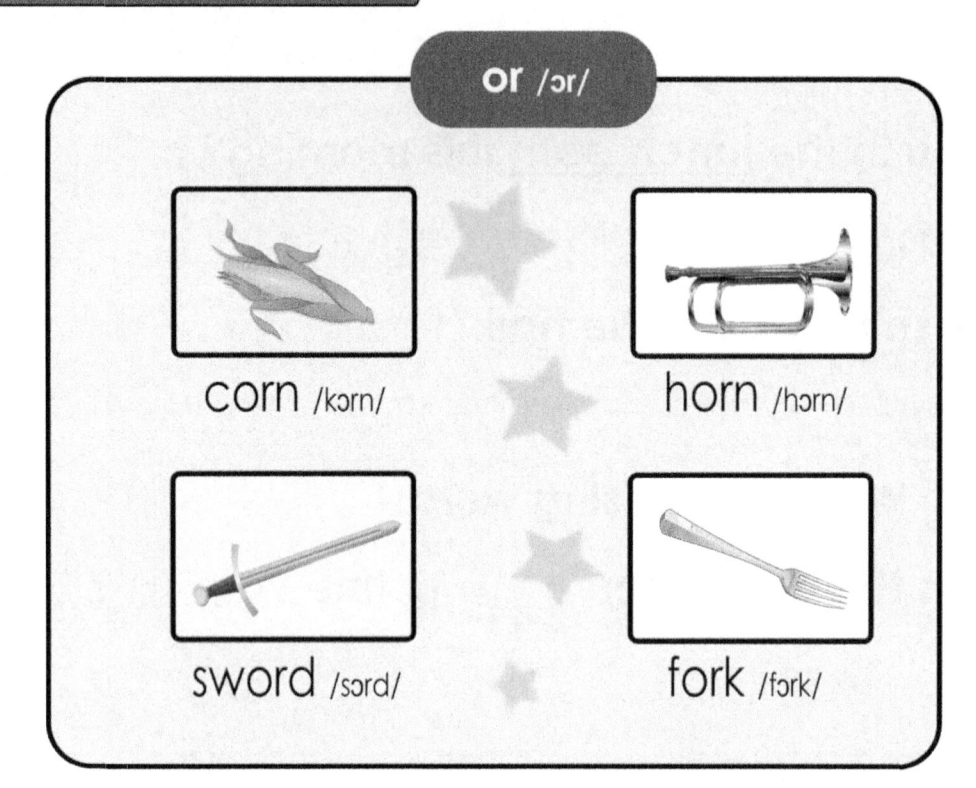

or /ɔr/

corn /kɔrn/

horn /hɔrn/

sword /sɔrd/

fork /fɔrk/

More words

horse

north

born

more

storm

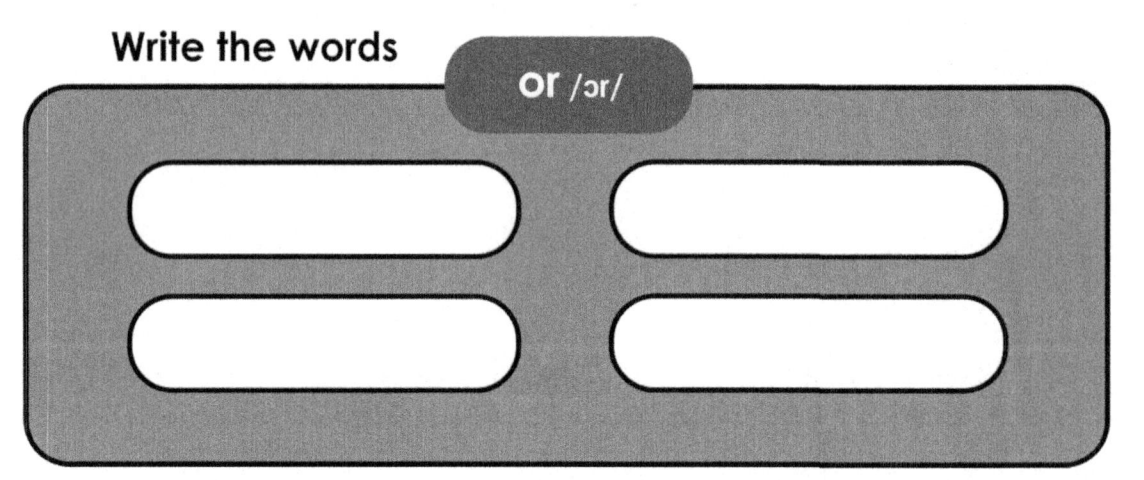

Write the words

or /ɔr/

Write the letters & Read the sentences!

He used a f_ _k to eat the c_ _n.

A st_ _m is coming from the n_ _th.

M_ _e h_ _ses were b_ _n.

Test

Complete the words

1. m_____m   3. c_____b   5. o_____e

2. l_____m   4. n_____e   6. c_____m

Write the answer next to the letter "A"

A: ___ 7. Where ___ you this morning?

a. was
b. were
c. are

A: ___ 8. I ___ the art room this morning.

a. were in
b. was at
c. was in

A: ___ 9. Were you in the science lab this morning?

a. No, I weren't. I was in the gym.
b. No, I wasn't. I was in the gym.
c. No I wasn't. I was in the gym.

A: ___ 10. ___ he in ___ this morning?

a. Was, the hall
b. Were, the hall
c. Was, hall

Answers on Page 306

Lesson 30

- Learn the words
- Learn the sentences
- Learn the phonics
- Test yourself!

Transportation

транспорт

Learn the words

1. **ride a motorcycle**
   їздити на мотоциклі
2. **take an airplane**
   летіти літаком
3. **take the ferry**
   переправлятися на поромі
4. **take a taxi**
   брати таксі
5. **catch a bus**
   сідати на автобус
6. **ride a bike**
   їздити на велосипеді
7. **take the subway**
   їздити на метро
8. **ride a scooter**
   їздити на скутері
9. **drive a car**
   водити машину
10. **take a train**
    їздити потягом

Write the missing letters!

1. r_d_ a mo_o_c_c_e
2. t_ _e a_ a_rpl_n_
3. t_k_ t_e f_r_y
4. _ak_ a t_x_
5. _a_c_ a b_s
6. _i_e a b_k_
7. _ak_ th_ s_b_a_
8. ri_ _ a sc_o_e_
9. d_i_e a _a_
10. _ _ke a tr_ _n

- 180 -

Have fun with the words!

take •	• a car
take • ——————	• a train
ride •	• a bus
ride •	• a motorcycle
catch •	• a taxi
ride •	• the subway
drive •	• a bike
take •	• a scooter

Write the 2 missing transportations!

1. _____

2. _____

Unscramble the letters!

1. tmeoyorclc   _____

2. crosoet   _____

Learn the sentences

How do you go there on <u>Mondays</u>?

I always <u>catch a bus</u> on Mondays.

I never <u>take the train</u>.

Write the missing words!

How _____ you go _____ on Mondays?

I always _____ the subway on _____ .

I _____ drive a _____ .

How does _____ go there _____ Tuesdays?

He _____ rides _____ motorcycle on _____ .

He never rides a _____ .

How _____ she _____ there _____ _____ ?

She _____ _____ the ferry _____ Wednesdays.

She _____ an _____ .

_____?
_____.
_____.

Learn the sentences

Does he <u>ride a scooter</u> there on <u>Sundays</u>?

Yes, he always does.

No, he never does. He always <u>rides a bike</u>.

Write the missing words!

Does _____ catch _____ bus _____ on Thursdays?
Yes, she always _____ .
No, she _____ does. She always _____ a train.

Do _____ ride a _____ there on Fridays?
Yes, I _____ _____ .
_____ , I never do. I _____ take a _____ .

Do _____ _____ a scooter there _____ Saturdays?
_____ , they _____ _____ .
No, they _____ do. They _____ take _____ subway.

_____?
_____.
_____.

Learn the phonics

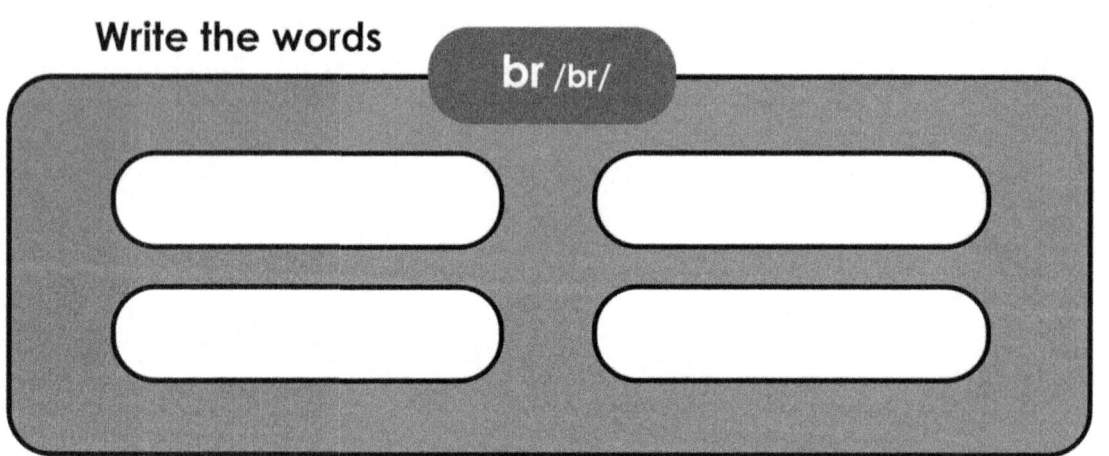

br /br/

broom /brum/

bread /brɛd/

bridge /brɪdʒ/

brick /brɪk/

More words

brain

bring

break

brown

bright

Write the words

br /br/

Write the letters & Read the sentences!

The _ _idge is made with _ _icks.

_ _ad likes to eat _ _own _ _ead.

I can _ _ing a _ _oom.

Test

Complete the words

1. f_____y   3. s_____y   5. t_____n

2. a_____e   4. m_____e   6. s_____r

Write the answer next to the letter "A"

A: ___ **7.** How do you go there on Sundays?

a. I always catch a bus at Sundays.
b. I alway ride a scooter on Sundays.
c. I always take the subway on Sundays.

A: ___ **8.** He never ___ a motorcycle.

a. riding
b. rides
c. ride

A: ___ **9.** Does she take the subway on Fridays?

a. Yes, she never does.
b. Yes, she always does.
c. Yes, she always dose.

A: ___ **10.** Do you ___ there on Mondays?

a. take a taxi
b. drive a motorcycle
c. take a airplane

Answers on Page 306

Lesson 31

- Learn the words
- Learn the sentences
- Learn the phonics
- Test yourself!

Fast food

фастфуд

Learn the words

1. **a cheeseburger**
Чізбургер

2. **onion rings**
цибулеві кільця

3. **fried chicken**
смажена курка

4. **chicken nuggets**
курячі нагетси

5. **french fries**
картопля фрі

6. **a taco**
тако

7. **a burrito**
буріто

8. **a pancake**
млинець

9. **a doughnut**
пончик

10. **a hot dog**
хот дог

Write the missing letters!

1. a c_ee_eb_r_e_

2. o_i_n r_n_s

3. _r__d c_ic_e_

4. ch_c__ n n_g_e_s

5. f_e_c_ f_i_s

6. a t_ _ _

7. a b_r_i_o

8. a p_n_a_ _

9. a d_u_h_ut

10. a h_t d_ _

- 186 -

Have fun with the words!

- taco
- french fries
- doughnut
- cheeseburger
- pancake

Write 4 more fast foods!

1. _____
2. _____
3. _____
4. _____

What were you eating?

_____

Learn the sentences

What were you eating <u>two</u> days ago?

I was eating <u>a cheeseburger</u>.

I wasn't eating <u>a pancake</u>.

Write the missing words!

What _____ you eating three _____ ago?

I was _____ _____ doughnut.

I _____ eating chicken _____.

_____ were you _____ four days _____?

I _____ _____ fried _____.

_____ wasn't _____ _____ taco.

What _____ _____ eating _____ days _____?

I _____ _____ _____ hot _____.

_____ _____ _____ onion _____.

_____?

_____.

_____.

Learn the sentences

Were you eating <u>a burrito</u> <u>four</u> days ago?

Yes, I was.

No, I wasn't. I was eating <u>chicken nuggets</u>.

Write the missing words!

Were you _____ a taco _____ days _____?

Yes, I _____.

No, _____ wasn't. I _____ eating _____ fries.

_____ you _____ a pancake seven _____ ago?

Yes, _____ was.

No, I _____. I _____ a _____ dog.

_____ you _____ rings _____ days ago?

Yes, _____ _____.

_____, I _____. I _____ _____ fried _____.

_____?
_____.
_____.

Learn the phonics

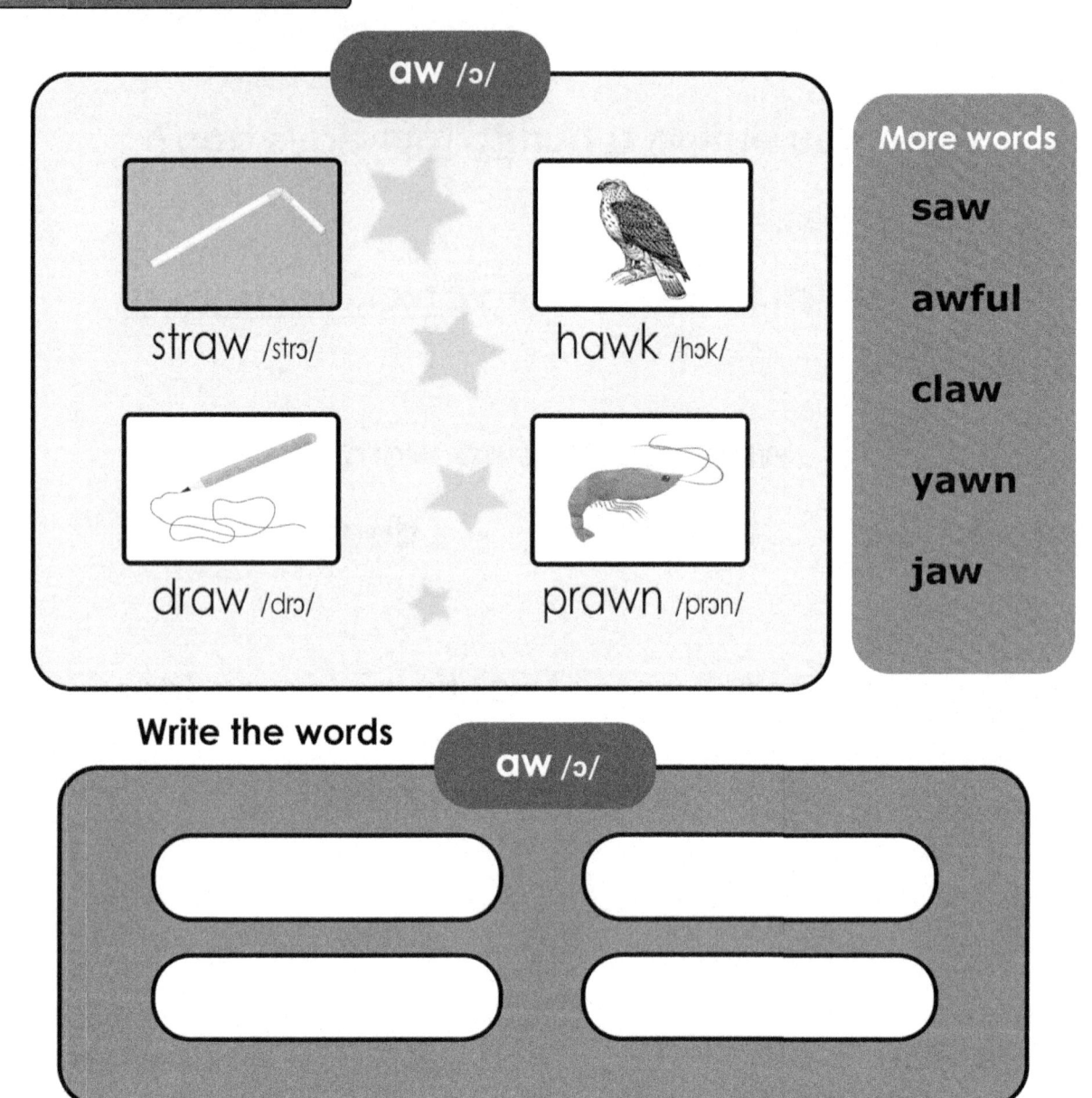

aw /ɔ/

straw /strɔ/

hawk /hɔk/

draw /drɔ/

prawn /prɔn/

More words

saw

awful

claw

yawn

jaw

Write the words

aw /ɔ/

Write the letters & Read the sentences!

The h_ _k has big cl_ _s.

I s_ _ some pr_ _ns.

His j_ _ opens wide when he y_ _ns.

Test

Complete the words

1. d_____t
2. c_____r
3. f_____s
4. o_____s
5. p_____e
6. b_____o

Write the answer next to the letter "A"

A: ___ **7.** What ___ you ___ two days ago?

a. were, eat
b. was, eating
c. were, eating

A: ___ **8.** I ___ eating chicken nuggets.

a. were
b. weren't
c. wasn't

A: ___ **9.** Were you eating a taco five days ago?

a. No, I wasn't. I was eaten a hot dog.
b. No, I wasnt. I was eating hot dog.
c. No, I wasn't. I was eating a hot dog.

A: ___ **10.** Were you eating fried ___ three ___ ago?

a. chicken, days
b. nuggets, days
c. chicken, day

Answers on Page 306

Lesson 32

- Learn the words
- Learn the sentences
- Learn the phonics
- Test yourself!

Landscapes

пейзажі

Learn the words

1. **mountain**
   гора
2. **forest**
   ліс
3. **beach**
   пляж
4. **river**
   річка
5. **volcano**
   вулкан
6. **island**
   острів
7. **jungle**
   джунглі
8. **waterfall**
   водоспад
9. **lake**
   озеро
10. **ocean**
    океан

Write the missing letters!

1. m_ _n_a_n
2. f_re_ _
3. b_ _c_
4. r_ _e_
5. v_l_a_o
6. i_l_n_
7. _u_g_e
8. w_ _e_fa_l
9. l_ _ _
10. o_e_ _

Have fun with the words!

Word Search

```
n u i j g l c p y l a k e e y w n s
z x c c f s f n e t z t z v q a q b
r l c l l o f b c j r a e u a t e b
g z a x j i r h h n a m l o v e k e
i s c a j s z e o w d o p v o r y a
u l y m u l j t s j c u y r l f m c
i r o i n a l b y t e n s l c a a h
o g c r g n o r i b u t p z a l v i
n l e d l d j d z o t a p h n l x f
v p a e e g d b q b p i d w o v e t
a r n p z r i v e r d n z z z n m s
a r a q k h n x k z c s e e g z u h
```

Word directions: → ↘ ↓

beach   **waterfall**

mountain   **island**

forest   **jungle**

river   **lake**

volcano   **ocean**

Learn the sentences

Where were you walking to yesterday?
Yesterday, we were walking to the <u>beach</u>.
We weren't walking to the <u>waterfall</u>.

Write the missing words!

Where _____ you walking _____ yesterday?
_____, we were _____ to _____ forest.
We _____ walking _____ the _____.

_____ were they _____ to _____?
Yesterday, _____ _____ walking to _____ jungle.
They weren't _____ to _____ _____.

Where _____ you _____ _____ _____?
_____, _____ were _____ _____ the _____.
We _____ _____ to _____ mountain.

_____?
_____.
_____.

Learn the sentences

Were they walking to the <u>river</u> yesterday?
Yes, they were.
No, they were walking to the <u>lake</u>.

Write the missing words!

Were they _____ to the _____ yesterday?

Yes, they _____ .

No, _____ were walking to _____ jungle.

_____ you walking _____ the ocean _____ ?

_____ , _____ were.

No, we _____ to the _____ .

_____ they _____ the volcano _____ ?

Yes, _____ _____ .

_____ , they _____ walking _____ the _____ .

_____ ?
_____ .
_____ .

Learn the phonics

cl /kl/

clam /klæm/

clap /klæp/

clothes /kloʊðz/

clock /klɑk/

More words

clown

class

club

clever

climb

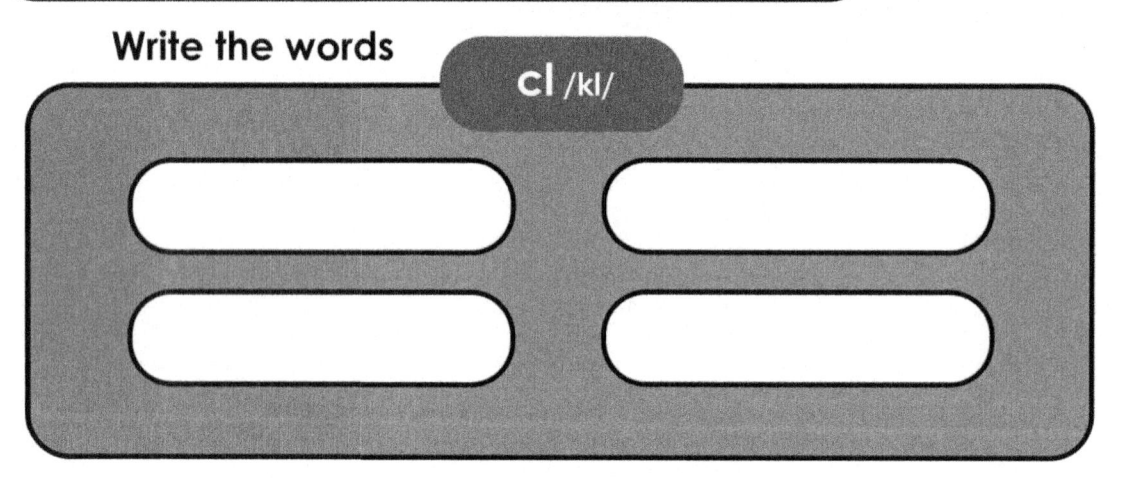

Write the words

cl /kl/

Write the letters & Read the sentences!

The people _ _apped for the _ _own.

This _ _ass is about _ _ocks.

I _ _imbed a tree and saw some _ _othes.

Test

Complete the words

1. m____n   3. r____r   5. o____n

2. b____h   4. j____e   6. w____l

Write the answer next to the letter "A"

A: ___ **7.** Where were you walking to yesterday?

a. I were walking to the forest.
b. We were walking to the forest.
c. We was walking to the forest.

A: ___ **8.** They ___ walking to the volcano.

a. werent'
b. wasn't
c. weren't

A: ___ **9.** Were you walking to the lake yesterday?

a. No, we were walking to the island.
b. No, they were walking to the island.
c. No, we were walking to island.

A: ___ **10.** Were they ___ to the ocean?

a. walk
b. walking
c. walks

Answers on Page 306

Lesson 33 — Homework

- Learn the words
- Learn the sentences
- Learn the phonics
- Test yourself!

домашнє завдання

Learn the words

1. **workbook** — збірник вправ
2. **vocabulary words** — лексика
3. **quiz** — вікторина
4. **science project** — науковий проект
5. **speech** — вимова
6. **article** — стаття
7. **poster** — плакат
8. **presentation** — презентація
9. **essay** — есе
10. **report** — звіт

Write the missing letters!

1. w_r_b_o_
2. vo_a_u_a_y w_ _ds
3. _u_ _
4. s_i_n_e p_o_e_t
5. s_ _e_h
6. a_t_c_e
7. p_s_ _r
8. p_e_e_t_o_
9. e_s_ _
10. r_ _or_

Have fun with the words!

Find the 8 homework words!

sausage quiz bedroom
chicken nuggets
ocean
pancake salad mountain
jungle beach essay taco
doughnut article lake
workbook
clothes presentation
report
waffles burrito draw bacon
forest
speech cheeseburger meat
pastries poster surf
essay fries
french write waterfall

Write the 8 shapes

1.
2.
3.
4.
5.
6.
7.
8.

Learn the sentences

Which homework have you already done?
I have already done the <u>report</u>.
However, I haven't done the <u>quiz</u> yet.

Write the missing words!

Which _____ have _____ already _____?
I _____ already done _____ presentation.
However, I _____ the _____ words yet.

_____ homework _____ you _____ done?
I have _____ the _____.
However, I _____ done _____ poster _____.

Which _____ you _____ _____?
I _____ already _____ _____ science _____.
_____, I _____ the _____ _____.

_____?
_____.
_____.

- 200 -

Learn the sentences

Have you done the <u>speech</u> yet?
Yes, I have already done it.
No, I haven't done it yet.

Write the missing words!

Have you _____ the workbook _____?
Yes, _____ have already _____ it.
No, I _____ done _____ yet.

_____ you _____ the article _____?
Yes, _____ have _____ done it.
_____, I _____ done _____ yet.

Have _____ _____ _____ _____ yet?
_____, I _____ already _____ _____.
No, I _____ _____ it _____.

_____?
_____.
_____.

Learn the phonics

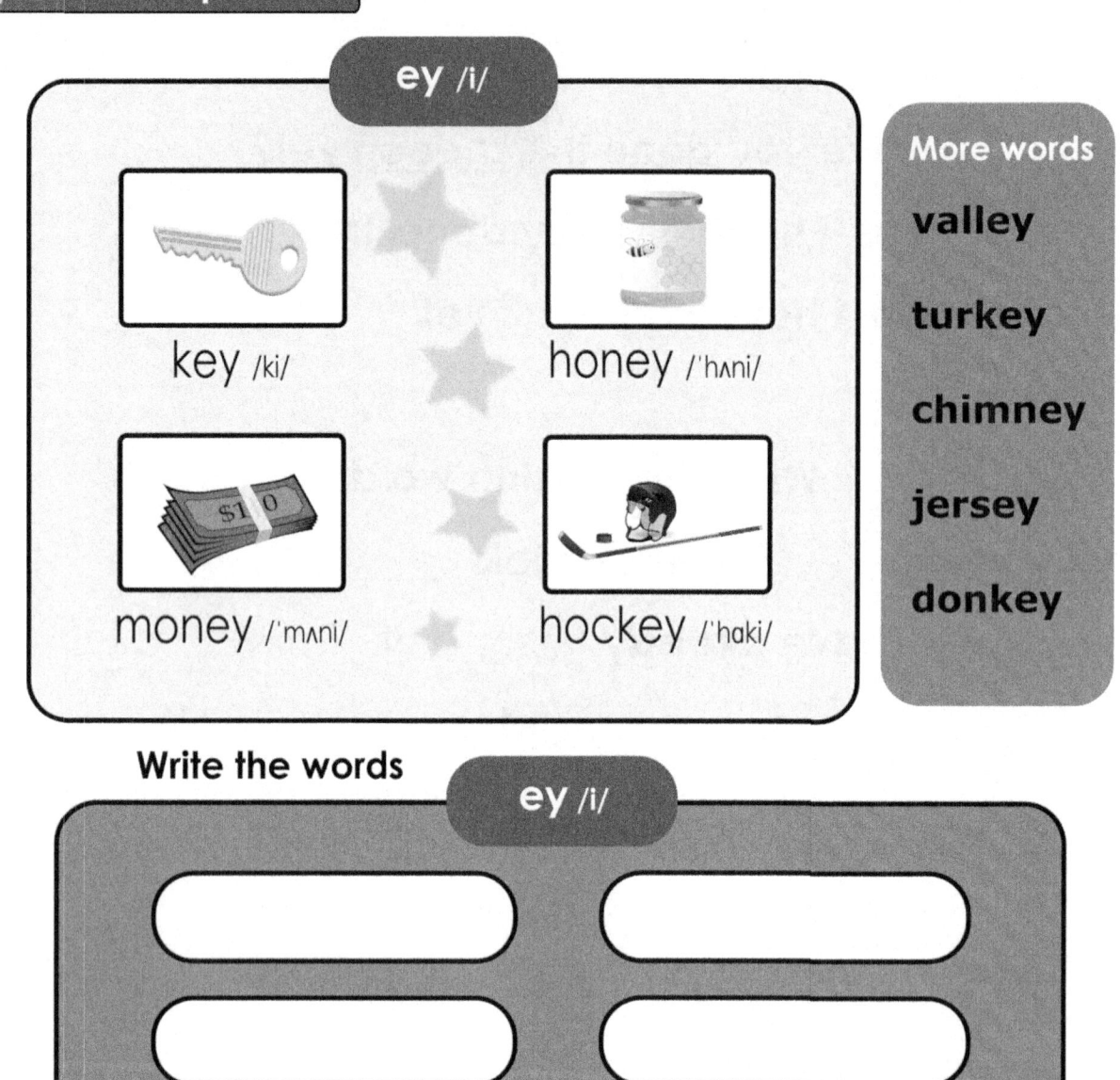

ey /i/

key /ki/

honey /ˈhʌni/

money /ˈmʌni/

hockey /ˈhaki/

More words

valley

turkey

chimney

jersey

donkey

Write the words

ey /i/

Write the letters & Read the sentences!

This jers_ _ is for the hock_ _ game.

There is a donk_ _ in the vall_ _.

That hon_ _ costs a lot of mon_ _.

Test

Complete the words

1. a_____e   3. q_____z   5. s_____h

2. p_____n   4. w_____k   6. r_____t

Write the answer next to the letter "A"

A: ___ **7.** Which homework ___ you already ___?

a. have, did
b. has, done
c. have, done

A: ___ **8.** However, I ___ done the quiz ___.

a. haven't, already
b. have, yet
c. haven't, yet

A: ___ **9.** Have you ___ the poster yet? Yes, I have already done ___.

a. did, it
b. done, it
c. done, yet

A: ___ **10.** Have you done the science project yet?

a. No, I haven't done it yet.
b. No, I have done it yet.
c. No, I haven't already done it.

Answers on Page 306

Lesson 34 — The calendar

- Learn the words
- Learn the sentences
- Learn the phonics
- Test yourself!

календар

Learn the words

1. **class** — заняття
2. **birthday** — день народження
3. **party** — вечірка
4. **competition** — змагання
5. **speech** — виступ
6. **test** — тест
7. **meeting** — зібрання
8. **recital** — концерт
9. **appointment** — зустріч
10. **day off** — вихідний

Write the missing letters!

1. _ i _ t _ d _ _
2. p _ _ t _
3. c _ m _ e _ it _ on
4. c _ _ s _
5. s _ _ e _ h
6. m _ e _ i _ _
7. r _ c _ t _ l
8. a _ p _ i _ t _ e _ t
9. t _ _ _
10. _ _ y o _ f

- 204 -

Have fun with the words!

- birthday
- party
- competition
- class
- speech
- meeting
- recital
- appointment
- test
- day off

Write the missing word:

Learn the sentences

When is your <u>brother</u>'s <u>birthday</u>?

My brother's birthday is on the <u>second</u> of <u>June</u>.

He hasn't prepared for his birthday yet.

Write the missing words!

When is _____ father's _____?

My _____ appointment is _____ the _____ of May.

He hasn't _____ for _____ appointment _____.

_____ _____ your _____ recital?

My friend's _____ is on _____ third _____ July.

She _____ prepared _____ _____ recital yet.

When _____ _____ sister's _____?

_____ _____ test is _____ the twentieth of _____.

She _____ prepared _____ _____ test _____.

_____?

_____.

_____.

Learn the sentences

Is your <u>aunt</u>'s <u>party</u> on the <u>first</u> of <u>February</u>?

Yes, her party is on that day.

No, my aunt has a <u>speech</u> on that day.

Write the missing words!

Is _____ mother's _____ on the tenth of _____?

Yes, _____ meeting is on _____ day.

No, my _____ has a _____ off on that _____.

_____ your _____ class on the _____ of April?

Yes, his _____ is _____ that day.

_____, my uncle _____ a _____ on that day.

Is _____ grandma's party _____ the _____ of May?

_____, her _____ is _____ that _____.

No, _____ has a _____ on _____ day.

_____?
_____.
_____.

Learn the phonics

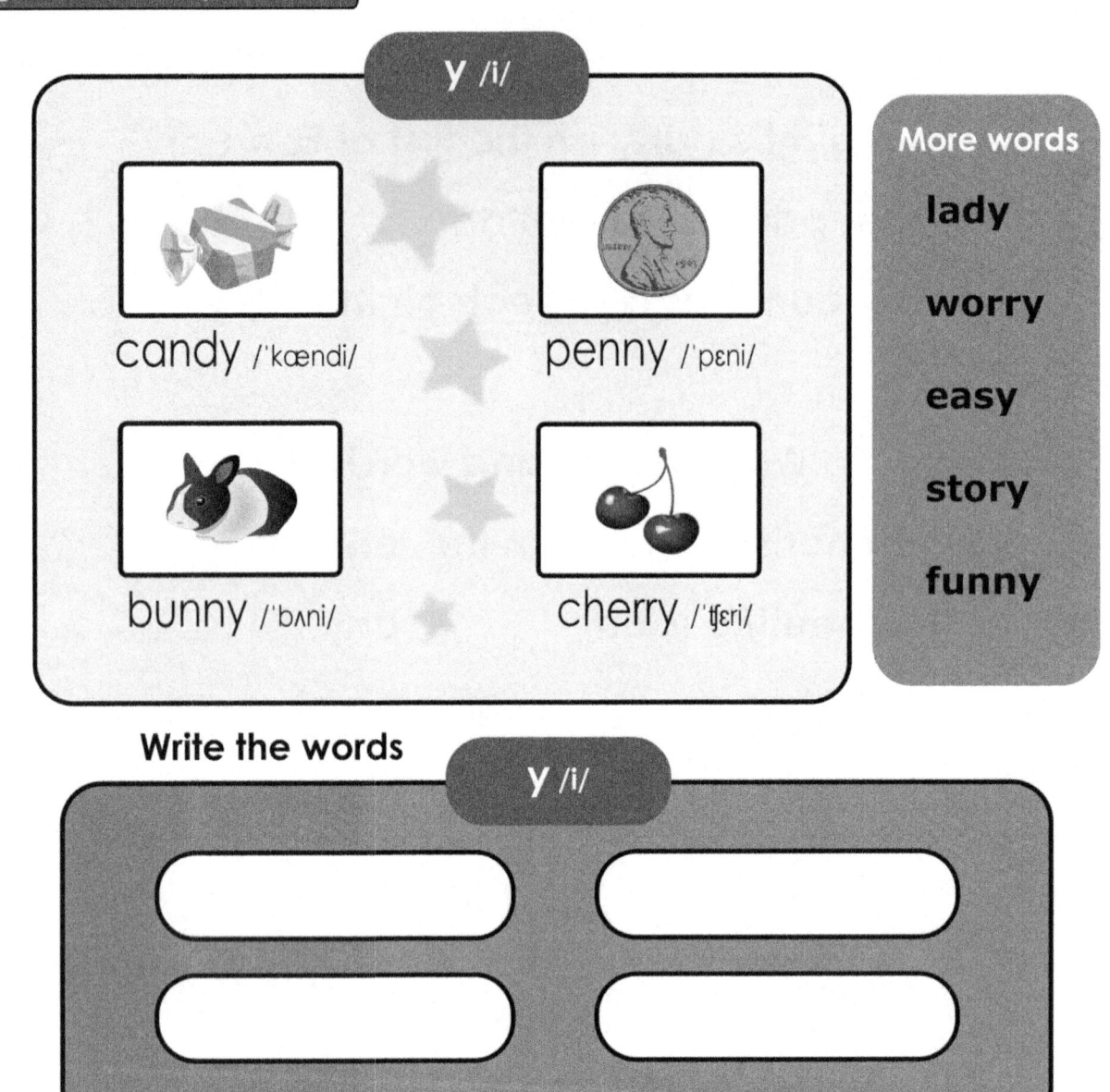

y /i/

candy /ˈkændi/

penny /ˈpɛni/

bunny /ˈbʌni/

cherry /ˈtʃɛri/

More words

lady

worry

easy

story

funny

Write the words

y /i/

Write the letters & Read the sentences!

This stor_ is reall_ funn_.

The lad_ ate the cherr_.

It is not eas_ to draw a bunn_.

Test

Complete the words

1. m_____g
2. a_____t
3. p_____y
4. r_____l
5. b_____y
6. c_____n

Write the answer next to the letter "A"

A: ___ **7.** When is ___ father's day off?

a. you're
b. your
c. you

A: ___ **8.** My aunt's appointment is ___ the third of October.

a. at
b. in
c. on

A: ___ **9.** She ___ prepared for her test yet.

a. hasn't
b. haven't
c. has

A: ___ **10.** Is your brother's class on the thirteenth of November?

a. Yes, her class is on that day.
b. Yes, his class isn't on that day.
c. Yes, his class is on that day.

Answers on Page 306

Lesson 35

- Learn the words
- Learn the sentences
- Learn the phonics
- Test yourself!

Camping

кемпінг

Learn the words

1. **a barbecue** — барбекю
2. **a gas bottle** — газовий балон
3. **sleeping bags** — спальні мішки
4. **plastic dishes** — пластиковий посуд
5. **fishing rods** — вудки
6. **binoculars** — бінокль
7. **a flashlight** — ліхтарики
8. **a tent** — намет
9. **a compass** — компас
10. **a cooler** — портативний холодильник

Write the missing letters!

1. b_r_e_u_
2. g_ _ b_t_le
3. s_e_pi_g b_ _s
4. p_a_t_c d_s_e_
5. f_s_i_g r_ _s
6. b_n_cu_a_s
7. f_a_h_i_ _t
8. t_ _ _
9. c_ _p_s_
10. co_l_ _

- 210 -

Have fun with the words!

Write the 3 missing words

1._____
2. _____
3. _____

- barbecue
- gas bottle
- sleeping bags
- compass
- plastic dishes
- flashlight
- cooler

1._____
2. _____
3. _____

- sleeping bags
- tent
- plastic dishes
- binoculars
- compass
- fishing rods
- barbecue

1._____
2. _____
3. _____

- cooler
- gas bottle
- flashlight
- plastic dishes
- fishing rods
- binoculars
- tent

1._____
2. _____
3. _____

- compass
- tent
- fishing rods
- barbecue
- cooler
- binoculars
- flashlight

1._____
2. _____
3. _____

- barbecue
- sleeping bags
- cooler
- tent
- flashlight
- plastic dishes
- gas bottle

1._____
2. _____
3. _____

- plastic dishes
- compass
- gas bottle
- sleeping bags
- binoculars
- fishing rods
- barbecue

Learn the sentences

What has he packed for the camping trip?

He has already packed <u>binoculars</u>.

However, he hasn't packed <u>a tent</u> yet.

Write the missing words!

What has he _____ for the _____ trip?

He _____ already packed _____ flashlight.

However, _____ hasn't packed _____ bags _____.

What _____ she _____ for the camping _____?

_____ has _____ packed _____ dishes.

However, she _____ a _____ yet.

_____ has he _____ for _____ camping _____?

He _____ already _____ _____ gas _____.

_____, he _____ packed _____ cooler _____.

_____?
_____.
_____.

Learn the sentences

Has she packed <u>a barbecue</u> yet?

Yes, she already has.

No, she hasn't yet.

Write the missing words!

Has she _____ a _____ yet?

Yes, _____ already _____ .

_____ , she hasn't _____ .

Has _____ packed _____ rods _____ ?

Yes, _____ already has.

_____ , he _____ yet.

_____ she _____ a _____ bottle _____ ?

_____ , _____ _____ has.

No, _____ _____ _____ .

_____ ?
_____ .
_____ .

Learn the phonics

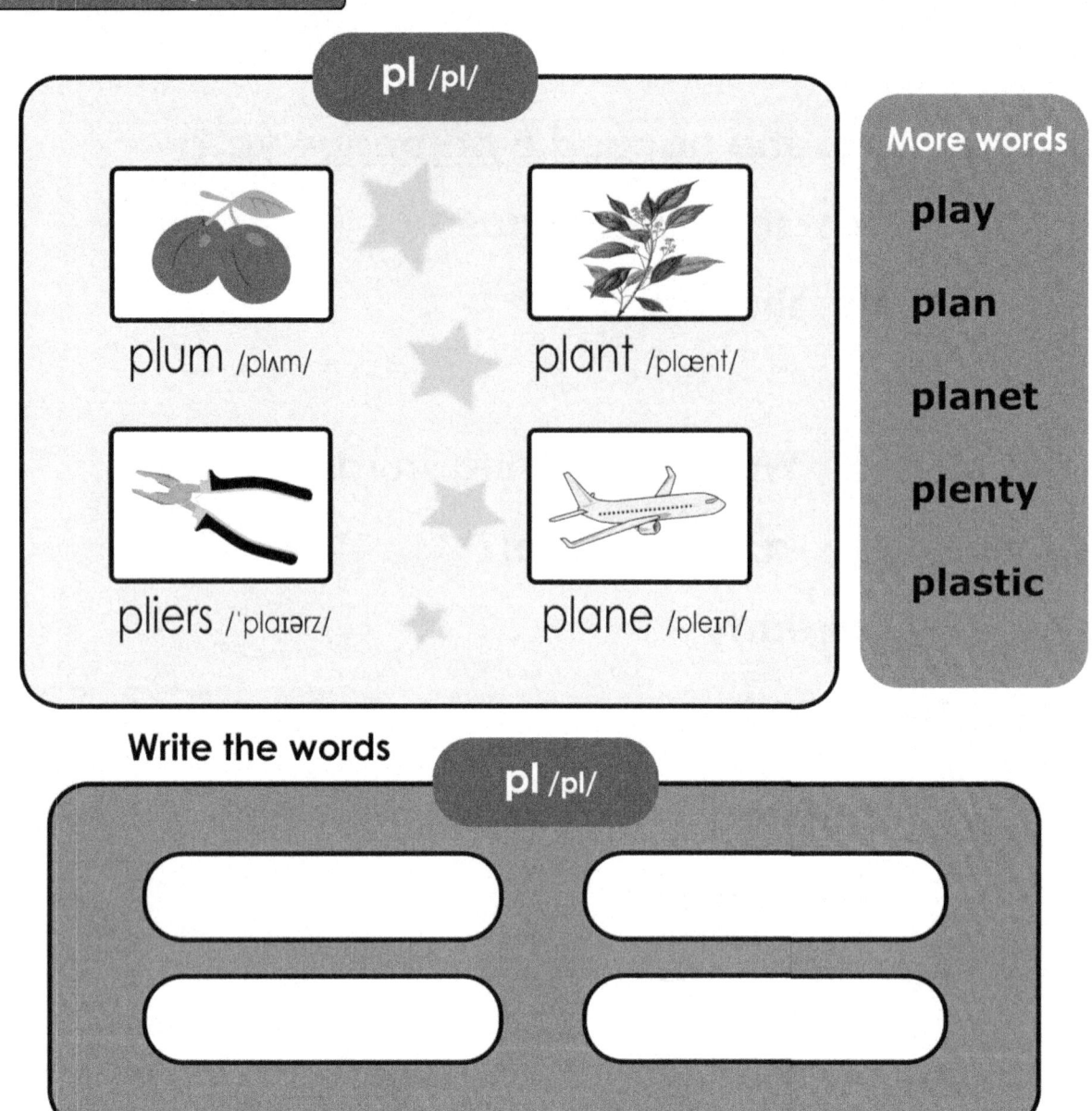

pl /pl/

plum /plʌm/

plant /plænt/

pliers /ˈplaɪərz/

plane /pleɪn/

More words

play

plan

planet

plenty

plastic

Write the words

pl /pl/

Write the letters & Read the sentences!

There are _ _enty of _ _ums by the _ _ant.

The toy _ _ane is made of _ _astic.

I _ _an to buy some new _ _iers.

Test

Complete the words

1. b_____s 3. p_____s 5. c_____r

2. c_____s 4. g_____e 6. b_____e

Write the answer next to the letter "A"

A: ___ **7.** What ___ she packed ___ the camping trip?

a. has, of
b. have, for
c. has, for

A: ___ **8.** He has already ___ the sleeping bags.

a. packed
b. packs
c. pack

A: ___ **9.** Has she packed a tent yet?

a. Yes, he already has.
b. No, she hasn't already.
c. Yes, she already has.

A: ___ **10.** Has he packed a ___ yet?

a. flashlight
b. sleeping bags
c. fishing rods

Answers on Page 306

Lesson 36 — Daily life

- Learn the words
- Learn the sentences
- Learn the phonics
- Test yourself!

повсякденне життя

Learn the words

1. **woken up** — прокинулись
2. **brushed my teeth** — почистили зуби
3. **done homework** — зробили домашнє завдання
4. **taken out the trash** — викинули сміття
5. **cooked dinner** — приготували обід
6. **eaten breakfast** — поснідали
7. **gone to school** — пішли до школи
8. **taken a shower** — прийняли душ
9. **gone shopping** — пішли за покупками
10. **gone to sleep** — пішли спати

Write the missing letters!

1. w_k_n u_
2. b_u_h_d m_t_e_ _
3. d_n_ h_m_w_ _k
4. t_k_n o_t t_e t_a_ _
5. c_o_e_ d_n_e_
6. _a_ _n b_e_k_a_t
7. g_ _e t_s_h_o_
8. t_ _e_ a s_o_e_
9. _on_ s_o_p_n_
10. g_n_ t_ s_ _e_

- 216 -

Have fun with the words!

Unscramble the words

1. brushed / already / teeth / had / I / my

    _____.

2. trash / the / taken / yet / out / hadn't / She

    _____.

3. he / had / done / already / What / o'clock / ten / by

    _____?

4. already / They / to / gone / school / had

    _____.

5. hadn't / shower / yet / a / I / taken

    _____.

6. already / sleep / to / she / Had / gone

    _____?

7. up / he / yet / hadn't / woken / No

    _____.

8. shopping / they / gone / Had / already

    _____?

Learn the sentences

What had you already done by <u>eight</u> o'clock?

I had already <u>brushed my teeth</u>.

I hadn't <u>taken out the trash</u> yet.

Write the missing words!

What _____ you already _____ by _____ o'clock?

I had _____ woken _____ .

I _____ a shower _____ .

_____ had he _____ done _____ nine _____ ?

He _____ already _____ homework.

_____ hadn't _____ _____ sleep yet.

What _____ she _____ by _____ o'clock?

_____ had _____ _____ shopping.

She _____ _____ dinner _____ .

_____ ?

_____ .

_____ .

Learn the sentences

Had you already <u>gone shopping</u>?

Yes, I already had.

No, I hadn't gone shopping yet.

Write the missing words!

Had you _____ taken _____ the _____?

_____, I _____ had.

No, I _____ out _____ trash yet.

Had _____ _____ brushed her _____?

_____, she already _____.

No, _____ hadn't _____ her teeth _____.

_____ he already _____ _____ school?

Yes, _____ _____ _____.

_____, he _____ gone _____ school _____.

_____?
_____.
_____.

Learn the phonics

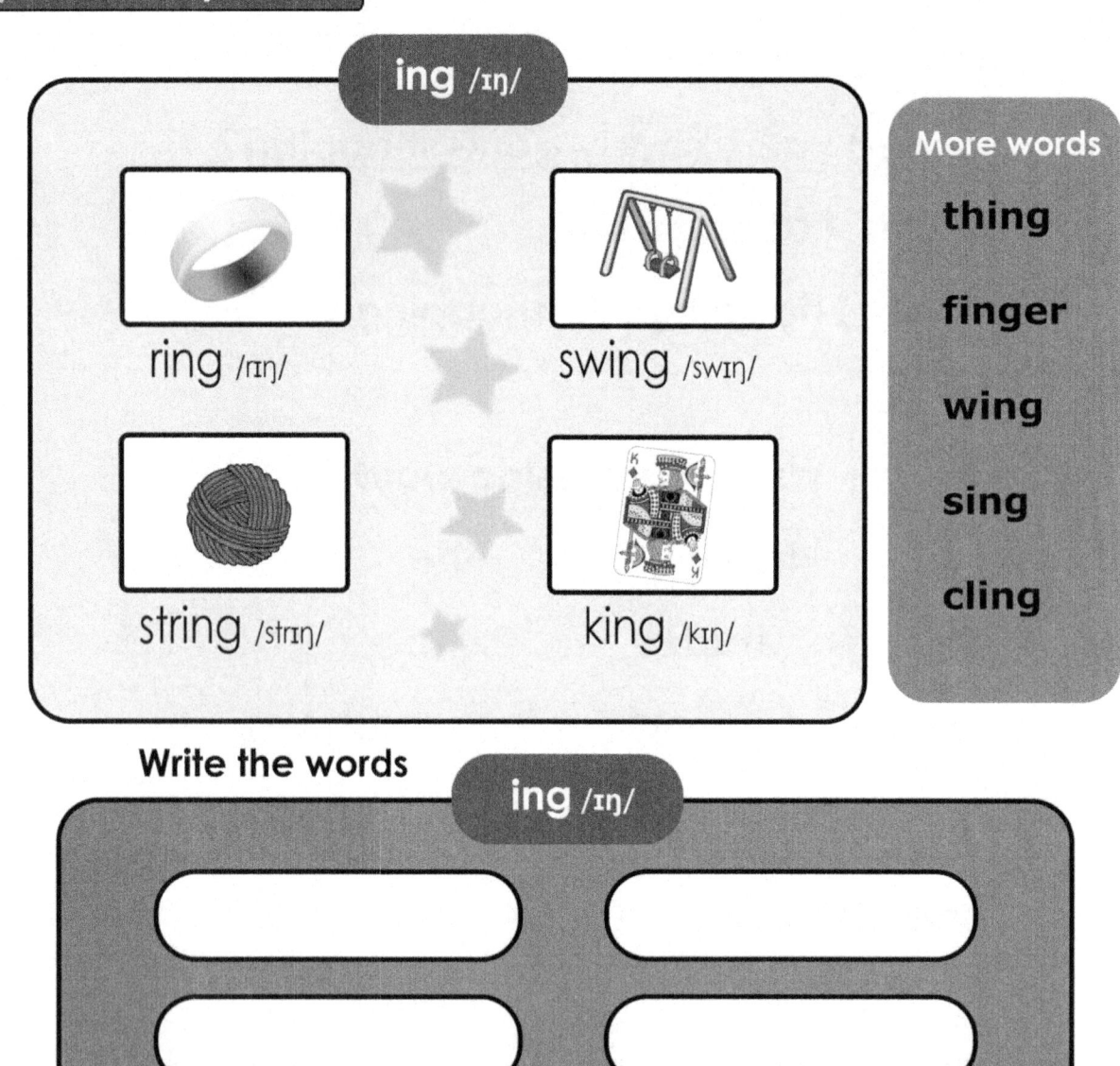

ing /ɪŋ/

ring /rɪŋ/

swing /swɪŋ/

string /strɪŋ/

king /kɪŋ/

More words

thing

finger

wing

sing

cling

Write the words

ing /ɪŋ/

Write the letters & Read the sentences!

This r_ _ _ is too small for my f_ _ _er.

The boy cl_ _ _s to the sw_ _ _.

The k_ _ _ can s_ _ _ very well.

Test

Complete the words

1. t_____h
2. b_____t
3. s_____r
4. s_____g
5. h_____k
6. d_____r

Write the answer next to the letter "A"

A: ___ **7.** What had you already ___ by nine o'clock?

a. did
b. done
c. doing

A: ___ **8.** She ___ gone to school yet.

a. haven't
b. had
c. hadn't

A: ___ **9.** Had you already ___ up?

a. gone
b. taken
c. woken

A: ___ **10.** Had you already cooked dinner?

a. No, I hadn't eaten dinner yet.
b. No, I hadn't cooked dinner yet.
c. No, I had cooked dinner yet.

Answers on Page 306

Lesson 37

- Learn the words
- Learn the sentences
- Learn the phonics
- Test yourself!

On the street

на вулиці

Learn the words

1. a bus
   автобус
2. a truck
   вантажівка
3. an ambulance
   швидка допомога
4. a fire engine
   пожежна машина
5. some traffic lights
   кілька світлофорів
6. a fire hydrant
   пожежний гідрант
7. a stop sign
   знак зупинки
8. a trash can
   сміттєвий бак
9. some shops
   кілька магазинів
10. a police car
    поліцейський автомобіль

Write the missing letters!

1. a _ u _
2. a t _ u _ _
3. a _ a _ b _ l _ n _ e
4. a _ ir _ e _ g _ _ e
5. _ o _ e t _ a f _ c li _ h _ s
6. a f _ _ e h _ d _ a _ t
7. a s _ o _ s _ _ n
8. a t _ a _ h c _ _
9. s _ m _ s _ o _ s
10. a po _ i _ _ c _ _

- 222 -

Have fun with the words!

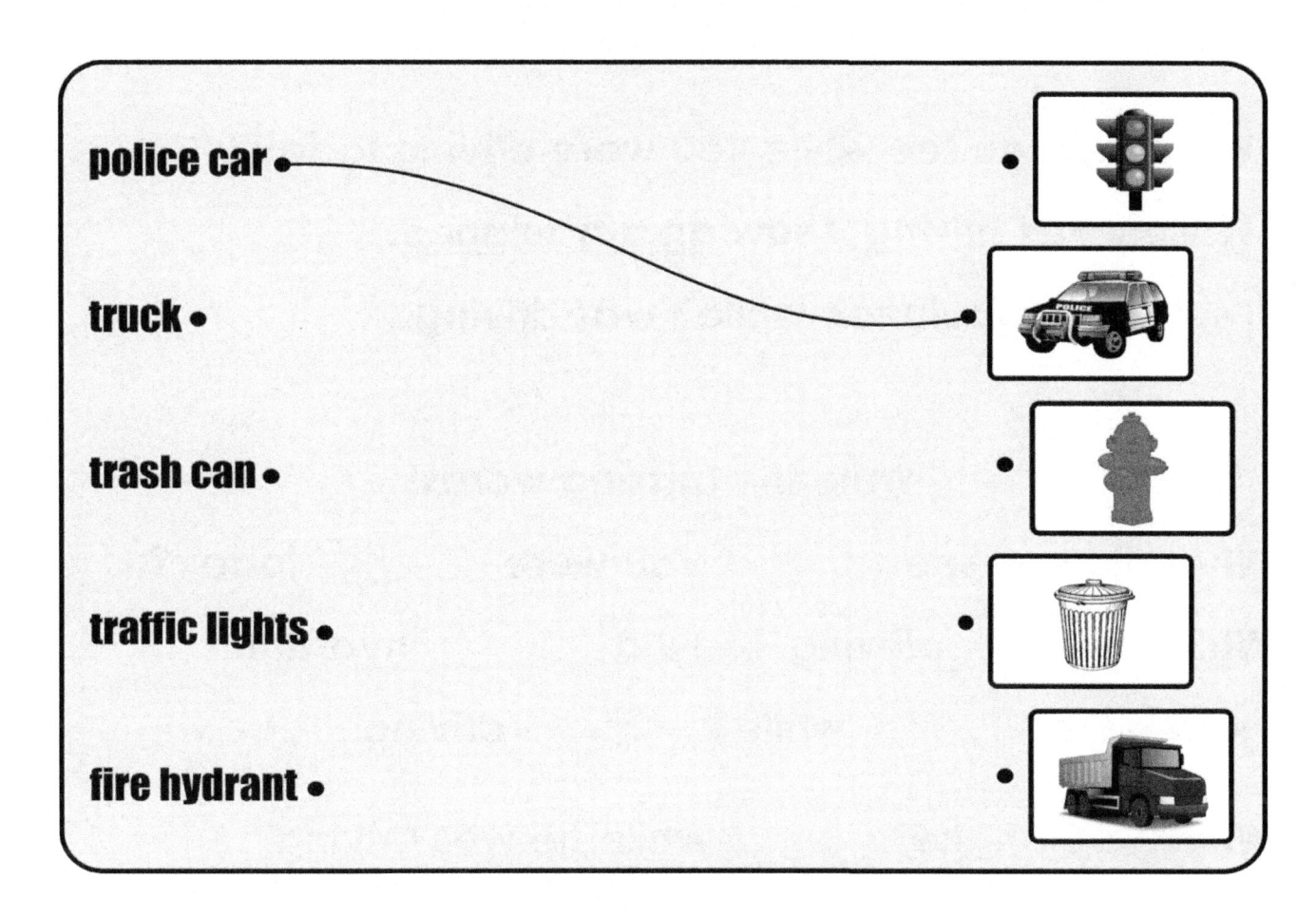

police car

truck

trash can

traffic lights

fire hydrant

Unscramble the letters!

1. BSU _____

2. IREF NEGIEN _____

3. HPSOS _____

4. MBALAECUN _____

5. TSPO GINS _____

Learn the sentences

What did you see while you were driving today?
While I was driving, I saw <u>an ambulance</u>.
I saw an ambulance while I was driving.

Write the missing words!

What did you see _____ you were _____ today?
While I _____ driving, I saw a _____ hydrant.
I saw a fire _____ while I _____ driving.

What _____ he _____ while he was driving _____?
_____ he was _____, he saw some _____ lights.
He saw _____ traffic _____ while he was _____.

What did _____ see _____ she was _____ today?
While she _____ driving, she _____ a police _____.
_____ saw a _____ car _____ she _____ driving.

_____?
_____.
_____.

Learn the sentences

Did you see <u>a truck</u> while you were driving?

Yes, I did. I saw <u>two</u> trucks.

No, I didn't. I didn't see any.

Write the missing words!

Did _____ see an _____ while you _____ driving?

Yes, I _____. I saw _____ ambulance.

No, I _____. I didn't see _____.

Did she see a stop _____ while _____ was _____?

Yes, _____ did. She _____ three _____ signs.

_____, I didn't. I _____ _____ any.

_____ he see a _____ while he _____ _____?

Yes, _____ _____. He _____ _____ buses.

No, _____ didn't. He _____ see _____.

_____?

_____.

_____.

Learn the phonics

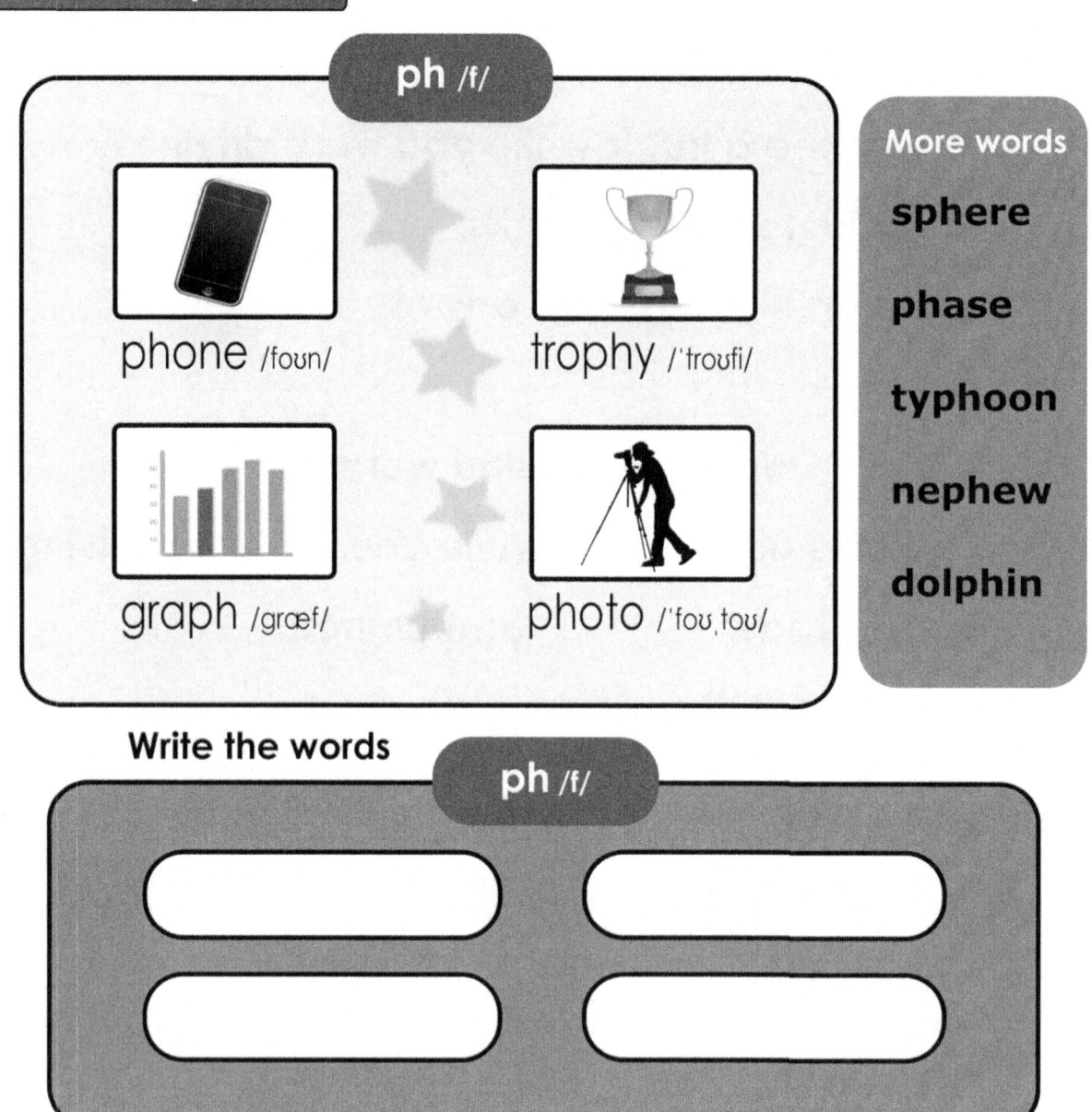

ph /f/

phone /foʊn/

trophy /ˈtroʊfi/

graph /græf/

photo /ˈfoʊˌtoʊ/

More words

sphere

phase

typhoon

nephew

dolphin

Write the words

ph /f/

Write the letters & Read the sentences!

My ne_ _ew wants a _ _one.

I took a _ _oto of a dol_ _in.

This gra_ _ is about ty_ _oons.

Test

Complete the words

1. t_____n   3. f_____t   5. a_____e

2. s_____n   4. p_____r   6. t_____k

Write the answer next to the letter "A"

A: ___ **7.** What ___ you see while you ___ driving today?

a. did, was
b. do, were
c. did, were

A: ___ **8.** While he was ___ he saw some traffic lights.

a. driving
b. driving,
c. driven,

A: ___ **9.** Did you see a fire engine while you were driving?

a. Yes, I did. I saw three fire engine.
b. Yes, I did. I saw one fire engine.
c. No, I did. I didn't see any.

A: ___ **10.** Did she see an ___ while she was driving?

a. ambulance
b. police car
c. bus

Answers on Page 306

Lesson 38

- Learn the words
- Learn the sentences
- Learn the phonics
- Test yourself!

Hobbies

хобі

Learn the words

1. **listen to music**
   слухати музику
2. **play video games**
   грати у відео ігри
3. **take photographs**
   Фотографувати
4. **do some gardening**
   займатися садівництвом
5. **go hiking**
   відправлятися в піший похід
6. **sing karaoke**
   співати в караоке
7. **go fishing**
   рибалити
8. **watch movies**
   дивитися фільми
9. **go camping**
   відправлятися в похід з палатками
10. **play chess**
    грати в шахи

Write the missing letters!

1. l_s_e_ t_ m_si_
2. p_a_ v_d_ _ g_m_s
3. t_ _e p_o_o_ ra_hs
4. d_ s_ _e g r_e_i g
5. _o h_ _i g
6. s_ _g k r_o_e
7. _o f_s_i_g
8. wa_c_ m_v_ _s
9. g_ c_m_ _n_
10. p_ _y c_e_ _

Have fun with the words!

Connect the words

sing • ────────────╮ • music

watch •   ╰• karaoke

listen to •   • chess

go •   • photographs

play •   • movies

do some •   • fishing

go •   • gardening

take •   • hiking

Learn the sentences

What do you like to do in your free time?
I like to <u>listen to music</u> in my free time.
I don't like to <u>go fishing</u>.

Write the missing words!

What do you _____ to _____ in your _____ time?
I like to _____ photographs _____ _____ free time.
I don't _____ to watch _____ .

What does _____ like _____ do in his free _____ ?
He likes _____ camping in _____ free time.
_____ like to sing _____ .

_____ do _____ to do in their _____ time?
They like to play _____ games in _____ free _____ .
They _____ to _____ hiking.

_____?
_____.
_____.

Learn the sentences

Do you like to <u>do some gardening</u> in your free time?
Yes, I really like to do some gardening.
No, I don't. I like to <u>play chess</u>.

Write the missing words!

Do you like to _____ to music in _____ free _____ ?
Yes, I _____ like _____ listen to _____ .
No, I _____ . I _____ to _____ movies.

Does he _____ to play _____ in _____ free time?
_____ , he really _____ to _____ chess.
No, _____ doesn't. He likes _____ go _____ .

Do they _____ to sing _____ in _____ free time?
Yes, _____ _____ like to _____ karaoke.
_____ , they _____ . _____ to go _____ .

_____ ?
_____ .
_____ .

Learn the phonics

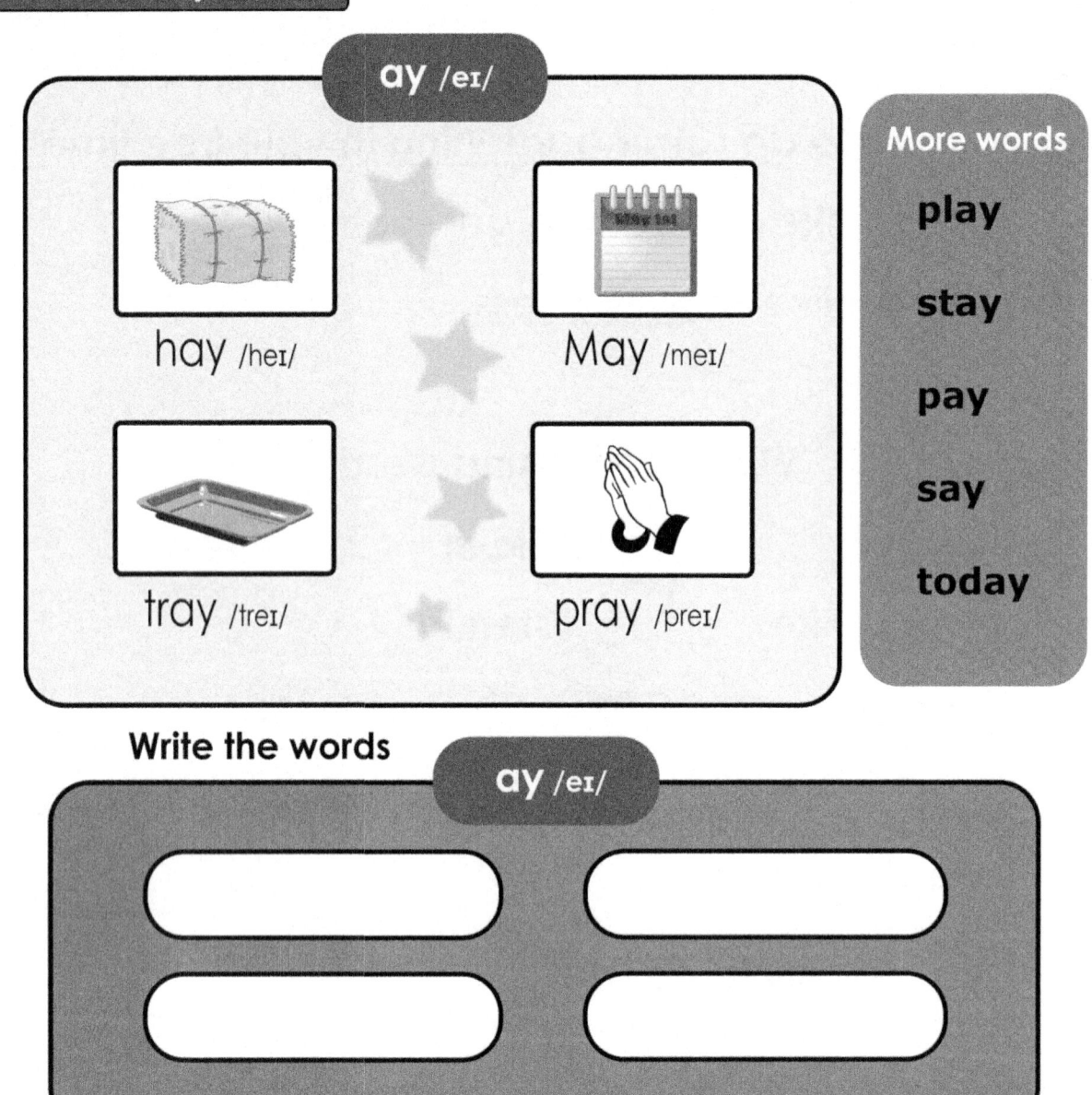

ay /eɪ/

hay /heɪ/

May /meɪ/

tray /treɪ/

pray /preɪ/

More words

play

stay

pay

say

today

Write the words

ay /eɪ/

Write the letters & Read the sentences!

I will p_ _ for the h_ _ tod_ _.

You can st_ _ here in M_ _.

They s_ _ to pr_ _ every d_ _.

Test

Complete the words

1. g_____g 3. k_____e 5. c_____g

2. p_____s 4. f_____g 6. h_____g

Write the answer next to the letter "A"

A: ___ 7. What do you like to do ___ your free time?

a. in
b. on
c. at

A: ___ 8. I like to listen ___ music in ___ free time.

a. to, me
b. to, my
c. the, my

A: ___ 9. He ___ like to go fishing.

a. don't
b. didn't
c. doesn't

A: ___ 10. Does she like to watch movies in her free time?

a. No, she doesn't. She likes to watch movies.
b. No, she doesn't. She like to play chess.
c. No, she doesn't. She likes to listen to music.

Answers on Page 306

Lesson 39 — In the bedroom

- Learn the words
- Learn the sentences
- Learn the phonics
- Test yourself!

в спальні

Learn the words

1. **pillow** — подушка
2. **bed** — ліжко
3. **blanket** — ковдра
4. **drawers** — шухляди
5. **mattress** — матрац
6. **alarm clock** — будильник
7. **lamp** — лампа
8. **bed sheets** — простирадло
9. **nightstand** — тумбочка
10. **wardrobe** — гардероб

Write the missing letters!

1. p_l_o_
2. b_ _
3. b_a_k_ _
4. d_a_e_s
5. m_t_r_s_
6. a_a_m _lo_ _
7. _a_ _
8. _e_ s_e_ _s
9. n_ _h_st_n_
10. w_ _d_o_e

Have fun with the words!

> **Find one mistake and write the sentence correctly**

Why is you going shopping now?
_____

I'm going shopping because I need a new bed sheets.
_____

My bed sheets is already ten years old.
_____

Why is she go shopping now?
_____

She's going shopping because she need a new pillow.
_____

Her pillow are already twelve years old.
_____

Are they gone to buy a new pillow?
_____

Yes, they are. My pillow is too old.
_____

Learn the sentences

Why are you going shopping now?

I'm going shopping because I need a new <u>lamp</u>.

My lamp is already <u>eight</u> years old.

Write the missing words!

Why _____ you _____ shopping _____?

I'm going _____ _____ I need a new _____ clock.

My alarm _____ is already five _____ old.

_____ is _____ _____ shopping now?

He's going _____ because he _____ new _____.

_____ drawers are _____ eleven years _____.

Why _____ they _____ _____ now?

They're going _____ _____ they _____ a new bed.

Their _____ _____ already _____ years _____.

_____?
_____.
_____.

Learn the sentences

Are you going to buy a new <u>nightstand</u>?

Yes, I am. My nightstand is too old.

No, I'm not. I don't need a new one.

Write the missing words!

Are you _____ to buy a _____ blanket?

Yes, I _____ . My blanket is _____ old.

No, I'm _____ . I _____ need _____ new one.

_____ she going to _____ a new _____ ?

Yes, _____ is. _____ wardrobe is too _____ .

No, _____ not. She doesn't need a new _____ .

_____ they _____ to _____ new _____ sheets?

Yes, _____ _____ . _____ bed _____ are too old.

_____ , they're not. They _____ need _____ ones.

_____?
_____.
_____.

Learn the phonics

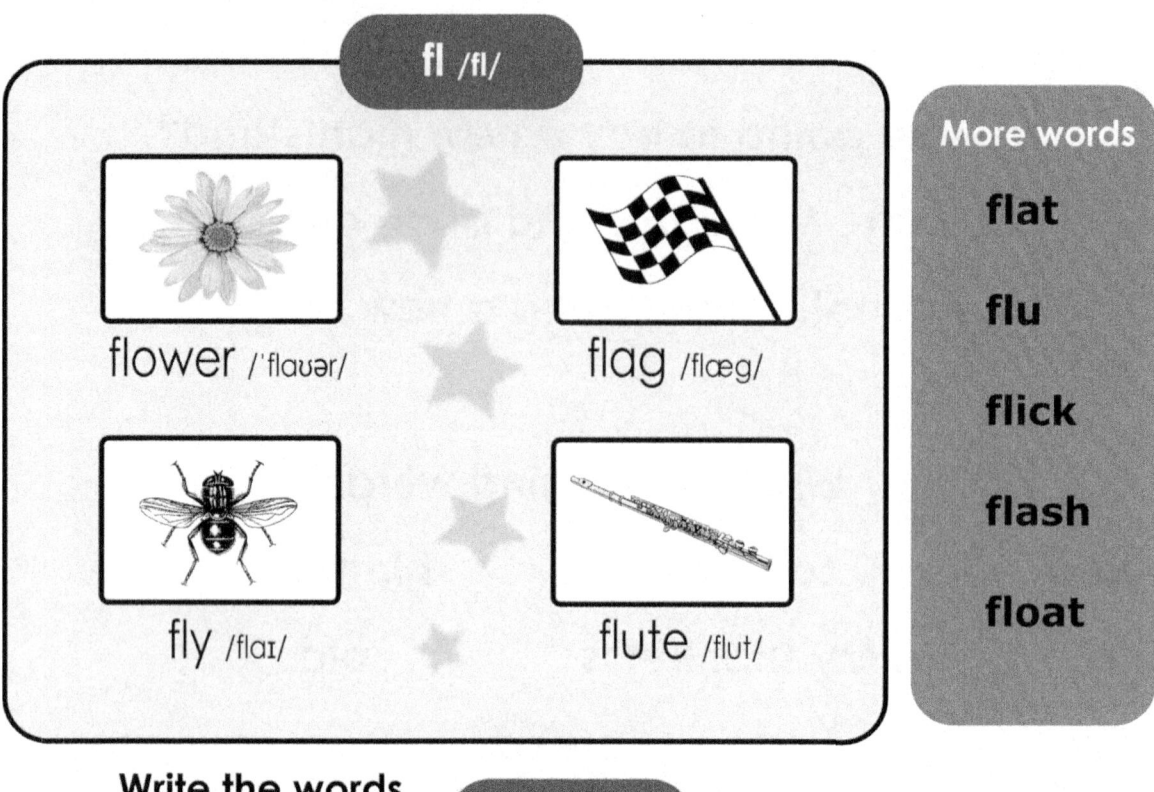

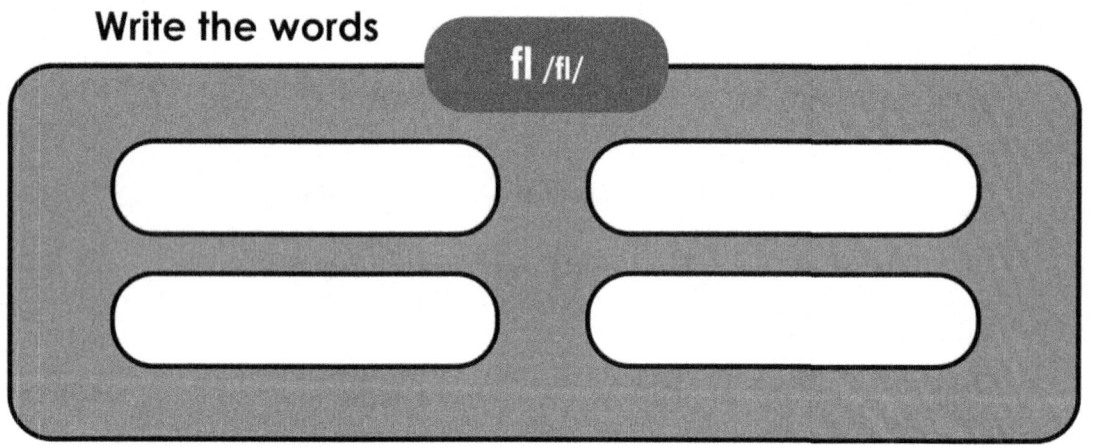

fl /fl/

flower /ˈflaʊər/

flag /flæg/

fly /flaɪ/

flute /flut/

More words

flat

flu

flick

flash

float

Write the words

fl /fl/

Write the letters & Read the sentences!

The _ _ower is _ _oating.

There is a _ _y on the _ _ute.

He _ _icked the _ _ame.

Test

Complete the words

1. w_____e
2. b_____t
3. m_____s
4. p_____w
5. d_____s
6. n_____d

Write the answer next to the letter "A"

A: ___ **7.** Why are you ___ shopping now?

a. go
b. going
c. going to

A: ___ **8.** I'm going shopping because I need a new ___.

a. bed
b. bed sheets
c. drawers

A: ___ **9.** Are you going to buy a new alarm clock?

a. No, I'm not. I need a new one.
b. No, I'm not. I don't need new ones.
c. No I'm not. I don't need a new one.

A: ___ **10.** Are you going to buy ___ bed sheets?

a. a new
b. new
c. old

Answers on Page 306

Lesson 40 — More places

- Learn the words
- Learn the sentences
- Learn the phonics
- Test yourself!

додаткові місця

Learn the words

1. **school** — школа
2. **library** — бібліотека
3. **police station** — міліція
4. **hospital** — лікарня
5. **train station** — залізнична станція
6. **factory** — фабрика, завод
7. **office** — офіс
8. **fire station** — пожежне депо
9. **clinic** — поліклініка
10. **bus stop** — автобусна зупинка

Write the missing letters!

1. s_h_o_
2. l_b_ar_
3. p_l_ _e s_at_o_
4. h_sp_ _a_
5. tr_ _n s_a_i_n
6. f_c_o_y
7. o_fi_ _
8. f_ _e _t_o_
9. c_i_i_
10. b_ _ s_o_

Have fun with the words!

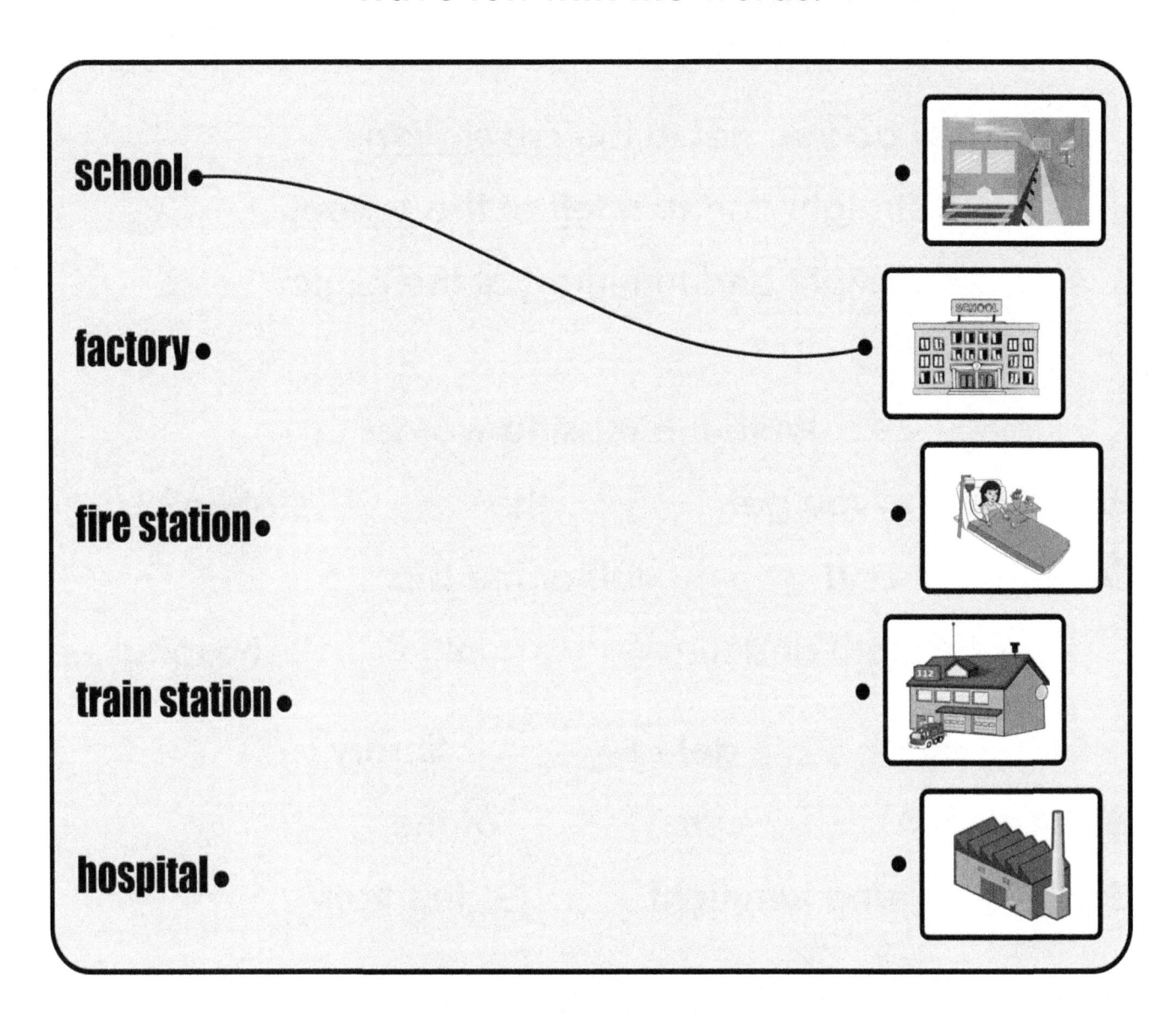

- school
- factory
- fire station
- train station
- hospital

Write 4 more places!

1. _____
2. _____
3. _____
4. _____

How do you get to the bus stop?

_____

Learn the sentences

How do you get to the <u>fire station</u>?

Go straight and turn <u>left</u> at the <u>school</u>.

Go straight and turn <u>right</u> at the <u>clinic</u>.

Write the missing words!

How _____ you get _____ the _____ station?

Go _____ and _____ left at the bus _____ .

_____ straight and turn _____ at _____ hospital.

_____ do _____ get to _____ library?

Go straight _____ turn _____ at the _____ .

Go _____ and turn right _____ the train _____ .

How _____ you _____ _____ clinic?

_____ straight and _____ left at the fire _____ .

Go _____ and turn _____ at the _____ .

_____?
_____.
_____.

- 242 -

Learn the sentences

Do you know how to get to the <u>bus stop</u>?
Yes, go straight and turn <u>right</u> at the <u>factory</u>.
No, I don't know how to get there.

Write the missing words!

Do you _____ how to _____ to the _____ stop?
Yes, go straight _____ turn _____ at the _____ .
_____ , I _____ know how to _____ there.

Do _____ know _____ to get to the _____ station?
_____ , go _____ and _____ left at the fire _____ .
No, _____ don't know _____ to get _____ .

_____ you _____ how to _____ to _____ clinic?
Yes, go _____ and _____ right _____ the hospital.
No, I _____ how _____ _____ there.

_____?
_____.
_____.

Learn the phonics

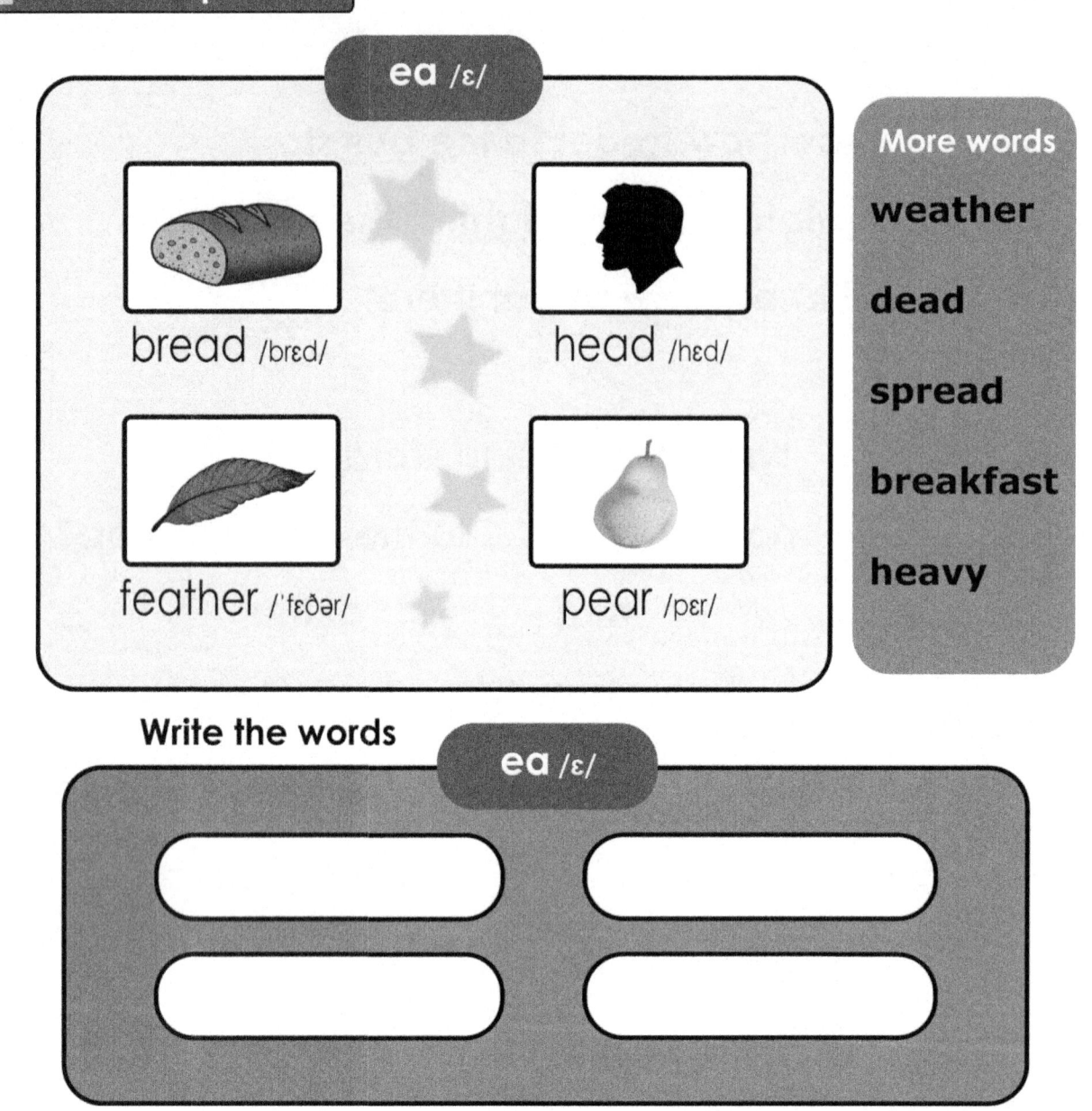

ea /ɛ/

bread /brɛd/

head /hɛd/

feather /ˈfɛðər/

pear /pɛr/

More words

weather

dead

spread

breakfast

heavy

Write the words

ea /ɛ/

Write the letters & Read the sentences!

We ate a p_ _r for br_ _kfast.

The f_ _ther is not h_ _vy.

I spr_ _d honey on my br_ _d.

Test

Complete the words

1. b_____p   3. c_____c   5. l_____y

2. h_____l   4. p_____n   6. f_____y

Write the answer next to the letter "A"

A: ___ **7.** How do you get to the train station?

a. Go straight and turn left at school.
b. Go straight and turn left at the school.
c. Get straight and turn right at the school.

A: ___ **8.** Go straight and ___ the fire station.

a. turn right into
b. turn right to
c. turn right at

A: ___ **9.** Do you know ___ get to the office?

a. how
b. how to
c. why to

A: ___ **10.** No, I don't know how to get ___.

a. there
b. their
c. here

Answers on Page 306

Lesson 41

- Learn the words
- Learn the sentences
- Learn the phonics
- Test yourself!

The face

обличчя

Learn the words

1. **chin**
   підборіддя
2. **nose**
   ніс
3. **eye**
   око
4. **eyebrow**
   брова
5. **eyelash**
   вія

6. **ear**
   вухо
7. **hair**
   волосся
8. **cheek**
   щока
9. **mouth**
   рот
10. **lip**
    губа

Write the missing letters!

1. c_i_
2. _o_e
3. e_ _
4. e_eb_o_
5. ey_l_s_

6. _a_
7. h_ _r
8. c_e_ _
9. m_u_ _
10. l_ _

Have fun with the words!

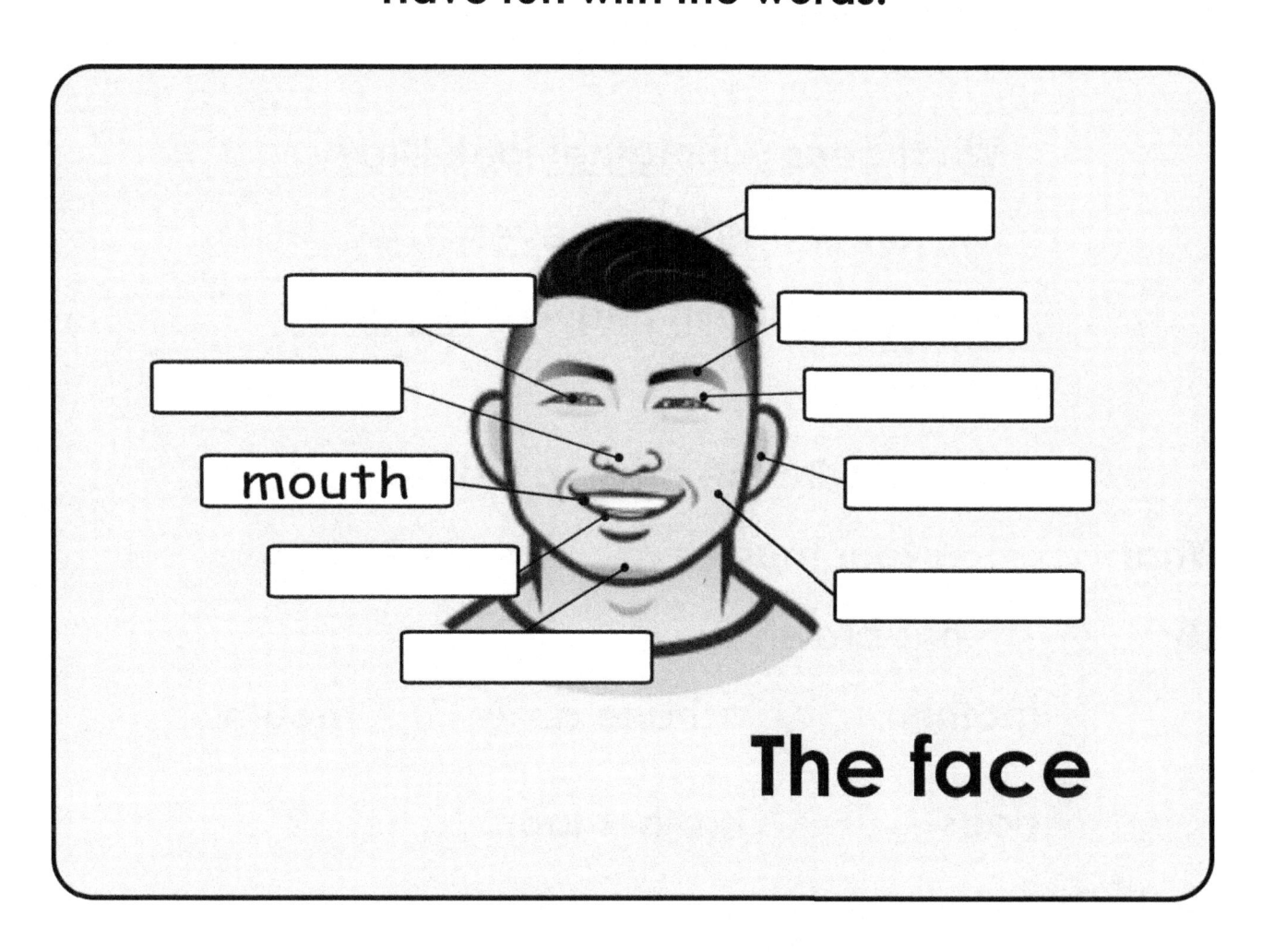

mouth

The face

Unscramble the letters!

1. UTOHM _____

2. ELSAYEH _____

3. RIHA _____

4. HICN _____

5. SONE _____

Learn the sentences

What does your <u>father</u> look like?

My father has <u>brown</u> <u>eye</u>s.

My father doesn't have a <u>big</u> <u>nose</u>.

Write the missing words!

What _____ your mother _____ like?

My _____ has brown _____ .

_____ mother _____ have a _____ mouth.

_____ does _____ brother look _____ ?

My brother _____ a _____ chin.

My _____ doesn't _____ blue _____ .

What _____ your _____ look _____ ?

My _____ has _____ eyelashes.

_____ aunt _____ a small _____ .

_____ ?

_____ .

_____ .

Learn the sentences

Does your <u>sister</u> have <u>long</u> <u>hair</u>?

Yes, she does.

No, she has <u>short</u> hair.

Write the missing words!

Does _____ uncle _____ big cheeks?

Yes, he _____.

No, he _____ small _____.

_____ your grandmother _____ green _____?

Yes, _____ _____.

_____, she has _____ eyes.

Does _____ grandfather _____ a small _____?

Yes, _____ _____.

_____, _____ has _____ big nose.

_____?
_____.
_____.

Learn the phonics

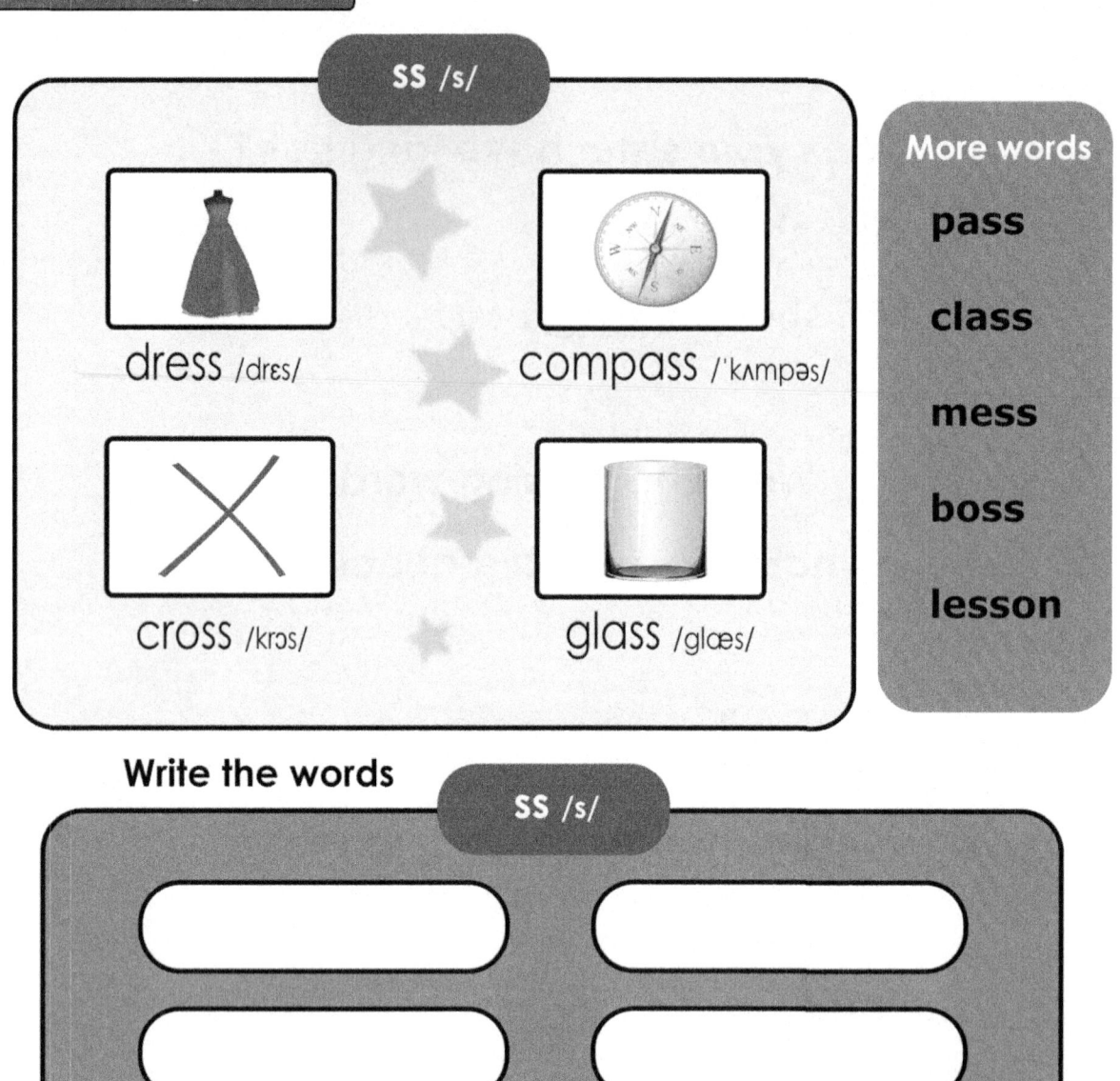

SS /s/

dress /drɛs/

compass /ˈkʌmpəs/

cross /krɔs/

glass /glæs/

More words

pass
class
mess
boss
lesson

Write the words

SS /s/

Write the letters & Read the sentences!

She wore a dre_ _ in cla_ _.

This le_ _on is about how to use a compa_ _.

My bo_ _ gave me this gla_ _.

Test

Complete the words

1. e _____ w
2. h _____ r
3. m _____ h
4. n _____ e
5. c _____ k
6. e _____ h

Write the answer next to the letter "A"

A: ___ **7.** What ___ your uncle look ___?

a. do, likes
b. does, like
c. did, liked

A: ___ **8.** My mother ___ long hair.

a. have
b. doesn't have
c. don't have

A: ___ **9.** Does your brother have blue eyes?

a. No, she has green eyes.
b. No, he have green eyes.
c. No, he has green eyes.

A: ___ **10.** Does your grandfather ___?

a. have a big nose
b. have big nose
c. has a big nose

Answers on Page 306

Lesson 42

- Learn the words
- Learn the sentences
- Learn the phonics
- Test yourself!

Personalities

риси характеру

Learn the words

1. **shy** — сором'язливий
2. **lazy** — лінивий
3. **outgoing** — товариський
4. **generous** — щедрий
5. **studious** — старанний
6. **interesting** — цікавий
7. **serious** — серйозний
8. **funny** — забавний
9. **smart** — розумний
10. **easygoing** — добродушно-веселий

Write the missing letters!

1. s_ _
2. l_z_
3. o_t_oi_ _
4. _e_e_o_s
5. s_u_i_u_
6. in_e_es_i_g
7. s_r_o_s
8. f_n_ _
9. s_a_ _
10. e_s_g_i_g

Have fun with the words!

shy
lazy
outgoing
generous
studious
interesting
serious
funny
smart
easygoing

s
m
a
r
t

Write the missing word:

Learn the sentences

What is your <u>friend</u> like?
My friend is a really <u>outgoing</u> person.
My friend isn't a <u>shy</u> person.

Write the missing words!

What _____ your father _____?
My father is a _____ easygoing _____.
My father _____ a _____ person.

_____ is _____ sister like?
My _____ is _____ really _____ person.
_____ sister isn't _____ studious _____.

What _____ your _____?
_____ grandfather _____ a _____ smart _____.
My _____ a _____.

_____?
_____.
_____.

- 254 -

Learn the sentences

Is your <u>mother</u> an <u>easygoing</u> person?
Yes, my mother is really easygoing.
No, my mother isn't easygoing.

Write the missing words!

Is _____ brother _____ interesting _____ ?
Yes, _____ brother is _____ interesting.
No, my _____ isn't _____ .

_____ your _____ a _____ person?
_____ , my aunt _____ really generous.
No, _____ aunt _____ generous.

Is _____ friend _____ studious _____ ?
Yes, _____ friend _____ really _____ .
_____ , my _____ isn't _____ .

_____?
_____.
_____.

Learn the phonics

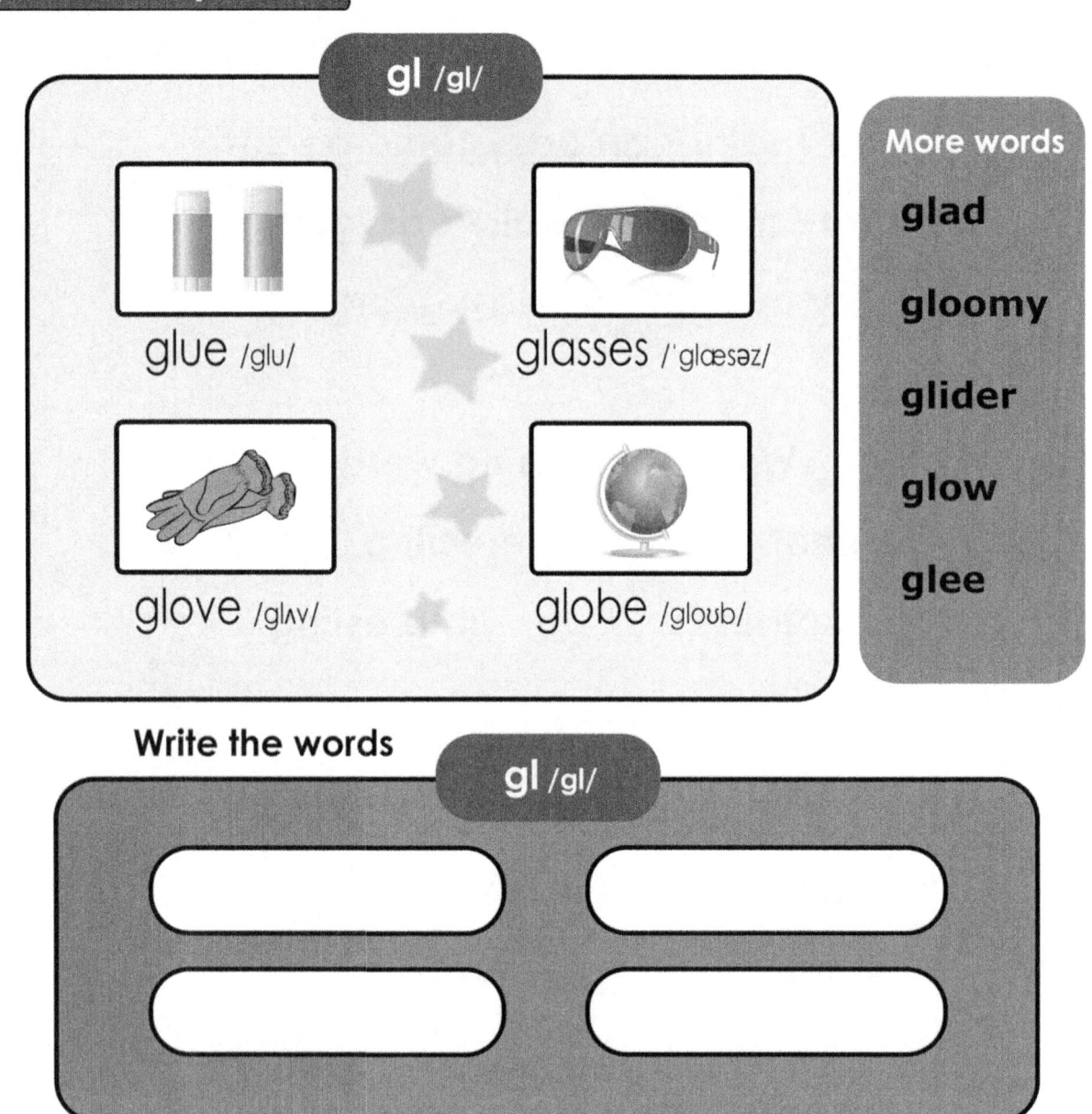

gl /gl/

glue /glu/

glasses /ˈglæsəz/

glove /glʌv/

globe /gloʊb/

More words

glad

gloomy

glider

glow

glee

Write the words

gl /gl/

Write the letters & Read the sentences!

I'm _ _ad I brought my _ _ider.

I can fix the _ _obe with _ _ue.

These _ _oves are _ _owing.

Test

Complete the words

1. l_____y
2. o_____g
3. g_____s
4. i_____g
5. s_____t
6. e_____g

Write the answer next to the letter "A"

A: ___ 7. What is your father like?

a. My father is really serious. My father isn't outgoing.
b. My father is real serious. My father isn't outgoing.
c. My father is really serious. My father is'nt outgoing.

A: ___ 8. What ___ your grandmother like? My grandmother is really shy.

a. does
b. is
c. do

A: ___ 9. Is your mother an ___ person? No, my mother is a ___ person.

a. easygoing, outgoing
b. lazy, studious
c. easygoing, smart

A: ___ 10. Is your brother a funny person?

a. Yes, my brother isn't really funny.
b. Yes, me brother is really funny.
c. Yes, my brother is really funny.

Answers on Page 306

Lesson 43 — Music

- Learn the words
- Learn the sentences
- Learn the phonics
- Test yourself!

музика

Learn the words

1. **beautifully** — красиво
2. **quietly** — тихо
3. **slowly** — повільно
4. **gracefully** — витончено
5. **well** — добре
6. **loudly** — гучно
7. **quickly** — швидко
8. **terribly** — жахливо
9. **correctly** — правильно
10. **badly** — погано

Write the missing letters!

1. be_u_if_l_y
2. _u_e_l_
3. sl_w_ _
4. g_a_e_u_l_
5. w_l_
6. l_ _d_y
7. q_i_k_y
8. _er_i_ly
9. c_r_ _c_l_
10. b_d_ _

- 258 -

Have fun with the words!

Write the 3 missing words

1._____
2._____
3._____

- beautifully
- well
- terribly
- quickly
- slowly
- badly
- quietly

1._____
2._____
3._____

- quickly
- gracefully
- terribly
- slowly
- loudly
- badly
- correctly

1._____
2._____
3._____

- slowly
- loudly
- quietly
- gracefully
- well
- correctly
- badly

1._____
2._____
3._____

- quietly
- correctly
- quickly
- loudly
- gracefully
- badly
- beautifully

1._____
2._____
3._____

- well
- gracefully
- terribly
- correctly
- quietly
- slowly
- beautifully

1._____
2._____
3._____

- badly
- correctly
- quickly
- well
- loudly
- terribly
- slowly

Learn the sentences

How does he play the <u>violin</u>?

He plays the <u>violin</u> <u>beautifully</u>.

He doesn't play the <u>violin</u> <u>badly</u>.

Write the missing words!

How _____ he _____ the guitar?

He _____ the _____ quickly.

He _____ play _____ guitar _____ .

_____ does _____ play _____ drums?

She plays _____ drums _____ .

_____ doesn't _____ the _____ correctly.

How _____ he _____ the _____ ?

_____ plays _____ piano gracefully.

He _____ _____ piano _____ .

_____ ?

_____ .

_____ .

Learn the sentences

Does she play the <u>piano</u> <u>well</u>?

Yes, she plays the piano very well.

No, she doesn't. She plays the piano <u>terribly</u>.

Write the missing words!

Does she _____ the _____ loudly?

_____, she plays _____ drums _____ loudly.

No, _____ doesn't. She _____ the drums _____.

_____ he _____ the _____ gracefully?

Yes, _____ plays _____ violin very _____.

_____, he _____. He _____ the violin _____.

Does _____ play _____ guitar _____?

_____, she _____ the _____ _____ well.

No, _____ _____. She _____ the _____ _____.

_____?
_____.
_____.

Learn the phonics

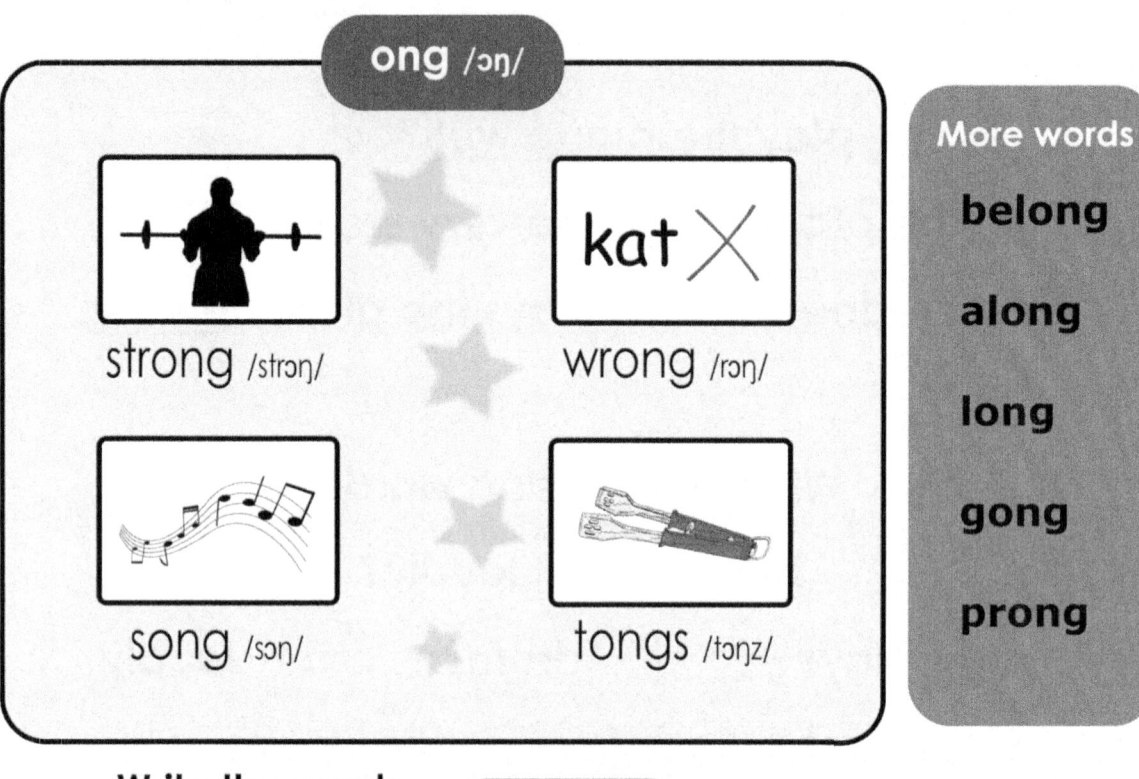

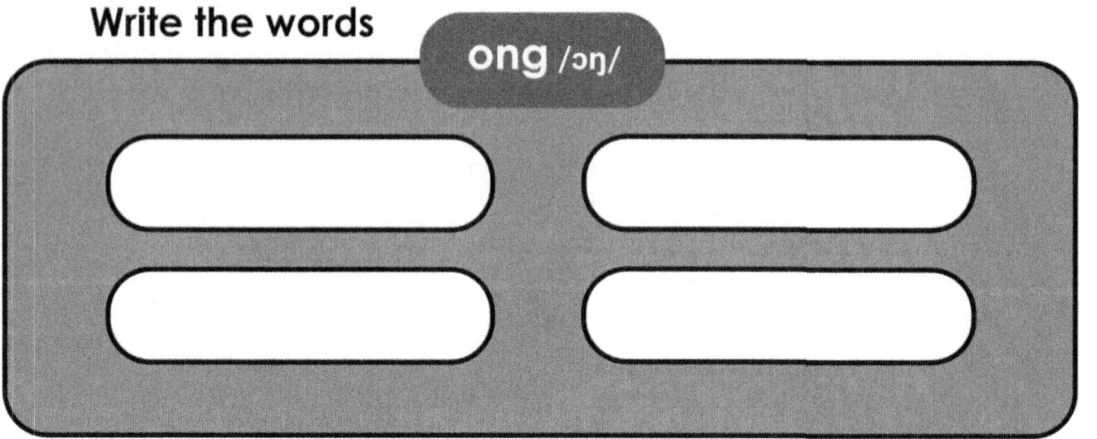

ong /ɔŋ/

strong /strɔŋ/

wrong /rɔŋ/ kat ✗

song /sɔŋ/

tongs /tɔŋz/

More words

belong

along

long

gong

prong

Write the words

ong /ɔŋ/

Write the letters & Read the sentences!

These t_ _ _s are too l_ _ _.

You can sing al_ _ _ to the s_ _ _.

This g_ _ _ bel_ _ _s to that str_ _ _ man.

Test

Complete the words

1. s_____y   3. w_____l   5. c_____y

2. l_____y   4. g_____y   6. t_____y

Write the answer next to the letter "A"

A: ___ 7. How ___ play the piano?

a. do he
b. does they
c. does she

A: ___ 8. How does he play the guitar?

a. He play the guitar loudly.
b. He plays the guitar badly.
c. He plays the guitar correct.

A: ___ 9. Does she ___ the violin well? Yes, she ___ the violin very well.

a. plays, plays
b. play, plays
c. plays, play

A: ___ 10. Does he play the drums quietly?

a. No, he doesn't. He plays the drums loudly.
b. No, he don't. He plays the drums loudly.
c. No, he doesn't. He play the drums loudly.

Answers on Page 306

Lesson 44

- Learn the words
- Learn the sentences
- Learn the phonics
- Test yourself!

Activities

діяльність

Learn the words

1. **play piano**
   грати на піаніно
2. **read books**
   читати книги
3. **play video games**
   грати у відео ігри
4. **surf the internet**
   шукати в Інтернеті
5. **take photographs**
   Фотографувати
6. **watch TV**
   дивитись телевізор
7. **sing songs**
   співати пісні
8. **study English**
   вивчати англійську
9. **play cards**
   грати в карти
10. **go shopping**
    ходити за покупками

Write the missing letters!

1. p_a_ p_ _n_
2. r_ _d b_o_s
3. _la_ v_d_o g_ _e_
4. s_ _f t_e i_t_r_e_
5. t_k_ p_ot_g_a_hs
6. w_t_h T_
7. s_ _g s_n_s
8. s_u_y E_ _l_s_
9. _l y c_ _ds
10. g_ s_op_i_g

Have fun with the words!

Connect the words

play •   • shopping

surf •   • cards

sing •   • photographs

go •   • the internet

watch •   • books

play •   • English

take •   • piano

study •   • songs

read •   • TV

Which activity is missing? _____

Learn the sentences

What have you been doing these days?
These days, I have been <u>reading books</u>.
I haven't been <u>singing songs</u>.

Write the missing words!

What _____ you _____ doing _____ days?
These _____, I've been _____ the internet.
I _____ been taking _____.

What have you been _____ these _____?
These days, we've _____ _____ video _____.
_____ haven't _____ going _____.

_____ have they _____ doing _____?
These days, _____ been _____ English.
They _____ _____ watching _____.

_____?
_____.
_____.

Learn the sentences

Have you been <u>playing piano</u>?
Yes, I have been.
No, I haven't been.

Write the missing words!

Have _____ been _____ cards?
Yes, _____ have _____ .
_____ , I _____ been.

_____ you _____ going _____ ?
_____ , we _____ been.
No, _____ haven't _____ .

Have _____ been _____ books?
Yes, they _____ _____ .
_____ , they _____ _____ .

_____?
_____.
_____.

Learn the phonics

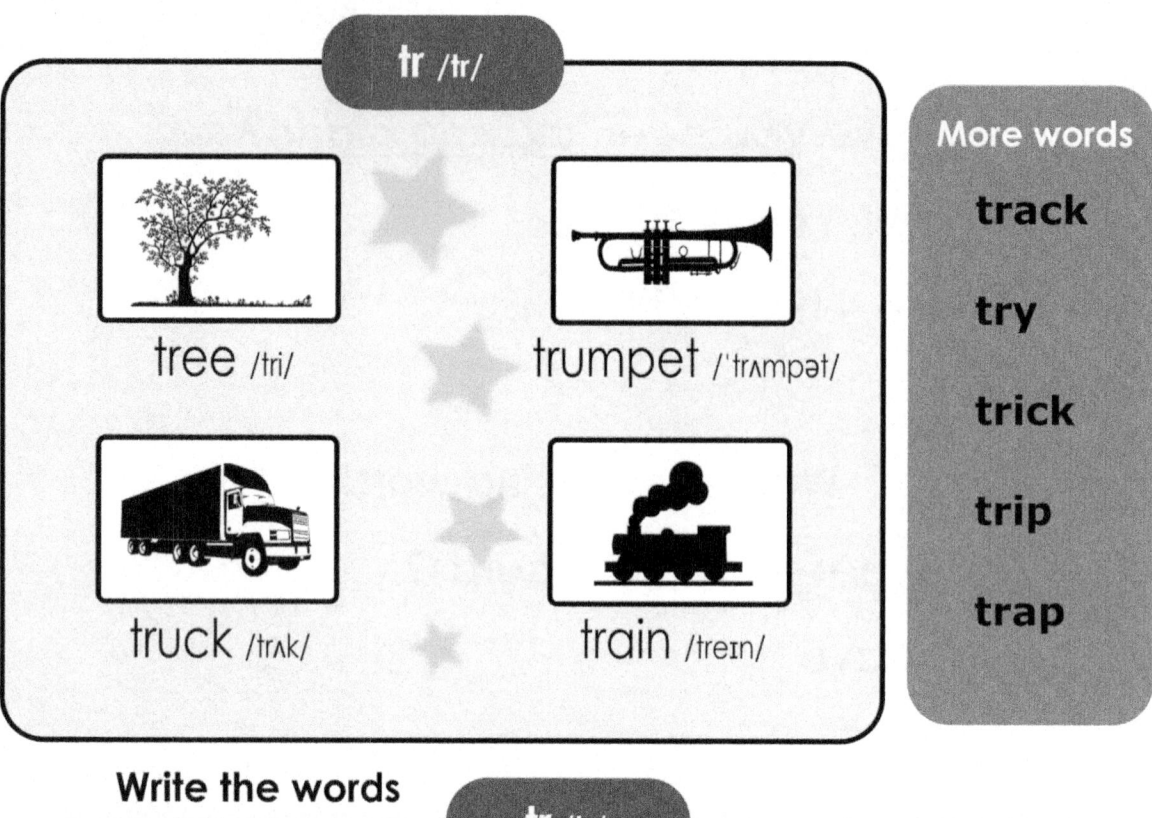

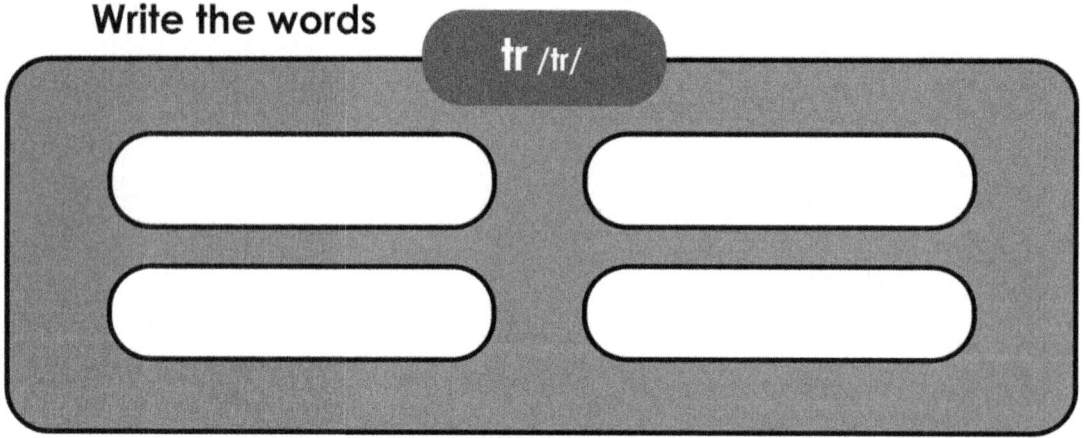

tr /tr/

tree /tri/

trumpet /ˈtrʌmpət/

truck /trʌk/

train /treɪn/

More words

track

try

trick

trip

trap

Write the words

tr /tr/

Write the letters & Read the sentences!

The _ _ain is on the _ _ack.

I _ _ied to learn the _ _umpet.

We saw many _ _ucks on our _ _ip.

Test

Complete the words

1. E_____h   3. b_____s   5. p_____s

2. s_____s   4. s_____g   6. i_____t

Write the answer next to the letter "A"

A: ___ **7.** What have you ___ doing lately?

a. be
b. been
c. being

A: ___ **8.** These days, I have been ___ video games.

a. playing
b. played
c. play

A: ___ **9.** Have you been watching TV?

a. Yes, I have.
b. Yes, I have been.
c. Yes, I been.

A: ___ **10.** ___ you been reading books? No, I ___ been.

a. Has, hasn't
b. Have, haven't
c. Are, aren't

Answers on Page 306

Lesson 45

- Learn the words
- Learn the sentences
- Learn the phonics
- Test yourself!

Outdoor activities

заходи на свіжому повітрі

Learn the words

1. **kayaking**
   каякінг
2. **going camping**
   відправлятися в похід з палатками
3. **flying a kite**
   запускати повітряного змія
4. **riding a horse**
   їздити верхи
5. **going hiking**
   відправлятися в піший похід
6. **skydiving**
   Затяжні стрибки з парашутом
7. **riding a bike**
   кататись на велосипеді
8. **snowboarding**
   сноубордінг
9. **going fishing**
   рибалити
10. **doing gardening**
    займатися садівництвом

Write the missing letters!

1. k_ya_i_g
2. g_i_g c_m_ _ng
3. f_y_ _g a _it_
4. r_ _i_g a h_ _s_
5. g_i_g h_ _i_g
6. s_y_i_i_g
7. r_d_n_ a b_ _e
8. s_o_b_a_di_g
9. _o_ng fi_h_n_
10. d_i_ _g_ _dni_g

- 270 -

Have fun with the words!

Unscramble the words

1. been / a / has / bike / She / spring / riding / this

   _____ .

2. doing / winter / been / this / What / he / has

   _____ ?

3. kite / hasn't / a / flying / He / been

   _____ .

4. she / Has / gardening / been / autumn / this / doing

   _____ ?

5. horse / a / been / riding / He's

   _____ .

6. she / What / been / winter / has / this / doing

   _____ ?

7. been / hasn't / No / she

   _____ .

8. he / summer / this / going / been / Has / fishing

   _____ ?

Learn the sentences

What has she been doing this <u>summer</u>?
She has been <u>riding a bike</u> this summer.
She hasn't been <u>flying a kite</u>.

Write the missing words!

What _____ he been _____ this winter?
He has _____ snowboarding this _____ .
He _____ been _____ a horse.

_____ has _____ been doing this _____ ?
She _____ been _____ gardening _____ autumn.
She _____ _____ skydiving.

What _____ he _____ _____ spring?
_____ has _____ going _____ this _____ .
He _____ _____ _____ fishing.

_____ ?
_____ .
_____ .

- 272 -

Learn the sentences

Has he been <u>going hiking</u> this <u>spring</u>?
Yes, he has been.
No, he hasn't been. He's been <u>riding a horse</u>.

Write the missing words!

Has she _____ kayaking _____ summer?
_____, she _____ been.
No, _____ hasn't _____. She's been _____ a bike.

_____ he been _____ hiking _____ winter?
Yes, he _____ _____.
No, he _____ been. _____ _____ snowboarding.

Has _____ been _____ fishing _____ _____?
_____, she _____ _____.
No, _____ hasn't _____. She's been _____ a kite.

_____?
_____.
_____.

Learn the phonics

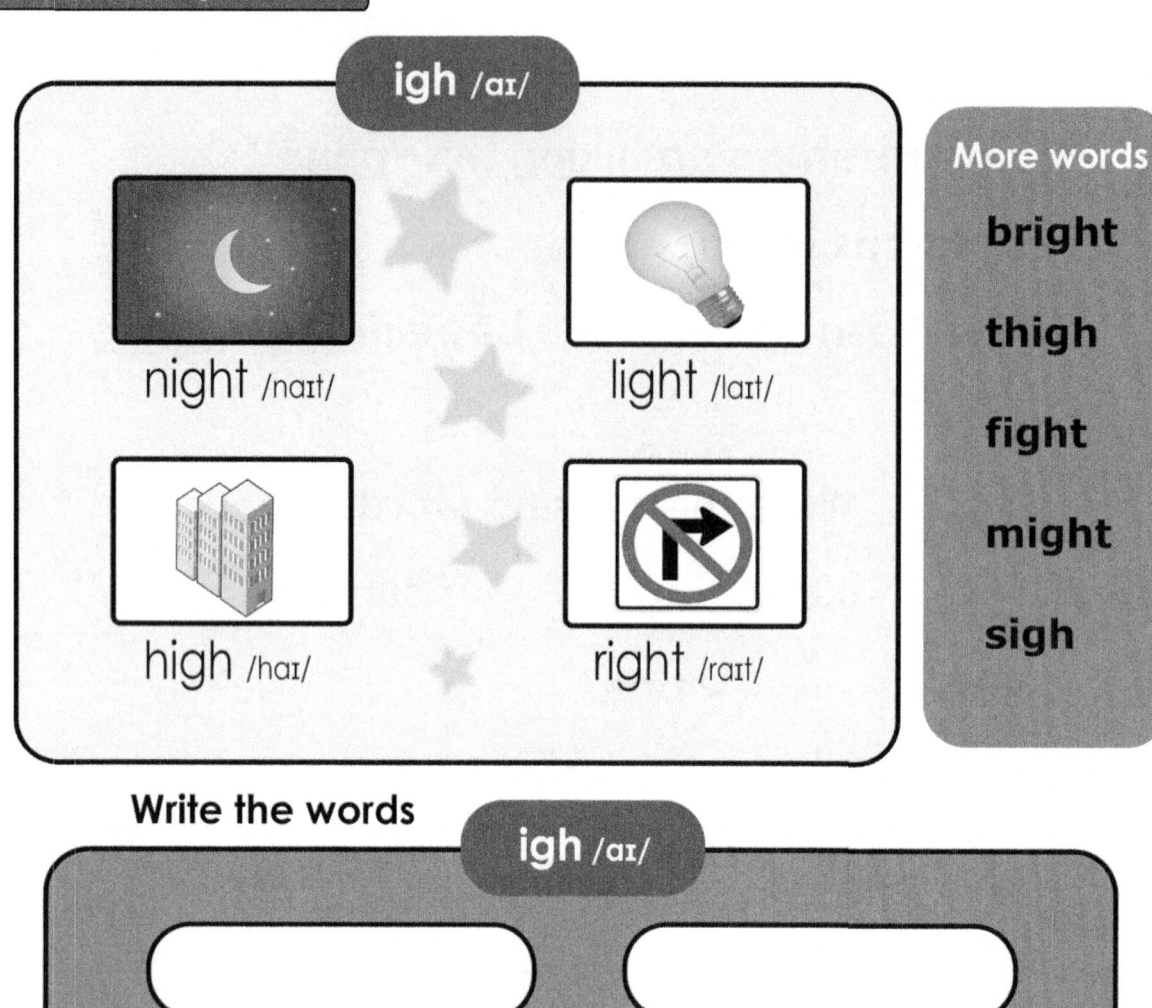

igh /aɪ/

night /naɪt/

light /laɪt/

high /haɪ/

right /raɪt/

More words
- bright
- thigh
- fight
- might
- sigh

Write the words

igh /aɪ/

Write the letters & Read the sentences!

We leave the br_ _ _t l_ _ _ts on at n_ _ _t.

This table m_ _ _t be too h_ _ _.

My th_ _ _ is hurting on the r_ _ _t side.

Test

Complete the words

1. h_____e
2. f_____g
3. c_____g
4. k_____g
5. g_____g
6. k_____e

Write the answer next to the letter "A"

A: ___ **7.** What ___ he been ___ this winter?

a. has, done
b. have, do
c. has, doing

A: ___ **8.** She has been ___ a kite this autumn.

a. flew
b. flying
c. flown

A: ___ **9.** Has she been kayaking this summer?

a. Yes, she has been.
b. Yes, she have been.
c. Yes, she has.

A: ___ **10.** Has he been snowboarding this winter?

a. No, he hasn't be. He's been skydiving.
b. No, he hasn't been. His been skydiving.
c. No, he hasn't been. He's been skydiving.

Answers on Page 306

Lesson 46 — Ocean life

- Learn the words
- Learn the sentences
- Learn the phonics
- Test yourself!

життя в океані

Learn the words

1. **dolphin** — дельфін
2. **seal** — тюлень
3. **whale** — кит
4. **octopus** — восьминіг
5. **shark** — акула
6. **jellyfish** — медуза
7. **tuna** — тунець
8. **salmon** — лосось
9. **crab** — краб
10. **squid** — кальмар

Write the missing letters!

1. d_l_h_n
2. s_ _l
3. w_a_e
4. o_t_p_s
5. s_a_ _
6. j_l_y_i_h
7. t_n_
8. s_l_ _n
9. c_ _b
10. s_ _i_

Have fun with the words!

Find the 8 ocean animals!

Write the 8 shapes

1.
2.
3.
4.
5.
6.
7.
8.

Learn the sentences

What do you hope to see one day?

I hope to see a <u>dolphin</u> one day.

I have always wanted to see a dolphin.

Write the missing words!

What do you _____ to see _____ day?

I hope _____ see a _____ one day.

I have _____ wanted to _____ a whale.

What _____ they hope _____ see one _____?

They _____ see an _____ one day.

They _____ always _____ to _____ an octopus.

_____ does he _____ to _____ one day?

He _____ to _____ a _____ one _____.

_____ has _____ wanted _____ see _____ seal.

_____?

_____.

_____.

Learn the sentences

Have you ever seen a <u>shark</u>?

Yes, I have. I saw one in the ocean.

No, I have never seen a shark.

Write the missing words!

Have you _____ seen _____ jellyfish?

_____, I have. I _____ one in the _____.

No, I have _____ seen a _____.

Has she _____ seen a _____?

Yes, she _____. She saw _____ in _____ ocean.

_____, she has never _____ _____ seal.

_____ you ever _____ _____ salmon?

Yes, we _____. We _____ one _____ the _____.

No, _____ have _____ _____ a _____.

_____?

_____.

_____.

Learn the phonics

sn /sn/

snail /sneɪl/

snow /snoʊ/

snack /snæk/

snake /sneɪk/

More words

snip

sneeze

sneak

snorkel

sniff

Write the words

sn /sn/

Write the letters & Read the sentences!

He has been _ _iffing and _ _eezing.

There aren't any _ _ails in the _ _ow.

The _ _ake ate my _ _ack.

Test

Complete the words

1. d_____n   3. o_____s   5. s_____d

2. j_____h   4. c_____b   6. t_____a

Write the answer next to the letter "A"

A: ___ **7.** What ___ she ___ see one day?

a. do, hope
b. does, hope to
c. does, hopes

A: ___ **8.** He has always ___ see a seal.

a. want to
b. wants to
c. wanted to

A: ___ **9.** ___ he ever seen a salmon?

a. Have
b. Has
c. Haves

A: ___ **10.** Have you ever seen a whale?

a. Yes, I have. I saw one in the ocean.
b. Yes, I have. I seen one in the ocean.
c. Yes, I have. I saw one at the ocean.

Answers on Page 306

Lesson 47 — In the bathroom

- Learn the words
- Learn the sentences
- Learn the phonics
- Test yourself!

у ванні

Learn the words

1. **shower** — душ
2. **bathtub** — ванна
3. **bath towel** — рушник
4. **bath mat** — килимок для ванної
5. **mirror** — дзеркало
6. **toilet** — туалет
7. **toilet paper** — туалетний папір
8. **sink** — раковина
9. **soap** — мило
10. **shelf** — полиця

Write the missing letters!

1. s_o_e_
2. b_t_t_b
3. _a_h t_ _e_
4. b_ _h m_ _
5. m_r_o_
6. t_ _le_
7. t_i_e_ p_p_ _
8. s_ _k
9. s_a_
10. s_e_ _

Have fun with the words!

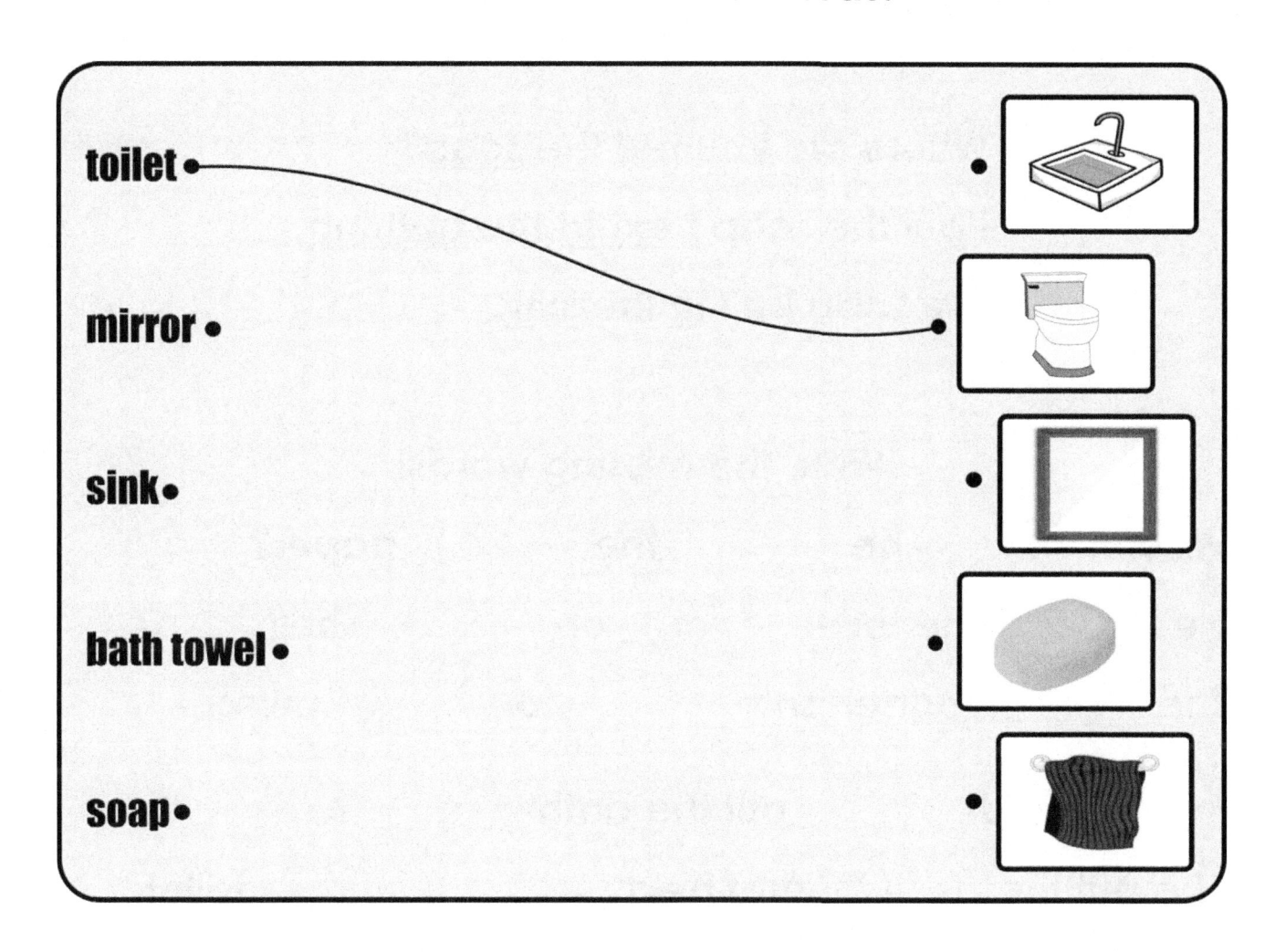

- toilet
- mirror
- sink
- bath towel
- soap

Unscramble the letters!

1. LHESF _____

2. TBHA MTA _____

3. HREWOS _____

4. LTOETI APREP _____

5. TBHUBTA _____

Learn the sentences

Where did you put the <u>soap</u>?

I put the soap <u>next to</u> the <u>bathtub</u>.

The soap isn't <u>in</u> the <u>sink</u>.

Write the missing words!

Where _____ he _____ the _____ paper?

He _____ the toilet _____ on _____ shelf.

The _____ paper isn't _____ to _____ mirror.

_____ did _____ put the bath _____ ?

She put the _____ mat next _____ _____ toilet.

The _____ isn't in _____ bathtub.

Where _____ you _____ _____ _____ ?

I _____ the soap _____ the _____ .

_____ soap _____ _____ _____ shower.

_____?

_____.

_____.

Learn the sentences

Did you put the <u>bath towel</u> <u>on</u> the <u>shelf</u>?

Yes, I did.

No, I didn't. I put it <u>next to</u> the <u>toilet</u>.

Write the missing words!

Did _____ put the _____ mat next to _____ sink?

Yes, she _____ .

No, _____ didn't. She _____ it _____ the bathtub.

Did he _____ the _____ paper on _____ shelf?

Yes, _____ did.

No, he _____ . _____ put it _____ the shower.

_____ you put the soap _____ to _____ mirror?

Yes, _____ _____ .

_____ , I _____ . I put _____ in _____ _____ .

_____?

_____.

_____.

Learn the phonics

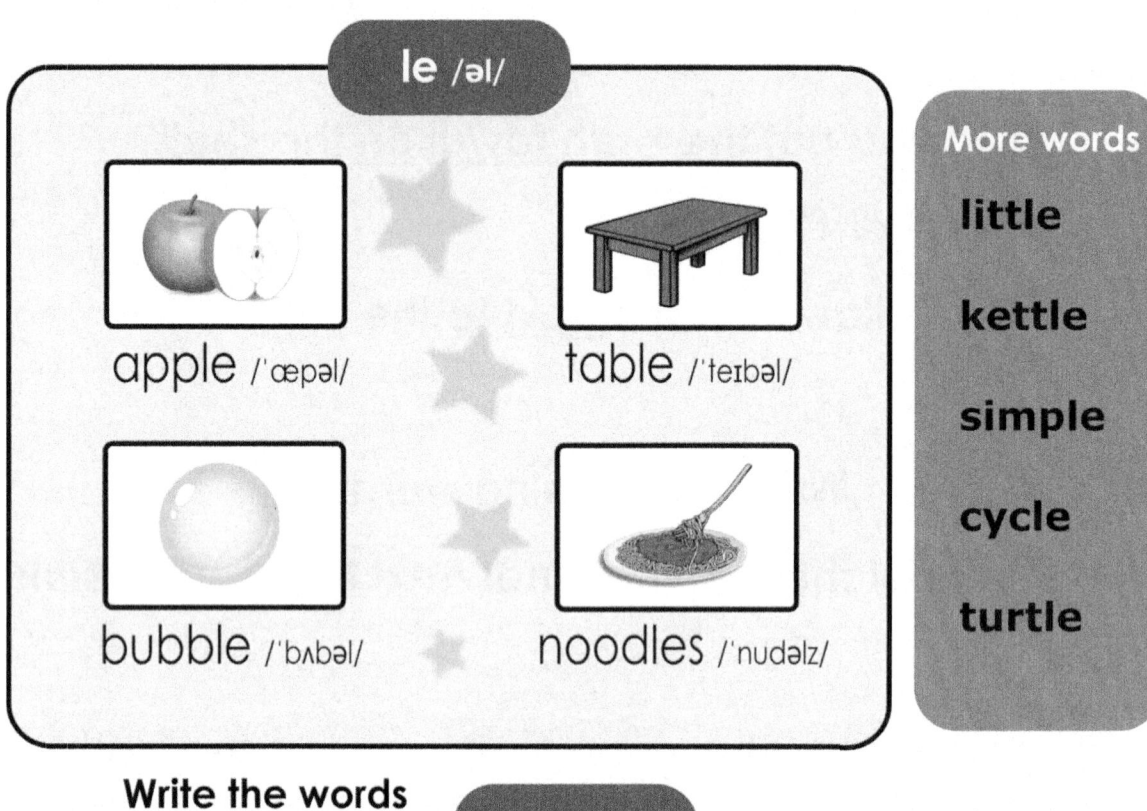

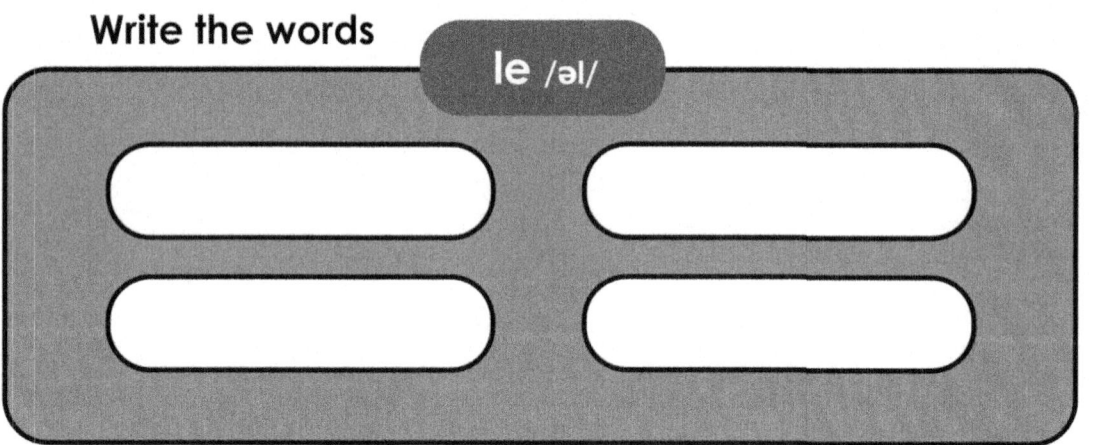

le /əl/

apple /ˈæpəl/

table /ˈteɪbəl/

bubble /ˈbʌbəl/

noodles /ˈnudəlz/

More words

little

kettle

simple

cycle

turtle

Write the words

le /əl/

Write the letters & Read the sentences!

I put the app_ _ on the tab_ _.

The turt_ _ looked at the bubb_ _.

This black kett_ _ is too litt_ _.

Test

Complete the words

1. m_____r 3. b_____b 5. s_____f

2. t_____t 4. s_____r 6. s_____p

Write the answer next to the letter "A"

A: ___ **7.** Where did you put the bath towel?

a. I put the bath towel next too the shower.
b. I put the bath towel next the shower.
c. I put the bath towel next to the shower.

A: ___ **8.** The bath mat ___ in the bathroom.

a. doesn't
b. isn't
c. aren't

A: ___ **9.** Did she put the soap in the sink?

a. No, she didn't. She put it on the shelf.
b. No, he didn't. He put it on the shelf.
c. No she didn't. She put it on the shelf.

A: ___ **10.** Did he ___ the bath towel on the shelf?

a. puts
b. put
c. putting

Answers on Page 306

Lesson 48

- Learn the words
- Learn the sentences
- Learn the phonics
- Test yourself!

Capital cities

столиці

Learn the words

1. **London**
   Лондон
2. **Madrid**
   Мадрид
3. **Paris**
   Париж
4. **Ottawa**
   Оттава
5. **Washington, D.C.**
   Вашингтон
6. **Cape Town**
   Кейптаун
7. **Wellington**
   Веллінгтон
8. **Canberra**
   Канберра
9. **Bangkok**
   Бангкок
10. **Beijing**
    Пекін

Write the missing letters!

1. L_n_o_
2. _a_r_d
3. P_ _i_
4. O_t_ _a
5. _a_ _in_to_, D. _.
6. C_p_ T_ _n
7. _e_li_g_o_
8. C_ _be_r_
9. _a_g_ _k
10. B_ _j_n_

- 288 -

Have fun with the words!

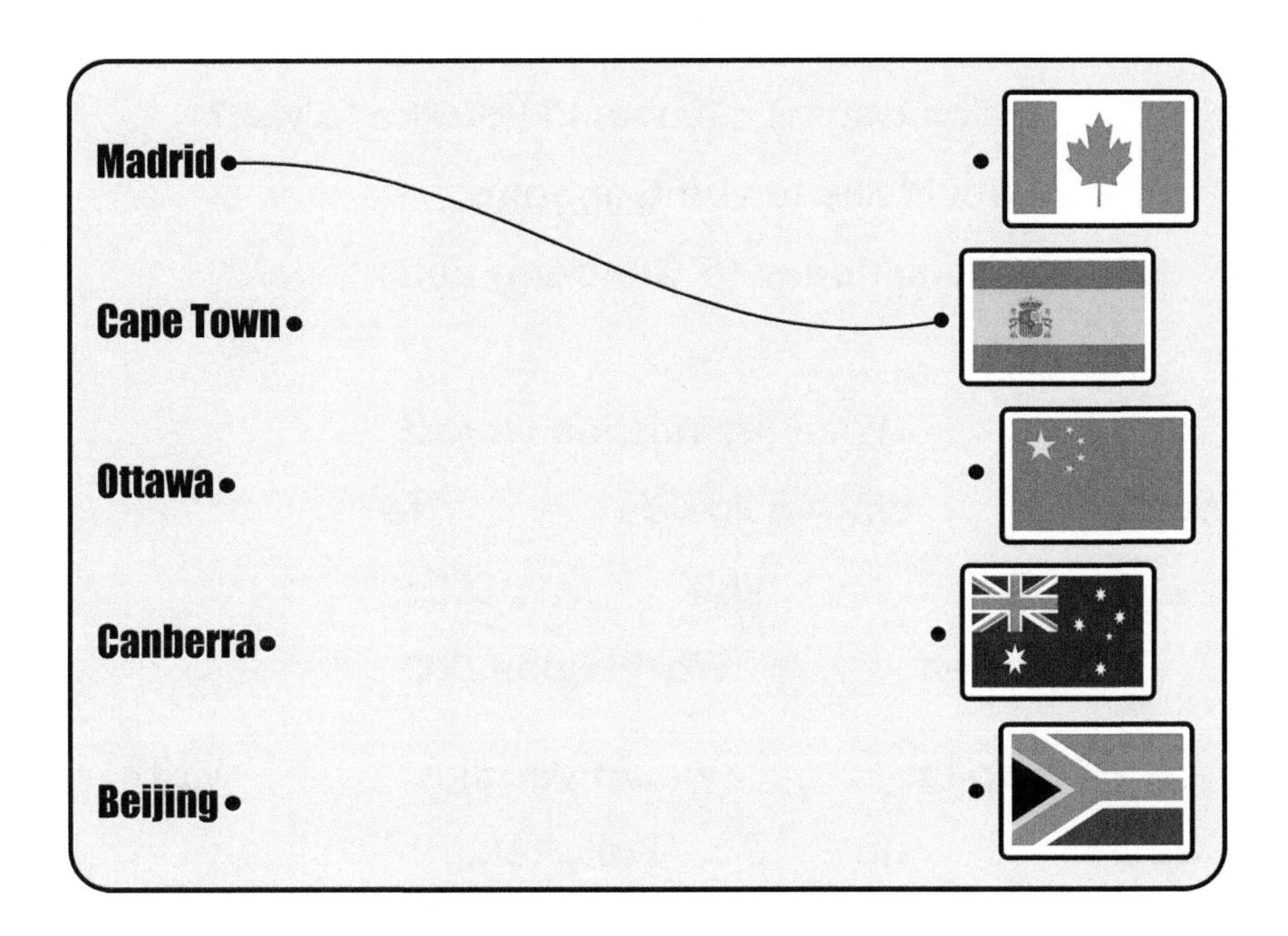

Madrid — (Spain flag)
Cape Town
Ottawa
Canberra
Beijing

Write 4 more capital cities!

1. _____
2. _____
3. _____
4. _____

What is the capital city of your country?

_____

Learn the sentences

Which capital city would you like to visit?
I would like to visit <u>Canberra</u>.
I haven't been to Canberra yet.

Write the missing words!

Which _____ city would you _____ to _____?
I _____ like _____ visit _____ D.C.
I _____ been _____ Washington D.C. _____.

_____ capital _____ would you like _____ visit?
I would _____ to _____ Bangkok.
_____ haven't _____ to _____ yet.

Which _____ would _____ like to _____?
I _____ _____ to visit _____ Town.
I _____ _____ to Cape _____ _____.

_____?
_____.
_____.

Learn the sentences

Would you like to visit <u>London</u>?

Yes, I would love to visit London.

No, I have already been there.

Write the missing words!

Would you _____ to _____ Paris?

Yes, I _____ love _____ visit _____.

No, _____ have _____ been _____.

_____ you like _____ visit _____?

Yes, _____ would _____ to _____ Ottawa.

_____, I _____ already _____ there.

Would _____ like _____ _____ Beijing?

Yes, I _____ love _____ _____.

_____, I _____ already _____ _____.

_____?
_____.
_____.

Learn the phonics

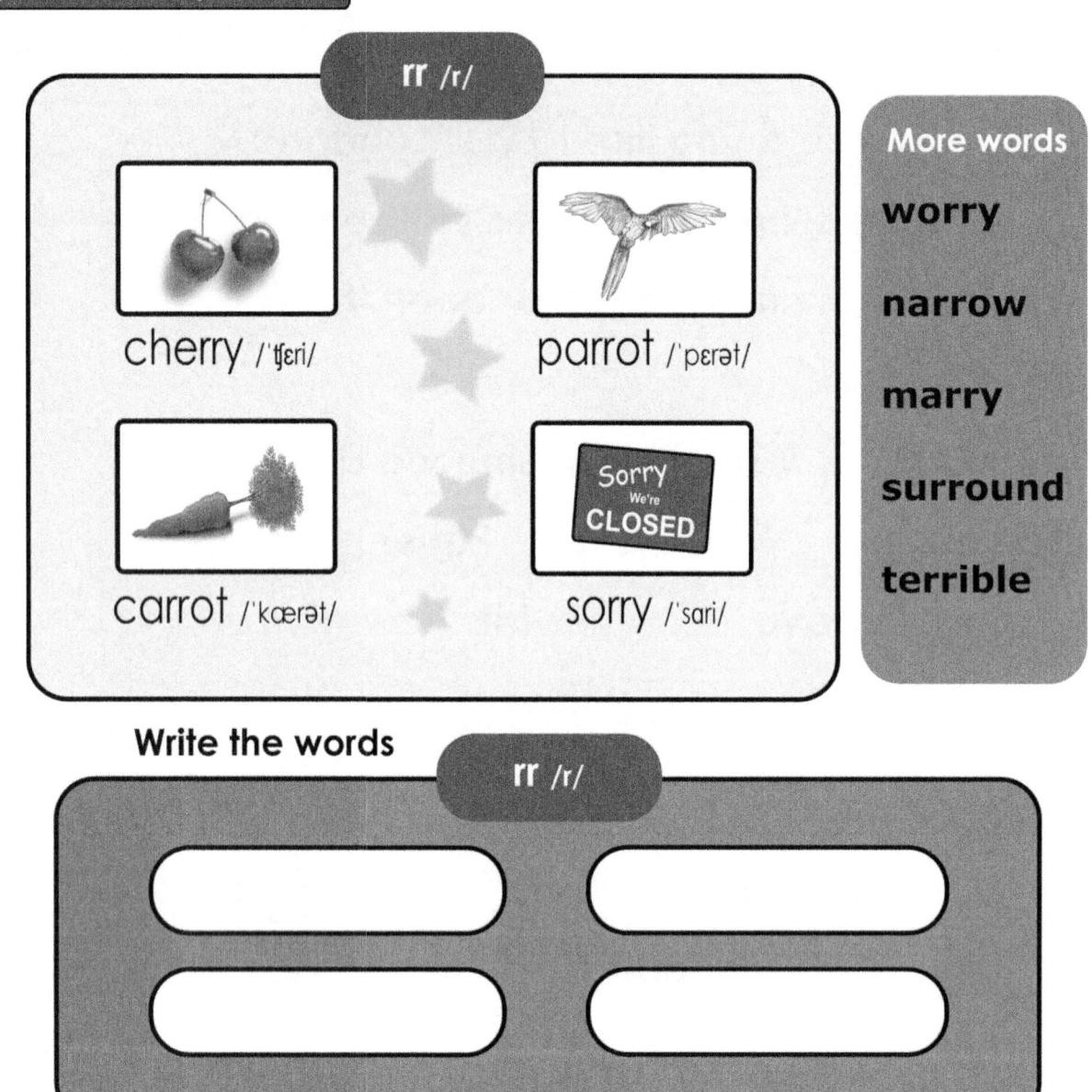

rr /r/

cherry /ˈtʃɛri/

parrot /ˈpɛrət/

carrot /ˈkærət/

sorry /ˈsɑri/

More words

worry

narrow

marry

surround

terrible

Write the words

rr /r/

Write the letters & Read the sentences!

That pa_ _ot eats che_ _ies.

I'm so_ _y I ate your ca_ _ot.

He is wo_ _ied about taking a fe_ _y.

Test

Complete the words

1. P_____s   3. B_____k   5. C_____a

2. O_____a   4. W_____n   6. L_____n

Write the answer next to the letter "A"

A: ___ 7. Which capital city ___ you like to visit?

a. would
b. could
c. should

A: ___ 8. I ___ been to Washington D.C. yet.

a. have
b. haven't
c. hasn't

A: ___ 9. Would you like to visit Cape Town?

a. Yes, I would to love visit Cape Town.
b. Yes, I would love to visit Cape Town.
c. Yes, I would love visiting Cape Town.

A: ___ 10. No, I have ___ been there.

a. already
b. all ready
c. yet

Answers on Page 306

Lesson 49

- Learn the words
- Learn the sentences
- Learn the phonics
- Test yourself!

In the toolbox

в ящику для інструментів

Learn the words

1. **a hammer**
   молоток
2. **a shovel**
   лопата
3. **a paintbrush**
   кисть
4. **a screwdriver**
   викрутка
5. **an electric drill**
   електрична дриль
6. **a tape measure**
   рулетка
7. **a wrench**
   гайковий ключ
8. **a ladder**
   драбина
9. **pliers**
   плоскогубці
10. **an axe**
    сокира

Write the missing letters!

1. h_m_e_
2. s_o_ _l
3. p_ _n_b_u_h
4. s_r_w_r_v_r
5. _le_t_ _c d_i_l
6. t_ _e m_ _su_e
7. _r_n_h
8. l_d_ _r
9. _li_r_
10. a_ _

- 294 -

Have fun with the words!

> **Find one mistake and write the sentence correctly**

Which tool should I uses to fix the table?
_____

You should use a electric drill.
_____

You should'nt use a wrench.
_____

Which tool should I use fix the chair?
_____

You should use a pliers.
_____

You shouldn't use tape measure.
_____

Should I use an axe to fix these shelf?
_____

No, he should use a screwdriver.
_____

Learn the sentences

Which tool should I use to fix the <u>chair</u>?

You should use <u>a screwdriver</u>.

You shouldn't use <u>a hammer</u>.

Write the missing words!

Which _____ should I _____ to fix _____ table?

You _____ use an _____ drill.

_____ shouldn't _____ pliers.

_____ tool _____ I use _____ fix the shelf?

You should _____ _____ ladder.

You _____ _____ an _____ .

Which _____ _____ I _____ to _____ the chair?

_____ should _____ a tape _____ .

You _____ _____ _____ shovel.

_____ ?

_____ .

_____ .

Learn the sentences

Should I use <u>pliers</u> to fix the <u>table</u>?

Yes, you should.

No, you should use <u>a wrench</u>.

Write the missing words!

Should I _____ a screwdriver to _____ the _____?

Yes, you _____.

No, _____ should _____ an electric _____.

_____ I use _____ paintbrush to fix _____ shelf?

Yes, _____ should.

No, you _____ use _____ axe.

Should I _____ a hammer _____ fix _____ table?

Yes, _____ _____.

_____, you _____ use _____ _____ measure.

_____?
_____.
_____.

Learn the phonics

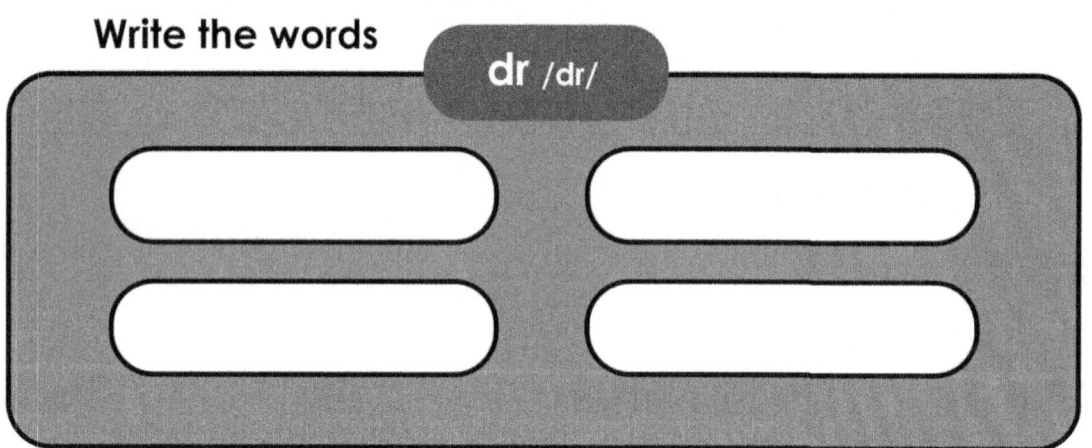

dr /dr/

drum /drʌm/

drop /drɑp/

drink /drɪŋk/

drill /drɪl/

More words
drive
dream
dry
dress
draw

Write the words

dr /dr/

Write the letters & Read the sentences!

My _ _eam is to play the _ _ums.

I _ _opped the _ _ink on your _ _ess.

The electric _ _ill is still not _ _y.

Test

Complete the words

1. w_____h 3. s_____l 5. s_____r

2. h_____r 4. p_____s 6. p_____h

Write the answer next to the letter "A"

A: ___ 7. Which tool should I use to fix the shelf?

a. You should use a axe to fix the shelf.
b. You should use an axe to fix the shelf.
c. You should use an axe fix the shelf.

A: ___ 8. You ___ use a ladder.

a. shouldnt'
b. should'nt
c. shouldn't

A: ___ 9. Should I use an ___ to fix the table?

a. electric drill
b. hammer
c. ladder

A: ___ 10. Should I use a tape measure to fix the chair?

a. Yes, I should.
b. Yes, you should.
c. Yes, you did.

Answers on Page 306

Lesson 50 — At the cinema

- Learn the words
- Learn the sentences
- Learn the phonics
- Test yourself!

в кінотеатрі

Learn the words

1. **exciting** — захоплюючий
2. **scary** — страшний
3. **romantic** — романтичний
4. **violent** — зі сценами насилля
5. **informative** — інформативний
6. **interesting** — цікавий
7. **boring** — нудний
8. **enjoyable** — приємний
9. **sad** — сумний
10. **funny** — смішний

Write the missing letters!

1. e_c_ti_g
2. s_a_ _
3. _o_a_t_c
4. v_ _l_n_
5. i_f_r_a_i_e
6. i_t_re_t_n_
7. _o_i_g
8. e_j_ _a_le
9. s_ _
10. f_n_ _

Have fun with the words!

Word Search

```
i z e q q e i q p q b p z v s i l n
e n x m k f n n i r t x u z i m c j
v m t v z k q j f u o i y a i r y d
s i y e i p e j o o m m d i z g q s
f e m b r o x x j y r c a p b g o c
m u j s v e l m c t a m c n r r m a
l f n t c p s e p i n b a q t s p r
x q j n f x w t n x t r l t e i a y
s n g y y p b n i t c i x e i f c g
v a w b o r i n g n e a n n p v o l
d c d s h w v f r g g a o g m b e c
f e p x a j y j l d v b t a x q b z
```

exciting   **interesting**

scary   **boring**

romantic   **enjoyable**

violent   **sad**

informative   **funny**

Learn the sentences

What did you think about the movie?
I thought the movie was <u>exciting</u>.
I didn't think the movie was <u>boring</u>.

Write the missing words!

What _____ you think _____ the _____?
I _____ the _____ was funny.
I didn't _____ the movie _____ _____.

_____ did he _____ about _____ movie?
He _____ _____ movie _____ scary.
He _____ think _____ _____ was enjoyable.

What _____ _____ think _____ the _____?
_____ thought _____ _____ was _____.
She _____ _____ the _____ _____ boring.

_____?
_____.
_____.

- 302 -

Learn the sentences

Did you think the movie was <u>romantic</u>?

Yes, I thought it was.

No, I thought it was <u>sad</u>.

Write the missing words!

Did you _____ the _____ was exciting?

Yes, _____ thought _____ was.

No, I _____ it was _____ .

Did _____ think _____ movie _____ informative?

_____ , she _____ it _____ .

No, _____ thought _____ was _____ .

_____ he _____ the _____ _____ boring?

Yes, _____ thought _____ _____ .

_____ , he _____ _____ was _____ .

_____?

_____.

_____.

Learn the phonics

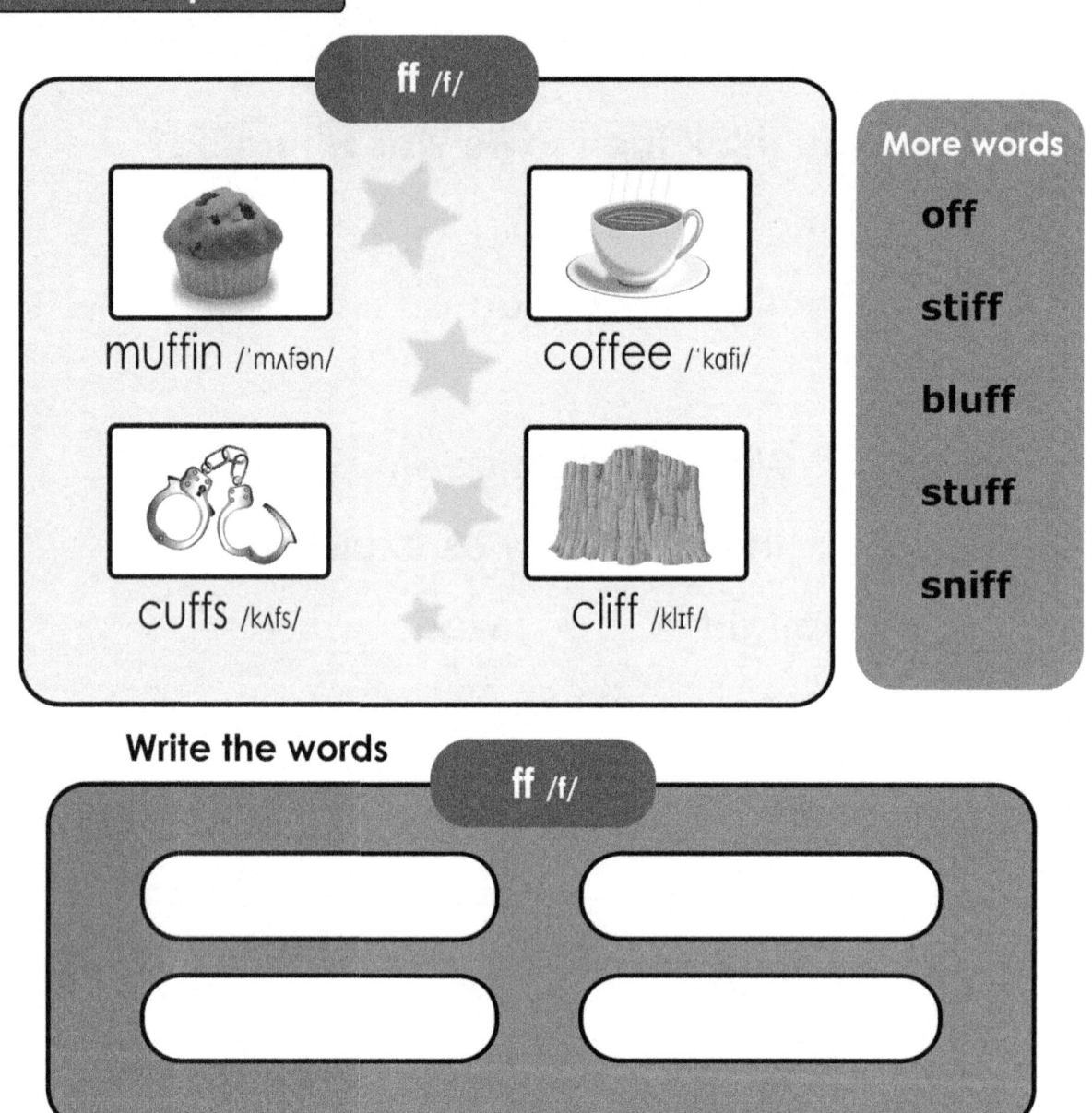

ff /f/

muffin /ˈmʌfən/

coffee /ˈkɑfi/

cuffs /kʌfs/

cliff /klɪf/

More words

off

stiff

bluff

stuff

sniff

Write the words

ff /f/

Write the letters & Read the sentences!

Don't fall o_ _ the cli_ _.

The dog is sni_ _ing the mu_ _ins.

These handcu_ _s are too sti_ _.

Test

Complete the words

1. v_____t 3. f_____y 5. s_____y

2. r_____c 4. e_____e 6. e_____g

Write the answer next to the letter "A"

A: ___ **7.** What did you think about the movie?

a. I thought movie was sad. I didn't think movie was scary.
b. I thought the movie was sad. I didn't thought the movie was scary.
c. I thought the movie was sad. I didn't think the movie was scary.

A: ___ **8.** What did he think ___ the movie?

a. around
b. about
c. above

A: ___ **9.** Did you think the movie was informative?

a. Yes, I thought it was.
b. Yes, I thought it is.
c. Yes, I thought it did.

A: ___ **10.** Did she ___ the movie was informative?

a. think
b. thought
c. thinks

Answers on Page 306

Answers

Test 1-5	Lesson 1	Lesson 2	Lesson 3	Lesson 4	Lesson 5
Question 1	pencil	computer	yellow	brother	star
Question 2	tape	globe	brown	sister	triangle
Question 3	marker	poster	orange	uncle	octagon
Question 4	eraser	bookshelf	green	aunt	rectangle
Question 5	crayon	whiteboard	black	father	heart
Question 6	whiteout	desk	purple	mother	diamond
Question 7	c	a	b	b	b
Question 8	b	b	c	c	c
Question 9	a	c	a	b	a
Question 10	b	a	b	a	c

Test 6-10	Lesson 6	Lesson 7	Lesson 8	Lesson 9	Lesson 10
Question 1	tiger	builder	strawberry	stomach	tennis
Question 2	bear	nurse	cherry	head	volleyball
Question 3	monkey	salesclerk	watermelon	foot	golf
Question 4	kangaroo	doctor	pineapple	finger	cricket
Question 5	lion	teacher	banana	shoulder	badminton
Question 6	crocodile	chef	lemon	neck	hockey
Question 7	a	B	b	c	a
Question 8	c	c	a	b	c
Question 9	b	b	c	b	a
Question 10	b	a	c	a	b

Test 11-15	Lesson 11	Lesson 12	Lesson 13	Lesson 14	Lesson 15
Question 1	store	blouse	geography	carrot	airplane
Question 2	cinema	sweater	computer	potato	dinosaur
Question 3	park	necktie	history	broccoli	robot
Question 4	restaurant	jacket	music	spinach	teddy bear
Question 5	supermarket	scarf	English	mushroom	ball
Question 6	gym	dress	science	onion	doll
Question 7	b	b	a	b	c
Question 8	b	b	b	c	b
Question 9	c	a	b	a	a
Question 10	a	a	c	c	b

Test 16-20	Lesson 16	Lesson 17	Lesson 18	Lesson 19	Lesson 20
Question 1	blender	angry	strawberry	cloudy	clock
Question 2	stove	sad	raspberry	sunny	armchair
Question 3	pan	bored	chocolate	freezing	bookcase
Question 4	toaster	tired	vanilla	rainy	sofa
Question 5	cupboard	energetic	cherry	warm	television
Question 6	refrigerator	frustrated	almond	cold	painting
Question 7	a	a	c	c	b
Question 8	b	c	b	a	c
Question 9	a	a	c	c	c
Question 10	c	b	a	c	a

Test 21-25	Lesson 21	Lesson 22	Lesson 23	Lesson 24	Lesson 25
Question 1	laundry	rabbit	swim	beef	Australia
Question 2	carpet	hamster	sing	chicken	Germany
Question 3	clothes	snake	read	salami	Mexico
Question 4	floor	mouse	cook	shrimp	England
Question 5	bedroom	turtle	write	bacon	Japan
Question 6	dinner	bird	draw	sausage	Russia
Question 7	a	a	c	a	b
Question 8	c	b	b	b	c
Question 9	c	c	a	c	a
Question 10	b	c	b	c	b

Test 26-30	Lesson 26	Lesson 27	Lesson 28	Lesson 29	Lesson 30
Question 1	Portuguese	bread	cupcakes	music room	ferry
Question 2	Vietnamese	water	pudding	lunchroom	airplane
Question 3	Spanish	salad	apple pie	computer lab	subway
Question 4	Hindi	juice	brownies	nurse's office	motorcycle
Question 5	Arabic	meat	waffles	office	train
Question 6	French	cola	pastries	classroom	scooter
Question 7	b	b	c	b	c
Question 8	c	c	c	c	b
Question 9	c	a	a	b	b
Question 10	b	b	b	a	a

Test 31-35	Lesson 31	Lesson 32	Lesson 33	Lesson 34	Lesson 35
Question 1	doughnut	mountain	article	meeting	binoculars
Question 2	cheeseburger	beach	presentation	appointment	compass
Question 3	french fries	river	quiz	party	plastic dishes
Question 4	onion rings	jungle	workbook	recital	gas bottle
Question 5	pancake	ocean	speech	birthday	cooler
Question 6	burrito	waterfall	report	competition	barbecue
Question 7	c	b	c	b	c
Question 8	c	c	c	c	a
Question 9	c	a	b	a	c
Question 10	a	b	a	c	a

Test 36-40	Lesson 36	Lesson 37	Lesson 38	Lesson 39	Lesson 40
Question 1	trash	trash can	gardening	wardrobe	bus stop
Question 2	breakfast	stop sign	photographs	blanket	hospital
Question 3	shower	fire hydrant	karaoke	mattress	clinic
Question 4	shopping	police car	fishing	pillow	police station
Question 5	homework	ambulance	camping	drawers	library
Question 6	dinner	truck	hiking	nightstand	factory
Question 7	b	c	a	b	b
Question 8	c	b	b	a	c
Question 9	c	b	c	c	b
Question 10	b	a	c	b	a

Test 41-45	Lesson 41	Lesson 42	Lesson 43	Lesson 44	Lesson 45
Question 1	eyebrow	lazy	slowly	English	horse
Question 2	hair	outgoing	loudly	songs	fishing
Question 3	mouth	generous	well	books	camping
Question 4	nose	interesting	gracefully	shopping	kayaking
Question 5	cheek	smart	correctly	photographs	gardening
Question 6	eyelash	easygoing	terribly	internet	kite
Question 7	b	a	c	b	c
Question 8	b	b	b	c	b
Question 9	c	c	b	a	a
Question 10	a	c	a	c	c

Test 46-50	Lesson 46	Lesson 47	Lesson 48	Lesson 49	Lesson 50
Question 1	dolphin	mirror	Paris	wrench	violent
Question 2	jellyfish	toilet	Ottawa	hammer	romantic
Question 3	octopus	bathtub	Bangkok	shovel	funny
Question 4	crab	shower	Wellington	pliers	enjoyable
Question 5	squid	shelf	Canberra	screwdriver	scary
Question 6	tuna	soap	London	paintbrush	exciting
Question 7	b	c	a	b	c
Question 8	c	b	b	c	b
Question 9	b	a	b	a	a
Question 10	a	b	a	b	a

Lee's EXCELLENT ENGLISH

The Bible of PHRASAL VERBS

Contents

Phrasal Verbs 1 – 18	Page 314
Test 1	Page 320
Phrasal Verbs 19 – 36	Page 322
Test 2	Page 328
Phrasal Verbs 37 – 54	Page 330
Test 3	Page 336
Phrasal Verbs 55 – 72	Page 338
Test 4	Page 344
Phrasal Verbs 73 – 90	Page 346
Test 5	Page 352
Phrasal Verbs 91 – 108	Page 354
Test 6	Page 360
Phrasal Verbs 109 – 126	Page 362
Test 7	Page 368
Phrasal Verbs 127 – 144	Page 370
Test 8	Page 376
Phrasal Verbs 145 – 162	Page 378
Test 9	Page 384
Phrasal Verbs 163 – 180	Page 386
Test 10	Page 392
Phrasal Verbs 181 – 198	Page 394
Test 11	Page 400
Phrasal Verbs 199 – 216	Page 402
Test 12	Page 408
Phrasal Verbs 217 – 234	Page 410
Test 13	Page 416
Phrasal Verbs 235 – 252	Page 418
Test 14	Page 424

Phrasal Verbs 253 – 270	Page 426
Test 15	Page 432
Phrasal Verbs 271 – 288	Page 434
Test 16	Page 440
Phrasal Verbs 289 – 306	Page 442
Test 17	Page 448
Phrasal Verbs 307 – 324	Page 450
Test 18	Page 456
Phrasal Verbs 325 – 342	Page 458
Test 19	Page 464
Phrasal Verbs 343 – 360	Page 466
Test 20	Page 472
Phrasal Verbs 361 – 378	Page 474
Test 21	Page 480
Phrasal Verbs 379 – 396	Page 482
Test 22	Page 488
Phrasal Verbs 397 – 414	Page 490
Test 23	Page 496
Phrasal Verbs 415 – 432	Page 498
Test 24	Page 504
Phrasal Verbs 433 – 450	Page 506
Test 25	Page 512
Phrasal Verbs 451 – 468	Page 514
Test 26	Page 520
Phrasal Verbs 469 – 486	Page 522
Test 27	Page 528
Phrasal Verbs 487 – 504	Page 530
Test 28	Page 536

Answers — Page 538

1 add to

Meaning: To join something together with another thing.

Example: I like to **add** milk **to** my coffee.

Fill in the blanks

I want to _____ some olives _____ the pizza. (add)

2 agree to + verb

Meaning: To consent to doing something.

Example: Peter **agreed to** wash the dishes.

Fill in the blanks

My sister _____ _____ help me with my math homework. (agreed)

3 agree with

Meaning: To share the same point of view with someone.

Example: I **agree with** you that it's too cold to swim.

Fill in the blanks

Dad doesn't _____ _____ us about getting a swimming pool. (agree)

4 arrive at

Meaning: To reach some kind of place.

Example: David will **arrive at** the train station in ten minutes.

Fill in the blanks

I _____ _____ the library thirty minutes ago. (arrived)

5 arrive in

Meaning: To reach a destination that has a name.

Example: We will be **arriving in** Japan soon.

Fill in the blanks

I just _____ _____ New York. (arrived)

6 ask for

Meaning: To request something from someone.

Example: Susan **asked** her mother **for** a new doll.

Fill in the blanks

You should _____ the teacher _____ help. (ask)

7 **be able to** + verb

Meaning: To have the ability to do something.

Example: They **were able to** book a hotel near the beach.

Fill in the blanks

I _____ _____ _____ watch TV after dinner. (am)

8 **be about to** + verb

Meaning: To indicate something will happen immediately.

Example: We'**re about to** watch a movie.

Fill in the blanks

She _____ _____ _____ start cooking dinner. (is)

9 **be afraid of**

Meaning: To feel frightened by something.

Example: My younger brother **is** still **afraid of** the dark.

Fill in the blanks

My mother _____ _____ _____ taking an airplane. (is)

10 be after

Meaning: To have something happen following something else.

Example: The English class **is after** lunch.

Fill in the blanks

Football season _____ _____ summer. (is)

11 be against

Meaning: To be in opposition of something.

Example: My wife **was** originally **against** camping, but I convinced her to go.

Fill in the blanks

Betty _____ _____ _____ the decision to replace the furniture. (has been)

12 be angry with

Meaning: To feel mad or frustrated at someone.

Example: The teacher **was angry with** me for not doing the homework.

Fill in the blanks

Ken will _____ very _____ _____ you for taking his bike. (be)

13 be born (in / on)

Meaning: To say the birthdate or birthplace of someone.

Example: My grandmother **was born** in Italy.

Fill in the blanks

Both children _____ _____ on the same day. (were)

14 be busy + verb+ing

Meaning: To be occupied doing something.

Example: I **am** too **busy** cooking dinner to answer any calls.

Fill in the blanks

Paul _____ _____ painting the bedroom, so he can't come out with us. (is)

15 be busy with

Meaning: To be occupied by something.

Example: Dad **was busy with** the broken letterbox.

Fill in the blanks

I'll _____ _____ _____ the science project today. (be)

16 be careful with

Meaning: To do something cautiously.

Example: You need to **be careful with** this hot coffee.

Fill in the blanks

The little girl _____ _____ _____ _____ the paint. (is being)

17 be different from

Meaning: To compare how two things are unlike.

Example: Your classroom **is different from** mine.

Fill in the blanks

Electric cars _____ very _____ _____ ones with combustion engines. (are)

18 be familiar to

Meaning: To be known by someone.

Example: Andy **is familiar to** everyone at school after winning the contest.

Fill in the blanks

These bands _____ not _____ _____ teenagers. (are)

Test 1 Write the answer next to the letter "A"

A: ___ **1.** She added soy sauce ___ the food.

a. in   b. to   c. for

A: ___ **2.** I didn't ___ to help organize the party.

a. agree   b. agreed   c. agreeing

A: ___ **3.** Frank agrees ___ me that we should get a dishwasher.

a. to   b. with   c. by

A: ___ **4.** Brad hasn't arrived ___ the tennis court yet.

a. on   b. to   c. at

A: ___ **5.** They will ___ in Sydney in about two hours.

a. meet   b. arrive   c. come

A: ___ **6.** I'm going to ask my father ___ some money to buy new furniture.

a. give   b. of   c. for

A: ___ **7.** I ___ able to find a cheap airplane ticket to Fiji.

a. haven't been   b. isn't   c. won't

A: ___ **8.** Luke is ___ to leave his home to help Ben.

a. around   b. abroad   c. about

A: ___ **9.** The children ___ afraid of the monster in the movie.

a. be   b. were   c. was

- 320 -

A: ___ **10.** The birthday party will ___ after school.

a. is   b. be   c. have

A: ___ **11.** My boss is ___ the idea of working on the weekend.

a. against   b. annoyed   c. avoid

A: ___ **12.** Mom was angry ___ my brother for not helping out with the chores.

a. to   b. with   c. about

A: ___ **13.** All my children were ___ in the same hospital.

a. born   b. birth   c. borned

A: ___ **14.** He's been busy ___ for the midterm exams.

a. prepare   b. prepared   c. preparing

A: ___ **15.** Abby and Max are busy ___ their newborn baby.

a. on   b. for   c. with

A: ___ **16.** Jasmine ___ always careful with the steak knives.

a. is   b. be   c. being

A: ___ **17.** Mary's new house is very different ___ her previous one.

a. for   b. from   c. of

A: ___ **18.** This story is really familiar ___ me.

a. with   b. for   c. to

19   be familiar with

Meaning: To know of something.

Example: Jasmine **is familiar with** the metro system in this city.

Fill in the blanks

I _____ not very _____ _____ the streets around this town. (am)

20   be famous for

Meaning: To be well known for something.

Example: She **is famous for** her books about wizards.

Fill in the blanks

The city of Naples _____ _____ _____ its delicious pizzas. (is)

21   be fit for

Meaning: To be appropriate for something.

Example: This video game **isn't fit for** young children.

Fill in the blanks

These shoes _____ not _____ _____ hiking in the mountain. (are)

22 be fond of

Meaning: To like something or someone very much.

Example: My parents **are fond of** black and white movies.

Fill in the blanks

We _____ not _____ _____ the hotel that we stayed at. (were)

23 be from

Meaning: To state where someone was born, lives or works.

Example: My Japanese teacher **is from** Tokyo.

Fill in the blanks

The new manager _____ _____ a much bigger company. (is)

24 be full of

Meaning: To contain as much of something as possible.

Example: The new library **will be full of** books for children.

Fill in the blanks

The park _____ _____ _____ people flying kites yesterday. (was)

25 be good / bad at

Meaning: To have either a high or low ability to do something.

Example: I didn't know you **were** so **good at** basketball.

Fill in the blanks

Even though I practice a lot, I _____ still _____ _____ playing guitar. (am)

26 be good / bad for

Meaning: To have either a beneficial or harmful effect.

Example: Eating too much junk food **is bad for** health.

Fill in the blanks

I think learning English _____ _____ _____ _____ you. (would be)

27 be in charge of

Meaning: To be responsible for something.

Example: You **are in charge of** feeding the pets in the morning.

Fill in the blanks

My sister and I _____ _____ _____ _____ washing the dishes. (were)

28 be in love with

Meaning: To love someone.

Example: I **have** never **been in love** with anyone.

Fill in the blanks

I think Stan _____ _____ _____ _____ your sister. (is)

29 be interested in

Meaning: To be curious about something.

Example: My son **isn't interested in** learning how to play piano.

Fill in the blanks

All the students _____ _____ _____ what the teacher was saying. (were)

30 be interested to + verb

Meaning: To be curious about doing something.

Example: I'm sure Lucy **will be interested to** help with the birthday party.

Fill in the blanks

I heard Tom _____ _____ _____ work with us on this project. (is)

31 be late for

Meaning: To arrive after the expected time.

Example: I just received a message from John that he **will be late for** dinner.

Fill in the blanks

You _____ _____ _____ _____ class two times this week. (have been)

32 be like

Meaning: To be similar to something else.

Example: This house **is like** that one I grew up in.

Fill in the blanks

It _____ _____ Janet to be late without calling first. (isn't)

33 be made from

Meaning: To say what material something is produced with.

Example: This wine **was made from** the grapes in South Australia.

Fill in the blanks

These tables and chairs _____ _____ _____ recycled wood. (were)

34 be made in

Meaning: To say where or when something was produced.

Example: Most of these toys **are made in** China.

Fill in the blanks

All the products _____ _____ _____ _____ a factory in Vietnam. (will be)

35 be made into

Meaning: To say what something is used for to make something else.

Example: This glass bottle **is going to be made into** a vase.

Fill in the blanks

These old tables _____ _____ _____ _____ benches. (will be)

36 be made of

Meaning: To say what material or materials something is produced with.

Example: These shoes **are made of** leather.

Fill in the blanks

It's best to take plates that _____ _____ _____ plastic for camping. (are)

Test 2 Write the answer next to the letter "A"

A: ___ **1.** The students aren't familiar ___ Greek history yet.

a. for   b. to   c. with

A: ___ **2.** This director is ___ for making horror movies.

a. familiar   b. famous   c. popular

A: ___ **3.** This video game isn't fit ___ young children.

a. to   b. for   c. of

A: ___ **4.** The teacher is ___ of all his grade five students.

a. fond   b. liked   c. teaching

A: ___ **5.** My ski coach ___ from Canada.

a. be   b. been   c. is

A: ___ **6.** That cupboard is ___ of clothes that I used to wear.

a. enough   b. full   c. lack

A: ___ **7.** Young kids are very good ___ skateboarding these days.

a. to   b. for   c. at

A: ___ **8.** I don't think those potato chips are very good ___ your health.

a. for   b. at   c. on

A: ___ **9.** Steven is ___ charge of taking out the trash.

a. in   b. on   c. take

A: ___ **10.** My friend is in love ___ this place and visits it every year.

a. for	b. with	c. by

A: ___ **11.** Susan is ___ in playing in a basketball team.

a. interest	b. interesting	c. interested

A: ___ **12.** I'm interested ___ learn more about those birds we saw in the forest.

a. in	b. to	c. for

A: ___ **13.** Why ___ you late for work yesterday?

a. are	b. were	c. was

A: ___ **14.** The second movie isn't ___ the first one.

a. like	b. haven't	c. as

A: ___ **15.** This fruit salad was ___ from fruit that was grown in the backyard.

a. made	b. making	c. make

A: ___ **16.** This electric guitar was made ___ the United States.

a. from	b. with	c. in

A: ___ **17.** This old wood will be made ___ a coffee table.

a. in	b. into	c. to be

A: ___ **18.** What is your belt made ___?

a. with	b. for	c. of

37 be on

Meaning: To say when something begins.

Example: There **are** no movies **on** at nine o'clock.

Fill in the blanks

My violin recital _____ _____ in the afternoon. (is)

38 be over

Meaning: To say when something finishes.

Example: I will come home as soon as the game **is over**.

Fill in the blanks

The class _____ _____ _____ in fifteen minutes. (will be)

39 be pleased with

Meaning: To be satisfied with how something is.

Example: She **was** very **pleased with** how the wedding cake tasted.

Fill in the blanks

We _____ _____ _____ our new home by the beach. (are)

40 be popular with

Meaning: To say who someone or something is liked by.

Example: This music **was** very **popular with** teenagers in the nineties.

Fill in the blanks

The movie _____ _____ _____ children all around the world. (is)

41 be proud of

Meaning: To feel a deep satisfaction for someone or something.

Example: I **am proud of** my daughter for trying her best.

Fill in the blanks

Your grandfather _____ _____ _____ you for not giving up. (is)

42 be proud to

Meaning: To feel a deep satisfaction to do something.

Example: My father said he **was proud to** walk me down the aisle.

Fill in the blanks

John _____ very _____ _____ be the coach of this football team. (is)

43 be ready for

Meaning: To be prepared for something.

Example: Are you **ready for** dinner yet?

Fill in the blanks

I didn't think Max _____ _____ _____ a promotion. (was)

44 be related to

Meaning: To have a relationship with someone or something.

Example: Scientists believe the recent floods **are related to** climate change.

Fill in the blanks

One of my classmates _____ _____ _____ the geography teacher. (is)

45 be rich / low in

Meaning: To contain a lot of or a little of something.

Example: Some green vegetables **are rich in** iron.

Fill in the blanks

She wants to eat more salad because it _____ _____ _____ calories. (is)

46 be satisfied with

Meaning: To be content with how something is.

Example: She **wasn't satisfied with** the car she was driving.

Fill in the blanks

The teacher _____ _____ _____ how the students are improving. (is)

47 be seated

Meaning: To be given a particular place to sit.

Example: We **were seated at** the back of the train.

Fill in the blanks

I don't want to _____ _____ too close to the front of the classroom. (be)

48 be sure that

Meaning: To be confident that something is true or correct.

Example: I **am sure that** you will do well on the math test.

Fill in the blanks

They _____ _____ _____ there would be more people at the show. (were)

49 be uncertain about

Meaning: To not be confident that something is true or correct.

Example: The builder **is uncertain about** when the house will be finished.

Fill in the blanks

We _____ still _____ _____ how we're going to travel. (are)

50 be used to

Meaning: To do something that is familiar or seems normal.

Example: He **is** already **used to** the spicy food here.

Fill in the blanks

My children _____ _____ _____ living in the city. (are)

51 be worried about

Meaning: To be concerned, nervous or uneasy about something.

Example: My mother **is worried about** driving in the storm.

Fill in the blanks

My uncle _____ not _____ _____ the economy. (is)

52 be worthy of

Meaning: To have enough value or merit to receive praise or a reward.

Example: Some people didn't think he **was worthy of** being promoted.

Fill in the blanks

She _____ certainly _____ _____ winning a gold medal. (is)

53 beg one's pardon

Meaning: To apologize for doing something wrong or making a mistake.

Example: I **beg** your **pardon** for interrupting the meeting.

Fill in the blanks

I _____ your _____, but I don't agree with your opinion. (beg)

54 begin with

Meaning: To start something in a particular way.

Example: The music teacher always **begins** the class **with** a song.

Fill in the blanks

I _____ the speech _____ a story about my childhood dreams. (began)

Test 3 Write the answer next to the letter "A"

A: ___ **1.** The fireworks are ___ at midnight.

a. off   b. start   c. on

A: ___ **2.** The class ___ over in twenty minutes.

a. will be   b. will   c. will been

A: ___ **3.** Dad was ___ with his Father's Day gift.

a. please   b. pleased   c. pleasing

A: ___ **4.** The movie is very ___ with both boys and girls.

a. famous   b. popular   c. liked

A: ___ **5.** The coach is very proud ___ his team's performance.

a. to   b. for   c. of

A: ___ **6.** My daughter was proud ___ make a speech about climate change.

a. of   b. to   c. in

A: ___ **7.** If you don't close the lid, the food will fall ___ of the lunchbox.

a. from   b. off   c. out

A: ___ **8.** I didn't know you're ___ to my neighbor.

a. related   b. relation   c. relating

A: ___ **9.** The doctor told me to eat food that is ___ in fat.

a. reduce   b. down   c. low

- 336 -

A: ___ **10.** My mother is ___ with the new oven that she bought.

a. satisfy						b. satisfying						c. satisfied

A: ___ **11.** I don't want to be ___ at the front of the cinema.

a. sat						b. seated						c. sit

A: ___ **12.** Justin isn't sure ___ he likes the university course he's studying.

a. that						b. which						c. where

A: ___ **13.** My parents are uncertain ___ which school I should attend.

a. for						b. about						c. on

A: ___ **14.** Jimmy is ___ to living in the city.

a. use						b. using						c. used

A: ___ **15.** Paula isn't worried ___ walking home at night.

a. by						b. about						c. for

A: ___ **16.** Sherry is certainly ___ of being the team captain.

a. worthy						b. worth						c. worth it

A: ___ **17.** I beg your ___, but you need to listen to me now.

a. please						b. pardon						c. forgiving

A: ___ **18.** I like to begin my day ___ a healthy breakfast.

a. have						b. eat						c. with

55 believe in

Meaning: To have the opinion that something is real.

Example: My brother doesn't **believe in** aliens.

Fill in the blanks

It's difficult to _____ _____ anything this reporter is saying. (believe)

56 belong to

Meaning: To be owned by someone.

Example: This luggage **belongs to** us.

Fill in the blanks

This notebook doesn't _____ _____ me. (belong)

57 blow away

Meaning: To be moved by wind.

Example: Hold onto the balloon so it doesn't **blow away**.

Fill in the blanks

The super typhoon _____ the clothes _____ during the night. (blew)

58 break one's promise

Meaning: To fail to do something that was assured, guaranteed or pledged.

Example: It's important that you don't **break** your **promise**.

Fill in the blanks

He has never _____ his _____ to you. (broken)

59 break down

Meaning: To stop functioning due to being broken.

Example: I'm worried that this car will **break down** during the road trip.

Fill in the blanks

The factory had to close due to the machinery _____ down. (breaking)

60 break into

Meaning: To enter a building or car illegally, usually with force.

Example: Someone **broke into** my car while I was shopping.

Fill in the blanks

There are reports of a person _____ _____ houses in this area. (breaking)

61 break into pieces

Meaning: To separate something into several parts.

Example: The vase fell and **broke into** several **pieces** during the earthquake.

Fill in the blanks

Please help me _____ the chocolate _____ small _____. (break)

62 break off

Meaning: To separate a part from a larger thing.

Example: You can **break** some bread **off** and feed it to the ducks.

Fill in the blanks

The stone has _____ _____ the ancient statue. (broken)

63 break out of

Meaning: To escape from a contained area.

Example: It was reported that two prisoners **broke out** of jail.

Fill in the blanks

One of the monkeys _____ _____ _____ its enclosure at the zoo. (broke)

64 break the rules

Meaning: To not follow or conform to the regulations.

Example: There were big fines for **breaking the rules** during the pandemic.

Fill in the blanks

Dad wasn't happy when he heard I'd _____ _____ school _____. (broken)

65 break up (with)

Meaning: To end a relationship.

Example: My sister cried for days after her boyfriend **broke up** with her.

Fill in the blanks

We thought they would never _____ up. (break)

66 bring down

Meaning: To make someone unhappy or depressed.

Example: The news about the war **brought** me **down**.

Fill in the blanks

Try not to _____ everyone _____ by talking about the stock market. (bring)

67 bring on

Meaning: To cause something typically unpleasant to happen.

Example: The heavy rains **brought on** flooding in the area.

Fill in the blanks

Firefighters are preparing for fires _____ _____ by the drought. (brought)

68 bring up (1)

Meaning: To start talking about a matter for discussion.

Example: The manager didn't **bring up** last month's decrease in sales.

Fill in the blanks

I will _____ the security concerns _____ at the next meeting. (bring)

69 bring up (2)

Meaning: To look after a child until they become an adult.

Example: I was **brought up** by my aunt because both my parents worked.

Fill in the blanks

My parents chose to _____ me _____ in the countryside. (bring)

70 build up (of)

Meaning: To become greater or larger in amount.

Example: The population growth was due to a **build up** of immigrants.

Fill in the blanks

_____ _____ an interest in soccer in the USA took some time. (Building)

71 burn down

Meaning: To have a building destroyed by fire.

Example: The factory **burned down** to the ground within hours.

Fill in the blanks

Locals worried homes would _____ _____ because of the wild fires. (burn)

72 burst in on

Meaning: To interrupt someone by suddenly entering the room.

Example: My mother **burst in on** me while I was dancing in my bedroom.

Fill in the blanks

You can't _____ _____ _____ people while they're in a meeting. (burst)

Test 4 Write the answer next to the letter "A"

A: ___ 1. My father doesn't believe ___ superstition, karma, or fate.

a. on b. in c. at

A: ___ 2. That pencil doesn't belong ___ you.

a. to b. for c. by

A: ___ 3. Put your rubbish in the box so that it doesn't blow ___.

a. over b. after c. away

A: ___ 4. You can believe him because he never ___ a promise.

a. stops b. breaks c. takes

A: ___ 5. The factory had to close for a day because the machine broke ___.

a. off b. down c. up

A: ___ 6. The museum was ___ into last night.

a. breaking b. broke c. broken

A: ___ 7. Break the vegetables into ___ and put it in the pot.

a. slices b. parts c. pieces

A: ___ 8. Some rocks broke ___ the cliff and landed on the road.

a. off b. down c. away

A: ___ 9. The hamster broke out ___ its cage and hid under the bed.

a. from b. of c. off

- 344 -

A: ___ **10.** If you break the ___ of the game, you can no longer play.

a. rules　　　　　　　　　　b. laws　　　　　　　　　　c. order

A: ___ **11.** I'm disappointed because my favorite band broke ___ today.

a. off　　　　　　　　　　　b. up　　　　　　　　　　　c. down

A: ___ **12.** This documentary about global warming is ___ me down.

a. taking　　　　　　　　　　b. bringing　　　　　　　　　c. pulling

A: ___ **13.** The lack of investments brought ___ an increase in unemployment.

a. on　　　　　　　　　　　b. to　　　　　　　　　　　c. with

A: ___ **14.** Don't ___ up anything about Frank's job this evening.

a. speak　　　　　　　　　　b. talk　　　　　　　　　　c. bring

A: ___ **15.** I would like to ___ my children up near the ocean.

a. grow　　　　　　　　　　b. bring　　　　　　　　　　c. raise

A: ___ **16.** The company needs to ___ up their inventory so that they can sell more.

a. grow　　　　　　　　　　b. make　　　　　　　　　　c. build

A: ___ **17.** The family couldn't do anything, but watch their house burn ___.

a. up　　　　　　　　　　　b. off　　　　　　　　　　　c. down

A: ___ **18.** My brother gets angry when I ___ in on him when the door is closed.

a. enter　　　　　　　　　　b. burst　　　　　　　　　　c. come

73 call back

Meaning: To return a phone call received by someone.

Example: I'll have Daniel **call** you **back** when he's out of the meeting.

Fill in the blanks

Do you have a number I can _____ you _____ on? (call)

74 call for

Meaning: To announce something to occur.

Example: The teachers are **calling for** a higher salary.

Fill in the blanks

The government _____ _____ people to get vaccinated. (called)

75 call on

Meaning: To visit someone at their location.

Example: The doctor **calls on** the patients who are too weak to travel.

Fill in the blanks

I will _____ _____ my nephew after work to make sure he's studying. (call)

76 care for

Meaning: To nurture or provide assistance to someone.

Example: It's very kind of you to **care for** your sister's child while she's away.

Fill in the blanks

Dad is _____ _____ the elderly neighbor by mowing her lawns. (caring)

77 carry on

Meaning: To continue doing something.

Example: The teacher **carried on** teaching despite the noise outside.

Fill in the blanks

The children can _____ _____ playing if they like. (carry)

78 carry out

Meaning: To start doing something that has been previously planned.

Example: We hope to begin **carrying out** the project next week.

Fill in the blanks

The installation of the new kitchen will be _____ _____ by Friday. (carried)

79 catch a bus

Meaning: To travel somewhere by bus.

Example: If you want to **catch a bus** to work, you'll need to leave earlier.

Fill in the blanks

_____ _____ _____ is more convenient than driving a car. (Catching)

80 catch a cold

Meaning: To become ill with the cold.

Example: I think my son **caught a cold** at the kindergarten.

Fill in the blanks

Wear a jacket so that you don't _____ _____ _____. (catch)

81 catch fire

Meaning: To begin to burn something.

Example: I'm worried the curtains in the kitchen will one day **catch fire**.

Fill in the blanks

The newspaper _____ _____ after it was placed by the campfire (caught).

82 catch up

Meaning: To reach the same standard of someone else.

Example: He'll need to **catch up** to the rest of the class after being absent.

Fill in the blanks

Jane is having trouble _____ _____ to the other students in class. (catching)

83 catch up with

Meaning: To make a plan to talk with someone.

Example: I will **catch up with** the boss on Monday to ask him about salaries.

Fill in the blanks

I haven't _____ _____ _____ Sam for over a year. (caught)

84 change...for

Meaning: To replace something for something else.

Example: The school is **changing** all the blackboards **for** whiteboards.

Fill in the blanks

I want to _____ this table _____ a bigger one. (change)

85 change into

Meaning: To become something different in some way.

Example: He **changed into** a responsible person after our daughter was born.

Fill in the blanks

They plan to _____ the hotel _____ an apartment building. (change)

86 change one's mind

Meaning: To adopt a different opinion or change a plan about something.

Example: I **changed** my **mind** about eating meat after talking with Janet.

Fill in the blanks

Why did you _____ your _____ about going camping this week? (change)

87 check in

Meaning: To report one's arrival at a place, typically a hotel or an airport.

Example: We are expected to **check** our bags **in** one hour before the flight.

Fill in the blanks

The hotel allowed us to _____ _____ thirty minutes early. (check)

88 check out

Meaning: To report one's exit of a place, typically a hotel.

Example: You should find out what time we need to **check out** tomorrow.

Fill in the blanks

We were charged a fee because we _____ _____ one hour late. (checked)

89 clean up

Meaning: To make a place tidy.

Example: You can watch TV after you **clean up** your toys.

Fill in the blanks

We spent the afternoon _____ the classroom _____. (cleaning)

90 clear away

Meaning: To remove something from a particular area.

Example: We should **clear** the old wood **away** before we try to sell the house.

Fill in the blanks

Please help me _____ the rubbish _____ before dinnertime. (clear)

Test 5 Write the answer next to the letter "A"

A: ___ **1.** Brad said he'll ___ you back after work.

a. shout				b. tell				c. call

A: ___ **2.** The factory workers were calling ___ safety improvements to the workplace.

a. to				b. for				c. on

A: ___ **3.** I'll call ___ my grandmother after school to make sure she's okay.

a. on				b. over				c. to

A: ___ **4.** I've been caring ___ these baby chicks for over a month.

a. for				b. on				c. of

A: ___ **5.** Please ___ on telling us about your vacation.

a. take				b. carry			c. bring

A: ___ **6.** They are going to carry ___ their plans to build a new playground.

a. in				b. on				c. out

A: ___ **7.** ___ a bus to the city is the easiest way.

a. Using			b. Catching			c. Grabbing

A: ___ **8.** I'm keeping my daughter at home after she ___ a cold on the weekend.

a. caught			b. found			c. made

A: ___ **9.** It's easy for houses to ___ fire during the summer months in this area.

a. burn				b. catch			c. start

A: ___ **10.** He couldn't catch ___ with the group after falling over.

a. out   b. on   c. up

A: ___ **11.** I caught up ___ Matthew yesterday and he said he's feeling better.

a. on   b. to   c. with

A: ___ **12.** I'm going to change my small cellphone ___ a bigger one.

a. for   b. into   c. of

A: ___ **13.** This kind of caterpillar doesn't change ___ a butterfly.

a. into   b. in   c. be

A: ___ **14.** I've already changed my ___ about going overseas.

a. mind   b. thought   c. head

A: ___ **15.** We've just ___ all the bags in at the counter.

a. put   b. brought   c. checked

A: ___ **16.** We still have one hour to ___ out of the hotel.

a. leave   b. check   c. sign

A: ___ **17.** My husband had already ___ up the house when I came home.

a. washed   b. cleaned   c. cleared

A: ___ **18.** The boys are ___ all the fallen leaves away.

a. clearing   b. cleaning   c. washing

91 clear up

Meaning: To offer an explanation to solve a problem.

Example: The teacher contacted the parents to **clear up** the issue.

Fill in the blanks

Thanks for _____ _____ everything at the meeting today. (clearing)

92 come about

Meaning: To say how something happened.

Example: The team's improvement **came about** because of the new coach.

Fill in the blanks

All the international sales _____ _____ because of our online store. (came)

93 come across

Meaning: To find someone or something by chance.

Example: I **came across** a new café while jogging yesterday.

Fill in the blanks

You may _____ _____ some kangaroos while hiking. (come)

94 come along (with)

Meaning: To accompany someone to go to a particular place.

Example: Would you like to **come along** with us to the beach?

Fill in the blanks

If you want to _____ _____, you'll need to bring a coat. (come)

95 come back (to)

Meaning: To return to a place.

Example: Adam will **come back** to the office to get the files.

Fill in the blanks

I want to _____ _____ to this forest in spring and see the flowers. (come)

96 come from

Meaning: To say where someone or something originated.

Example: My mother **comes from** a small town in France.

Fill in the blanks

These dumplings _____ _____ the new Chinese restaurant. (came)

97 come in

Meaning: To enter a room.

Example: Please **come in** and make yourself at home.

Fill in the blanks

He hasn't _____ _____ to the restaurant yet. (come)

98 come out

Meaning: To say when or where something is publicly released.

Example: He's excited because the new movie will be **coming out** tomorrow.

Fill in the blanks

Her new book will _____ _____ next Sunday. (come)

99 come over

Meaning: To visit someone's place.

Example: Come over and see our new swimming pool.

Fill in the blanks

I invited the neighbors to _____ _____ for a barbecue this weekend. (come)

100 come together

Meaning: To gather as a group.

Example: The veterans **come together** once a year to have a meal.

Fill in the blanks

The friends will be _____ _____ to play boardgames this evening. (coming)

101 come true

Meaning: To become real.

Example: My father's dream of skydiving **came true** on his fiftieth birthday.

Fill in the blanks

If you work hard, your dream job will _____ _____ one day. (come)

102 come up with

Meaning: To think of a new idea.

Example: We need to **come up with** a new way of marketing our products.

Fill in the blanks

I _____ _____ _____ ideas on how to reduce my carbon footprint. (came)

103 compare to

Meaning: To consider how two things are similar or different.

Example: Taiwan is quite a big place **compared to** Singapore.

Fill in the blanks

If you _____ today's sales _____ yesterday's, we did very well. (compare)

104 compare with

Meaning: To compare the differences and similarities of two things.

Example: How does your new job **compared with** your old one?

Fill in the blanks

I _____ this gym _____ others, and this one offers more classes. (compared)

105 connect to

Meaning: To bring two things together.

Example: You can **connect** the electric drill **to** this power cord.

Fill in the blanks

The device isn't _____ _____ the internet right now. (connected)

106 consider + verb+ing

Meaning: To think about doing something.

Example: You could **consider exercising** more if you want to lose weight.

Fill in the blanks

I've been _____ taking some German classes before I travel. (considering)

107 cut down on

Meaning: To reduce the amount of something.

Example: You need to **cut down on** the amount of fried food you're eating.

Fill in the blanks

After I started _____ _____ _____ junk food, I felt better. (cutting)

108 cut up

Meaning: To chop something into small pieces.

Example: Please help me **cut** these carrots **up** and put them in the pot.

Fill in the blanks

I _____ some fruit _____ for the smoothie. (cut)

Test 6 Write the answer next to the letter "A"

A: ___ 1. I'm glad to hear you both have cleared ___ the issue.

a. over						b. away						c. up

A: ___ 2. The increase in fuel costs came ___ because of low supply.

a. around					b. about					c. up

A: ___ 3. We came ___ a baby giraffe at the zoo today.

a. over						b. across					c. along

A: ___ 4. My daughter came ___ with me to the hospital yesterday.

a. along					b. across					c. to

A: ___ 5. Why did you ___ back to the office?

a. arrive					b. return					c. come

A: ___ 6. He speaks Portuguese because he ___ from Brazil.

a. was born					b. comes					c. lives

A: ___ 7. More tourists will be ___ in when summer begins.

a. coming					b. come						c. came

A: ___ 8. A new song came ___ today, which surprised all the fans.

a. up						b. out						c. over

A: ___ 9. Are you coming ___ for lunch today?

a. over						b. after					c. across

A: ___ **10.** The family likes to come ___ at my home at least once a month.

a. over	b. along	c. together

A: ___ **11.** If you study every day, your dream to become a doctor will come ___.

a. true	b. real	c. by

A: ___ **12.** Have you come ___ with a better way to store the meat?

a. up	b. on	c. by

A: ___ **13.** What's the weather like there ___ to where you used to live?

a. comparison	b. compared	c. comparing

A: ___ **14.** Compared ___ other parks in the area, this one is about the same.

a. which	b. with	c. by

A: ___ **15.** This computer doesn't connect ___ the printer.

a. to	b. on	c. in

A: ___ **16.** You should consider ___ in a hotter area of the country.

a. lived	b. live	c. living

A: ___ **17.** I'm cutting ___ on coffee because I haven't been sleeping well.

a. off	b. down	c. lower

A: ___ **18.** You need to cut ___ the fruit first before blending it.

a. down	b. up	c. in

109 depend on (1)

Meaning: To determine something in consideration of something else.

Example: Whether we go camping or stay at a hotel will **depend on** the price.

Fill in the blanks

Which school you attend will _____ _____ the area we move to. (depend)

110 depend on (2)

Meaning: To need someone or something for support.

Example: Jason no longer **depends on** his parents for money.

Fill in the blanks

The coach _____ _____ me to score the winning goal. (depended)

111 devote to

Meaning: To decide what something will be used for.

Example: I always **devote** one hour in the morning **to** exercise.

Fill in the blanks

He has _____ his life _____ finding a cure for cancer. (devoted)

112 die of

Meaning: To have life end because of something, typically a disease.

Example: The animals seemed to have **died of** something in the water.

Fill in the blanks

My grandfather didn't _____ _____ cancer. (die)

113 die out

Meaning: To go extinct.

Example: Some frogs are **dying out** because of climate change.

Fill in the blanks

The dinosaurs _____ _____ 65 million years ago. (died)

114 divide into

Meaning: To separate something into parts or groups.

Example: The teacher **divided** the class **into** six groups of four.

Fill in the blanks

We plan to _____ this room _____ two areas. (divide)

115 do one a favor

Meaning: To help someone in some way.

Example: Do me **a favor** and take out the garbage.

Fill in the blanks

Can you please _____ me _____ _____ and set the table? (do)

116 do one's best

Meaning: To try to accomplish something in the best way.

Example: I **did** my **best** on the project, but didn't get a high grade.

Fill in the blanks

As long as you _____ your _____, I'll be proud of you. (do)

117 do one's homework

Meaning: To complete a task, typically assigned by a teacher.

Example: You must **do** your **homework** before watching TV.

Fill in the blanks

Have you _____ your _____ that's due tomorrow? (done)

118 do (some / any) shopping

Meaning: To buy things, typically for common household goods.

Example: Mom hasn't **done** any **shopping** this week.

Fill in the blanks

I need to _____ some _____ this afternoon. (do)

119 do (some / any) sightseeing

Meaning: To go out and see famous sites.

Example: We'll mostly be **doing some sightseeing** in Europe.

Fill in the blanks

She plans to _____ some _____ on her day off. (do)

120 do (some / any) washing

Meaning: To wash the clothes.

Example: I don't have to **do** any **washing** because Dad promised he'd do it.

Fill in the blanks

He needs to _____ some _____, so he'll be arriving later. (done)

121 do / play sport

Meaning: To participate in a sport.

Example: Are you **doing** any **sport** this year?

Fill in the blanks

I didn't _____ much _____ last year. (play)

122 do well

Meaning: To find success, typically financially.

Example: I heard your brother's new restaurant is **doing** really **well**.

Fill in the blanks

I am glad to see you're _____ _____ at school this semester. (doing)

123 don't have to

Meaning: To not have an obligation to do something.

Example: The teacher said we **don't have to** make a presentation anymore.

Fill in the blanks

James _____ _____ _____ wash the dishes tonight. (doesn't)

124 dream of

Meaning: To think about something you would really like to happen.

Example: I **dream of** living by the beach one day.

Fill in the blanks

My sister _____ _____ being a doctor when she was a child. (dreamed)

125 dress up

Meaning: To wear nice or fancy clothes, typically for a special occasion.

Example: Jessica **dressed up** as a princess for her birthday party.

Fill in the blanks

You'll need to _____ _____ for dinner this evening. (dress)

126 drop in

Meaning: To visit someone in an informal manner.

Example: I going to **drop in** on the way home to borrow your lawn mower.

Fill in the blanks

Thanks for _____ _____ and bringing a pizza. (dropping)

Test 7 Write the answer next to the letter "A"

A: ___ **1.** Going to the beach will ___ on the weather.

a. dampen   b. deepen   c. depend

A: ___ **2.** Sasha depends ___ her job to pay for living expenses.

a. on   b. for   c. to

A: ___ **3.** The teacher will devote one hour a week ___ playing a game.

a. at   b. to   c. for

A: ___ **4.** The birds in this area are ___ of a new virus.

a. dying   b. died   c. dead

A: ___ **5.** Many animals have died ___ because of loss of habitat.

a. over   b. about   c. out

A: ___ **6.** The office space will be divided ___ three areas.

a. onto   b. into   c. to

A: ___ **7.** Could you ___ me a favor and mop the floor?

a. make   b. do   c. help

A: ___ **8.** You did your ___, so you should be happy with yourself.

a. best   b. hardest   c. most

A: ___ **9.** I haven't ___ my homework yet.

a. do   b. did   c. done

A: ___ **10.** My father and I did some ___ this morning.

a. buying   b. shopping   c. purchasing

A: ___ **11.** We didn't have much chance to ___ any sightseeing during the work trip.

a. go   b. get   c. do

A: ___ **12.** I will have done the ___ by this weekend.

a. wash   b. washing   c. washed

A: ___ **13.** Gerrard doesn't do any ___ at the moment.

a. sport   b. sports   c. sporting

A: ___ **14.** My brother is doing really ___ in science class.

a. well   b. good   c. better

A: ___ **15.** Your father ___ have to work today, so he can play with you.

a. don't   b. doesn't   c. isn't

A: ___ **16.** My wife ___ of opening her own café one day.

a. hopes   b. wishes   c. dreams

A: ___ **17.** What will you be ___ up as for Halloween this year?

a. wearing   b. dressing   c. being

A: ___ **18.** Thank you for ___ in on your way home to see me.

a. dropping   b. visiting   c. coming

127 earn a living

Meaning: To say how someone makes money.

Example: My father **earns a living** by fixing old furniture.

Fill in the blanks

I hope to _____ _____ _____ in the tourism industry. (earn)

128 end up

Meaning: To say how something eventually concludes.

Example: We **ended up** staying home and watching a movie.

Fill in the blanks

Which dress did you _____ _____ buying for the wedding? (end)

129 enjoy oneself

Meaning: To have a good time.

Example: I'm sure he will **enjoy himself** at the summer camp.

Fill in the blanks

I didn't think I'd _____ _____ at the party, but it was actually fun. (enjoy)

130 fall asleep

Meaning: To begin sleeping.

Example: I didn't **fall asleep** until two o'clock in the morning.

Fill in the blanks

My baby brother always _____ _____ in the car. (falls)

131 fall behind

Meaning: To fail to keep up with someone else.

Example: The teacher gave me extra homework so that I don't **fall behind**.

Fill in the blanks

I was sick for a week and have now _____ _____ in math. (fallen)

132 fall ill

Meaning: To become sick.

Example: A lot of children in the same classroom have **fallen ill** this week.

Fill in the blanks

You should stay away from me so that you don't _____ _____. (fall)

133 fall in love with

Meaning: To be very attracted to someone or something.

Example: When did you **fall in love with** your wife?

Fill in the blanks

I _____ _____ _____ _____ this city because of the restaurants. (fell)

134 fall off

Meaning: To unintentionally drop off something.

Example: Your pencil case **fell off** the desk.

Fill in the blanks

Wear a helmet in case you _____ _____ your bike. (fall)

135 fall over

Meaning: To unintentionally fall to the ground.

Example: Paul **fell over** and hurt his knee.

Fill in the blanks

I _____ _____ many times when I was learning to ski. (fell)

136 feed on

Meaning: To eat something that provides nourishment.

Example: Koalas **feed on** eucalyptus leaves.

Fill in the blanks

The goat was _____ _____ the plants in the backyard. (feeding)

137 feel like

Meaning: To have the urge or desire to do something.

Example: I **feel like** eating ice cream today.

Fill in the blanks

My friend _____ _____ playing video games, so we stayed home. (felt)

138 figure out

Meaning: To think about a problem with the intention of solving it.

Example: We need to **figure out** where we're going to eat dinner.

Fill in the blanks

I can't _____ _____ how to fix the kitchen sink. (figure)

139 fill in for

Meaning: To replace someone to do their work for a short time.

Example: Justin said that he'll be able to **fill in for** me until I get to work.

Fill in the blanks

Another doctor will be _____ _____ _____ the regular one today. (filling)

140 fill out

Meaning: To add information to a document.

Example: The bank manager helped us **fill** the loan application **out**.

Fill in the blanks

I've already _____ _____ the first page of the document. (filled)

141 fill up

Meaning: To make something become full.

Example: Stop at the next gas station so we can **fill up** the car.

Fill in the blanks

I had _____ the room _____ with balloons before she came home. (filled)

142 fix up

Meaning: To repair something or make a problem right.

Example: Please **fix** the pictures **up** before posting them on the website.

Fill in the blanks

Dad has _____ _____ all the old chairs. (fixed)

143 fold up

Meaning: To bend something tightly to make it smaller in size.

Example: I still need to **fold up** the bed sheets.

Fill in the blanks

Please _____ your clothes _____ before putting them away. (fold)

144 follow up (with)

Meaning: To take appropriate action in response to something.

Example: I will **follow up** with the shop to see if they've sent the product.

Fill in the blanks

You'll need to _____ _____ with Sam to see if he's done the project. (follow)

Test 8 Write the answer next to the letter "A"

A: ___ **1.** He's been earning a ___ by exporting wine from his home country.

a. living   b. money   c. life

A: ___ **2.** I ___ up ordering a pizza for dinner.

a. finished   b. ended   c. decided

A: ___ **3.** The children ___ themselves at the birthday party.

a. liked   b. enjoyed   c. found

A: ___ **4.** The baby took a while to ___ asleep last night.

a. go   b. be   c. fall

A: ___ **5.** If you don't start studying, you'll fall ___ again.

a. behind   b. over   c. back

A: ___ **6.** You've ___ ill because you didn't wear a coat when you went outside.

a. fell   b. fallen   c. falling

A: ___ **7.** My parents fell ___ love with each other in high school.

a. over   b. on   c. in

A: ___ **8.** He hurt his knee after he fell ___ his skateboard.

a. on   b. off   c. down

A: ___ **9.** I almost ___ over while walking in high heels today.

a. fall   b. fallen   c. fell

A: ___ **10.** Pandas mostly feed ___ bamboo.

a. on							b. of							c. to

A: ___ **11.** I don't feel ___ going out tonight.

a. as							b. for							c. like

A: ___ **12.** Can you ___ out what time it is in Canada right now?

a. think						b. figure						c. tell

A: ___ **13.** I need to find someone to fill ___ me while I go to the dentist.

a. up for						b. in for						c. for

A: ___ **14.** You'll need to ___ out this form before you can join the fitness center.

a. write						b. copy							c. fill

A: ___ **15.** We should fill ___ the car before we leave.

a. up							b. in							c. out

A: ___ **16.** The teacher told me to fix ___ the grammar in my essay.

a. in							b. up							c. on

A: ___ **17.** You don't have to ___ up my shirts.

a. line							b. roll							c. fold

A: ___ **18.** I'm going to ___ up with Cathy to find out what happened to the order.

a. follow						b. chase						c. call

145 forget to

Meaning: To fail to remember to do something.

Example: Bryan **forgot to** hang the clothes up on the line, so they're still wet.

Fill in the blanks

Don't _____ _____ turn off the lights before you leave the house. (forget)

146 freak out

Meaning: To become crazy or excited about something.

Example: My mother **freaked out** when she saw a big spider in the car.

Fill in the blanks

I was _____ _____ when my favorite actor walked by. (freaking)

147 freshen up

Meaning: To wash oneself to feel more comfortable.

Example: I want to go home and **freshen up** before we go out for dinner.

Fill in the blanks

If you need to _____ _____, you can use this bathroom. (freshen)

148 get along (with)

Meaning: To have a good relationship with someone.

Example: I'm so glad you two are both **getting along** again.

Fill in the blanks

It's important to try to _____ _____ with the neighbors. (get)

149 get...back

Meaning: To retrieve something that went missing.

Example: Please try to **get** my favorite book **back** from your sister.

Fill in the blanks

Have you _____ the test results _____ from the doctor yet? (gotten)

150 get back from

Meaning: To return from a place.

Example: When you **get back from** school, we can play basketball together.

Fill in the blanks

My dad hasn't _____ _____ _____ his business trip yet. (gotten)

151 get better

Meaning: To improve at something.

Example: I noticed William's English is **getting better**.

Fill in the blanks

If you want to _____ _____ at playing flute, you need to practice more. (get)

152 get down to

Meaning: To begin something with intent.

Example: Dad finally **got down to** fixing the fence today.

Fill in the blanks

I plan to _____ _____ _____ planting some seeds this weekend. (get)

153 get dressed

Meaning: To wear clothes.

Example: It's time to go to school, so hurry up and **get dressed**.

Fill in the blanks

He hadn't _____ _____ cold weather, so he was uncomfortable. (gotten)

154 get...from

Meaning: To buy or obtain something from a particular place.

Example: I was able to **get** some cheap clothes **from** the night market.

Fill in the blanks

I'll be _____ some frozen vegetables _____ the supermarket. (getting)

155 get home

Meaning: To return to the place one lives.

Example: Don't wait up because I'll be **getting home** late tonight.

Fill in the blanks

What time will you _____ _____ this evening? (get)

156 get in

Meaning: To arrive at a destination.

Example: The flight has been delayed, so I won't be **getting in** until ten o'clock.

Fill in the blanks

The boss usually _____ _____ earlier than everyone else. (gets)

157 get in touch with

Meaning: To contact someone.

Example: You need to **get in touch with** your mother about the wedding.

Fill in the blanks

I still haven't _____ _____ _____ _____ Kim regarding the email. (gotten)

158 get into the habit of

Meaning: To become used to something.

Example: You'll need to **get into the habit of** sleeping early every day.

Fill in the blanks

I _____ _____ _____ _____ _____ eating fruit for breakfast. (got)

159 get married

Meaning: To marry someone.

Example: They are planning to **get married** in summer.

Fill in the blanks

She doesn't want to _____ _____ for another five years. (get)

- 382 -

160 get off (1)

Meaning: To escape punishment or consequence for doing something wrong.

Example: You were lucky to **get off** so easily for not doing the homework.

Fill in the blanks

She _____ _____ lightly after being caught cheating in the test. (got)

161 get off (2)

Meaning: To leave a mode of transportation.

Example: I need to **get off** at the next station.

Fill in the blanks

Check the road before _____ _____ the bus. (getting)

162 get on

Meaning: To enter a mode of transportation.

Example: Show your ticket when you **get on** the train.

Fill in the blanks

Have you _____ _____ the ferry yet? (gotten)

Test 9 Write the answer next to the letter "A"

A: ___ 1. I forgot ___ call my mother for her birthday.

a. to   b. about   c. of

A: ___ 2. My daughter freaked ___ when we gave her a new car.

a. on   b. out   c. over

A: ___ 3. I'm going to the bathroom to ___ up before we go out.

a. fresh   b. freshing   c. freshen

A: ___ 4. I have always ___ along with my parents.

a. get   b. gotten   c. got

A: ___ 5. He's going to his brother's house to get his bike ___.

a. back   b. over   c. around

A: ___ 6. I'll be ___ back from overseas at the end of the month.

a. gotten   b. got   c. getting

A: ___ 7. Helen is getting ___ at playing drums.

a. more good   b. better   c. well

A: ___ 8. Let's get ___ to business and discuss the new products.

a. down   b. up   c. over

A: ___ 9. We can go out as soon as Charles gets ___.

a. dress   b. dressing   c. dressed

- 384 -

A: ___ **10.** Did you get these waffles ___ the bakery?

a. from   b. off   c. by

A: ___ **11.** What time will you ___ home tonight?

a. been   b. back   c. get

A: ___ **12.** We'll start the meeting as soon as Brenda ___ in.

a. gotten   b. gets   c. get

A: ___ **13.** I haven't gotten in ___ with Stacy for a while.

a. talk   b. touch   c. reach

A: ___ **14.** I'm trying to get into the ___ of drinking more water.

a. hand   b. habitat   c. habit

A: ___ **15.** My sister's getting ___ this weekend.

a. married   b. marriage   c. marry

A: ___ **16.** The lawyer believes I can get ___ with a small fine.

a. over   b. out   c. off

A: ___ **17.** When you ___ off the bus, call me and I'll pick you up.

a. get   b. come   c. go

A: ___ **18.** She still hasn't ___ on the train yet.

a. got   b. gotten   c. getting

163 get out of

Meaning: To leave a situation you don't want to be part of.

Example: I need an excuse to **get out of** violin class this afternoon.

Fill in the blanks

Don't try to _____ _____ _____ washing the dishes this time. (get)

164 get ready for

Meaning: To prepare for something.

Example: It's time to **get** the children **ready for** bed.

Fill in the blanks

I'm _____ _____ _____ the concert. (getting)

165 get ready to + verb

Meaning: To prepare to do something.

Example: I'm **getting ready to** leave for work, so I can't talk right now.

Fill in the blanks

Let's _____ _____ _____ watch the movie. (get)

166 get rid of

Meaning: To be free or dispose of something.

Example: I'm **getting rid of** all my old furniture.

Fill in the blanks

I want to _____ _____ _____ all my old shirts. (get)

167 get through

Meaning: To overcome a difficult situation or challenge.

Example: It was difficult to **get through** the novel for English class.

Fill in the blanks

Once I've _____ _____ this document, I'll call you back. (gotten)

168 get to

Meaning: To arrive at a place.

Example: We should **get to** the airport in ten minutes.

Fill in the blanks

I can't _____ _____ the office until after lunch. (get)

169 get to know

Meaning: To become acquainted with something or someone.

Example: Once you **get to know** this place, you'll end up loving it.

Fill in the blanks

I _____ _____ _____ him at the café where we both used to work. (got)

170 get together

Meaning: To meet with someone.

Example: Do you want to **get together** later to discuss the situation?

Fill in the blanks

We'll be _____ _____ at the library to study for the test. (getting)

171 get up

Meaning: To wake up and get out of bed.

Example: I've been **getting up** too late these days.

Fill in the blanks

What time do we need to _____ _____ in the morning? (get)

172 give...a call

Meaning: To call someone by phone.

Example: I'll **give** Susan **a call** regarding the order.

Fill in the blanks

Could you please _____ me _____ _____ back in twenty minutes? (give)

173 give a talk (on)

Meaning: To deliver a speech on a particular subject.

Example: The professor is going to **give a talk** on impressionism in painting.

Fill in the blanks

What will you be _____ _____ _____ on today? (giving)

174 give back

Meaning: To return something.

Example: Please **give** my black pencil **back**.

Fill in the blanks

Mom will _____ _____ my cellphone when I get better grades. (give)

175 give birth (to)

Meaning: To have a baby.

Example: My friend **gave birth** to twin girls.

Fill in the blanks

She will be _____ _____ at the end of this month. (giving)

176 give in (to)

Meaning: to finally agree or yield to what someone wants.

Example: My husband always **gives in** to our daughter.

Fill in the blanks

I always _____ _____ to my boss when he asks me to work overtime. (give)

177 give off

Meaning: To emit or radiate something.

Example: These flowers **give off** a lovely scent.

Fill in the blanks

I think the stove is _____ _____ some gas. (giving)

178 give rise to

Meaning: To cause something to happen.

Example: His controversial comments **gave rise to** protests on the street.

Fill in the blanks

The unattended landfill _____ _____ _____ an increase in rodents. (gave)

179 give up

Meaning: To stop making an effort and quit something.

Example: It's important not to **give up** when learning a new skill.

Fill in the blanks

My son has _____ _____ trying to learn to play golf. (given)

180 give way

Meaning: To break under pressure.

Example: That bridge could **give way** at any moment.

Fill in the blanks

The fence _____ _____ after the tree fell on it. (gave)

Test 10 Write the answer next to the letter "A"

A: ___ 1. I was able to get out ___ doing the speech in geography class.

a. with   b. of   c. for

A: ___ 2. You should have already ___ ready for school by now.

a. got   b. getting   c. gotten

A: ___ 3. Daniel's getting ___ to go to the job interview.

a. ready   b. prepare   c. done

A: ___ 4. I'll be getting ___ of all the toys that the kids no longer play with.

a. by   b. rid   c. out

A: ___ 5. Getting ___ this text book in one week won't be easy.

a. on   b. finished   c. through

A: ___ 6. Can you get ___ the office before the meeting starts?

a. on   b. to   c. at

A: ___ 7. I never had the chance to get to ___ my grandfather.

a. realize   b. know   c. understand

A: ___ 8. We can ___ together as soon as I finish my homework.

a. getting   b. gotten   c. get

A: ___ 9. I set your alarm clock so that you'll get ___ for work on time.

a. up   b. by   c. on

- 392 -

A: ___ **10.** Zach said he'll give the accountant a ___ about this letter.

a. talk   b. phone   c. call

A: ___ **11.** I've been asked to give a ___ to the science class on how to prevent accidents.

a. advice   b. talk   c. phone

A: ___ **12.** Geoffrey hasn't ___ my electric drill back yet.

a. give   b. given   c. gave

A: ___ **13.** My aunt will give birth ___ her third child next month.

a. to   b. for   c. of

A: ___ **14.** You shouldn't give ___ to your mother all the time.

a. on   b. in   c. up

A: ___ **15.** These flowers give ___ a lovely scent.

a. to   b. out   c. off

A: ___ **16.** The sharp increase in profits gave ___ to discussions about wages.

a. rise   b. raise   c. risen

A: ___ **17.** I was surprised to hear that he gave ___ on his studies.

a. against   b. over   c. up

A: ___ **18.** The garage roof gave ___ during the hurricane.

a. way   b. away   c. off

181 go ahead

Meaning: To start doing something.

Example: You can **go ahead** and read out the letter.

Fill in the blanks

We told Tim not to drive, but he _____ _____ anyway. (went)

182 go against

Meaning: To oppose or resist something.

Example: One of my coworkers **went against** my idea to expand the factory.

Fill in the blanks

I won't do anything that _____ _____ my values. (goes)

183 go away

Meaning: To leave a place.

Example: You should **go away** from here when the roadworkers arrive.

Fill in the blanks

I _____ _____ after the protest became violent. (went)

- 394 -

184 go back (to)

Meaning: To return to a place.

Example: Steven has decided to **go back** to university this year.

Fill in the blanks

I'll _____ _____ to the hotel and get your coat. (go)

185 go bad

Meaning: To no longer be fresh enough to eat or drink.

Example: The milk will **go bad** if you don't put it back in the refrigerator.

Fill in the blanks

I think the cheese has _____ _____. (gone)

186 go by

Meaning: To pass something or someone without stopping.

Example: I **went by** the park, but didn't see anyone there.

Fill in the blanks

I _____ _____ the zoo every day, but have never visited it. (go)

187 go down (to)

Meaning: To go from one place to another.

Example: I'm **going down** to Joseph's house now.

Fill in the blanks

I plan to _____ _____ to your area sometime this year. (go)

188 go for a walk / run

Meaning: To go outside for the purpose of walking or running.

Example: I usually **go for a run** after the kids fall asleep.

Fill in the blanks

My grandmother still _____ _____ _____ _____ every morning. (goes)

189 go home

Meaning: To return to one's place of residence.

Example: I will **go home** straight after the work is done here.

Fill in the blanks

Cathy _____ _____ as soon as the meeting ended. (went)

190 go on (with)

Meaning: To proceed to do something.

Example: Please **go on** with the story.

Fill in the blanks

I can't _____ _____ working at this company anymore. (go)

191 go out (1)

Meaning: To leave one's home to have fun, typically in a social environment.

Example: I'll be **going out** with my cousin to see a movie this weekend.

Fill in the blanks

We _____ _____ to see the fireworks last night. (went)

192 go out (2)

Meaning: To say the fire, power or light has extinguished or stopped.

Example: Put some more wood on the fire before it **goes out**.

Fill in the blanks

The lights have _____ _____ in the living room. (gone)

193 go shopping

Meaning: To go to a place where goods are sold with the intention to buy.

Example: Next time you **go shopping**, please get some bread.

Fill in the blanks

I'll be _____ _____ this afternoon, so let's write a shopping list. (going)

194 go swimming

Meaning: To go somewhere to swim.

Example: I had never **gone swimming** in the ocean before.

Fill in the blanks

The hotel had a swimming pool that we _____ _____ in every day. (went)

195 go to bed

Meaning: To get into one's bed and fall asleep.

Example: The kids can **go to bed** at eleven o'clock on the weekend.

Fill in the blanks

I've been _____ _____ _____ too late these days. (going)

196 go to school

Meaning: To attend a school to study.

Example: Sharon decided to get a job, so she no longer **goes to school**.

Fill in the blanks

Do you still want to _____ _____ _____ in London? (go)

197 go to the movies

Meaning: To see a movie at the cinema.

Example: We decided to **go to the movies** because of the rainy weather.

Fill in the blanks

We'll be _____ _____ _____ _____ for Valentine's Day. (going)

198 go to work

Meaning: To go to one's place of employment.

Example: I have to **go to work** early today.

Fill in the blanks

My father sometimes _____ _____ _____ on Saturdays. (goes)

Test 11 Write the answer next to the letter "A"

A: ___ **1.** My mother went ___ and washed your clothes.

a. ahead					b. along					c. across

A: ___ **2.** I didn't expect so many politicians would go ___ more funding for education.

a. off					b. behind					c. against

A: ___ **3.** We decided to go ___ when the dark clouds in the sky appeared.

a. over					b. by						c. away

A: ___ **4.** Do you think you'll go ___ to work when you feel better?

a. back					b. return					c. over

A: ___ **5.** The bread has ___ bad, so don't eat it.

a. going					b. gone					c. went

A: ___ **6.** I went ___ the house, but her car wasn't in the driveway.

a. beside					b. by						c. over

A: ___ **7.** I will go ___ to the beach with the children on Sunday.

a. forward				b. there					c. down

A: ___ **8.** My father has been going ___ a run before work almost every day.

a. for					b. to						c. with

A: ___ **9.** Mom wants us to ___ home after the movie ends.

a. been					b. go						c. go to

A: ___ **10.** The group had decided to ___ on with the first plan.

a. do   b. go   c. start

A: ___ **11.** We didn't ___ out last night because we were all too tired.

a. go   b. gone   c. went

A: ___ **12.** The power went ___ during the big storm.

a. cut   b. out   c. over

A: ___ **13.** I haven't gone ___ this week, so there's not much food in the refrigerator.

a. shops   b. shop   c. shopping

A: ___ **14.** ___ swimming every day has really improved my health.

a. Go   b. Gone   c. Going

A: ___ **15.** He should start ___ to bed earlier from now on.

a. goes   b. going   c. goes

A: ___ **16.** My child won't be going ___ school today.

a. with   b. at   c. to

A: ___ **17.** Peter only ___ to the movies about once a year.

a. go   b. goes   c. gone

A: ___ **18.** Dad doesn't have to go to ___ today.

a. job   b. working   c. work

199 go up

Meaning: To increase in amount.

Example: The population didn't **go up** last year in this country.

Fill in the blanks

The price of houses in this area has _____ _____ a lot. (gone)

200 grow up

Meaning: To become older and develop into an adult.

Example: I can't believe how much you've **grown up** since last time I saw you.

Fill in the blanks

My father _____ _____ in Italy before he moved to New Zealand. (grew)

201 hand down

Meaning: To pass something to a successor or someone younger.

Example: My first skateboard was **handed down** from my older brother.

Fill in the blanks

You can _____ your school uniform _____ to your sister. (hand)

202 hand in

Meaning: To give something to a person of authority.

Example: The geography essay needs to be **handed in** by Friday.

Fill in the blanks

The teacher let me _____ the math homework _____ one day later. (hand)

203 hand out

Meaning: To distribute something to a group of people.

Example: They were **handing out** free samples of their skin products.

Fill in the blanks

Could you help me _____ _____ these gifts to the children? (hand)

204 happen to be

Meaning: To say something happened by chance.

Example: My birthday **happens to be** on your wedding day.

Fill in the blanks

My favorite band _____ _____ _____ performing tonight. (happens)

205 have a baby

Meaning: To give birth.

Example: I heard your sister **had a baby** last year.

Fill in the blanks

My wife wants to _____ _____ _____ before she's thirty years old. (have)

206 have a connection with

Meaning: To share a special relationship with someone or something.

Example: She **has a connection with** Chris because they're both vegans.

Fill in the blanks

I _____ _____ _____ _____ this city because Mom was born here. (have)

207 have a drink of

Meaning: To drink a beverage.

Example: You should **have a drink of** this delicious smoothie.

Fill in the blanks

I haven't _____ _____ _____ _____ water today. (had)

208 have a good time

Meaning: To enjoy oneself.

Example: I hope you **have a good time** on the vacation.

Fill in the blanks

We _____ _____ _____ _____ visiting all the sites in Paris. (had)

209 have a word with

Meaning: To speak with someone about a particular topic.

Example: I **had a word with** your teacher about your poor grades.

Fill in the blanks

The manager wants to _____ _____ _____ _____ you after lunch. (have)

210 have breakfast

Meaning: To eat a meal in the morning.

Example: I didn't have time to **have breakfast** this morning.

Fill in the blanks

My father and I _____ _____ at the café on Sundays. (have)

211 have an effect on

Meaning: To influence someone or something in some way.

Example: This TV show **had an effect on** my choice to study medicine.

Fill in the blanks

Regular exercise _____ _____ _____ _____ how well you sleep. (has)

212 have fun

Meaning: To do something that is enjoyable.

Example: Did you **have fun** with your friends today?

Fill in the blanks

We _____ so much _____ playing board games on the weekend. (had)

213 have a cough

Meaning: To persistently cough for a period of time.

Example: My daughter is staying home today because she **has a cough**.

Fill in the blanks

How long have you _____ _____ _____ for? (had)

214 have lessons / classes in

Meaning: To attend a class on a particular subject.

Example: I **have** extra **lessons in** math with a tutor.

Fill in the blanks

I'm thinking about _____ _____ _____ Spanish. (having)

215 have nothing to do with

Meaning: To be unrelated or irrelevant to someone or something.

Example: These floods **have nothing to do with** climate change.

Fill in the blanks

This article _____ _____ _____ _____ _____ what happened here. (has)

216 have on

Meaning: To be committed to a scheduled arrangement.

Example: I **have** something **on** tomorrow, so I can't meet you.

Fill in the blanks

Do you _____ anything _____ this evening? (have)

Test 12 Write the answer next to the letter "A"

A: ___ **1.** The price of fruit and vegetables has ___ up a lot this year.

a. gone   b. grown   c. flown

A: ___ **2.** When I ___ up, I want to be a doctor.

a. get   b. rise   c. grow

A: ___ **3.** I'm going to ___ down this car to my nephew.

a. hand   b. provide   c. offer

A: ___ **4.** The teacher gave me until Friday to ___ in the report.

a. put   b. give   c. hand

A: ___ **5.** Clowns were handing ___ balloons to the kids at the department store.

a. up   b. in   c. out

A: ___ **6.** My aunt ___ to be the new art teacher at your school.

a. causes   b. happens   c. happy

A: ___ **7.** My biggest regret is not ___ a baby when I was younger.

a. have   b. had   c. having

A: ___ **8.** Jordan had a ___ with his coworker because they both love baseball.

a. connection   b. contact   c. communication

A: ___ **9.** You should drop by my home and ___ a drink of coffee with me.

a. drink   b. get   c. have

A: ___ **10.** Did you have a good ___ during the summer holidays?

a. time   b. occasion   c. situation

A: ___ **11.** You should have a ___ with your son about his behavior at school.

a. note   b. word   c. letter

A: ___ **12.** My parent will be coming over to have ___ tomorrow.

a. break fast   b. a breakfast   c. breakfast

A: ___ **13.** Traveling overseas had a big ___ on my daughter.

a. effect   b. affect   c. feeling

A: ___ **14.** It looks like you all were having a lot of ___ at the park today.

a. funny   b. fun   c. happiness

A: ___ **15.** The doctor asked me how long I have had ___ for.

a. coughed   b. been coughing   c. a cough

A: ___ **16.** I don't have any classes ___ physics this semester.

a. in   b. on   c. for

A: ___ **17.** His speech had nothing to ___ with any particular political party.

a. do   b. make   c. be

A: ___ **18.** We don't have anything ___ this weekend, so you should come over for dinner.

a. for   b. in   c. on

217 have to + verb

Meaning: To must do something.

Example: My cousin **has to** leave at seven o'clock to get to school on time.

Fill in the blanks

We won't _____ _____ do homework after dinner if we do it now. (have)

218 have to do with

Meaning: To be related or associated to something.

Example: This lesson **has to do with** the midterm test, so concentrate.

Fill in the blanks

The documentary _____ _____ _____ _____ how ducks migrate. (has)

219 hear about

Meaning: To learn something about someone or something.

Example: I **heard about** your performance at the school concert.

Fill in the blanks

The manager hasn't _____ _____ any new employees coming. (heard)

220 hear from

Meaning: To be contacted by someone.

Example: I haven't **heard from** Lucy for a long time.

Fill in the blanks

You won't _____ _____ Chris until he comes back from his trip. (hear)

221 hear of

Meaning: To know about something.

Example: I've never **heard of** this man before.

Fill in the blanks

Have you ever _____ _____ this college before? (heard)

222 help oneself to

Meaning: To serve oneself to something, typically food or drinks.

Example: Please **help** yourself **to** the cheese and crackers.

Fill in the blanks

He _____ himself _____ the restaurant's salad bar. (helped)

223 help out

Meaning: To do something to assist another person.

Example: I can **help out** with the party invitations.

Fill in the blanks

You can _____ me _____ and vacuum the carpet. (help)

224 help...with

Meaning: To provide assistance to someone in some way.

Example: Please **help** Joe **with** his English homework.

Fill in the blanks

Could you please _____ me _____ setting the table? (help)

225 hinder from

Meaning: To stop or prevent someone from doing something.

Example: Not learning the local language may **hinder** you **from** finding a job.

Fill in the blanks

Being homeschooled has never _____ me _____ opportunities. (hindered)

226 hold a meeting

Meaning: To organize a meeting at a particular place and time.

Example: You need to **hold a meeting** on the new advertisement design.

Fill in the blanks

I'll _____ _____ _____ with everyone from the sales department. (hold)

227 hold down

Meaning: To restrain someone or something from moving.

Example: The police officer **held down** the thief until more help arrived.

Fill in the blanks

Use the pegs to _____ _____ the tent so that it doesn't move. (hold)

228 hold on

Meaning: To stop and wait for someone or something.

Example: Hold on for a minute so that I can get my umbrella.

Fill in the blanks

If you can _____ _____ for five minutes, I can help you. (hold)

229 hold one's breath

Meaning: To stop breathing for a short time.

Example: The children are learning to **hold** their **breath** under water.

Fill in the blanks

I always _____ my _____ when I walk pass a person smoking. (hold)

230 hold out

Meaning: To continue to survive a difficult situation.

Example: The group that was trapped in a cave **held out** until help arrived.

Fill in the blanks

We need to _____ _____ until the typhoon ends before going home. (hold)

231 hurry off

Meaning: To quickly leave from a place.

Example: The students **hurried off** before the teacher could talk to them.

Fill in the blanks

I'm sorry, but I have to _____ _____ and pick up Tom from school. (hurry)

232 hurry up

Meaning: To do something quicker.

Example: You'll need to **hurry up** if you want to complete the test on time.

Fill in the blanks

We need to _____ _____ because the train is about to leave. (hurry)

233 join in

Meaning: To participate in an activity with other people.

Example: Would you like to **join in** our game of basketball?

Fill in the blanks

My sisters never let me _____ _____ their games. (join)

234 jump into

Meaning: To begin working on or participating in something with enthusiasm.

Example: Ruby **jumped into** the coloring book as soon as I gave it to her.

Fill in the blanks

Joe and Chris will _____ _____ designing new advertisements today. (jump)

Test 13 Write the answer next to the letter "A"

A: ___ 1. You ___ to put your toys away before dinner.

a. must					b. force				c. have

A: ___ 2. This book has to do ___ life during the Great Depression.

a. of					b. with					c. about

A: ___ 3. I haven't heard anything ___ a new space movie.

a. of					b. about				c. from

A: ___ 4. Have you heard ___ your sister this week?

a. from					b. of					c. by

A: ___ 5. I've never heard ___ this illness before.

a. for					b. from					c. of

A: ___ 6. You can ___ yourself to anything in the office.

a. hand					b. give					c. help

A: ___ 7. The students help ___ with cleaning the schoolyard.

a. out					b. up					c. in

A: ___ 8. I'm happy to help you ___ some of the chores.

a. for					b. with					c. of

A: ___ 9. Not sleeping well can ___ an athlete from performing at the highest quality.

a. hinder				b. harm					c. hurt

- 416 -

A: ___ **10.** The manager is going to ___ a meeting regarding the supply issues.

a. hold   b. make   c. keep

A: ___ **11.** I had to hold ___ the dog while the vet gave him an injection.

a. up   b. on   c. down

A: ___ **12.** ___ on for five minutes and I'll help you with the heavy furniture.

a. Stay   b. Wait   c. Hold

A: ___ **13.** The crowd held their ___ during the penalty shootout.

a. hands   b. breath   c. heads

A: ___ **14.** We may need to ___ out until the rain stops.

a. keep   b. hold   c. stay

A: ___ **15.** Why did you hurry ___ home after the meeting?

a. off   b. away   c. up

A: ___ **16.** You need to ___ up and packs your bags.

a. quicken   b. run   c. hurry

A: ___ **17.** Mike hasn't been ___ in class discussions.

a. entering   b. joining   c. coming

A: ___ **18.** I'm eager to ___ into a new project as soon as I can.

a. start   b. go   c. jump

235 keep one's promise

Meaning: To fulfill something that was promised.

Example: My uncle didn't **keep** his **promise** to take me surfing.

Fill in the blanks

It's important to _____ your _____ to your friends. (keep)

236 keep a record (of)

Meaning: To maintain important information.

Example: The teacher **keeps a record** of every student's test results.

Fill in the blanks

I've _____ _____ _____ of how many calories I ate this week. (kept)

237 keep alive

Meaning: To prolong something that may end.

Example: The machine is **keeping** my grandmother **alive**.

Fill in the blanks

The aim of the festival is to _____ cultural traditions _____. (keep)

238 keep away from

Meaning: To avoid going near someone or something.

Example: You should **keep away from** the slippery rocks.

Fill in the blanks

Please _____ _____ _____ the broken slide at the park. (keep)

239 keep busy

Meaning: To be occupied doing something.

Example: The manager has **kept** us **busy** by having us call customers.

Fill in the blanks

The baby is _____ me _____ all day. (keeping)

240 keep calm

Meaning: To remain in control and not show strong emotions.

Example: You need to **keep calm** and step away from the snake.

Fill in the blanks

It was difficult for me to _____ the students _____ in class today. (keep)

241 keep fit

Meaning: To maintain a healthy body by exercising.

Example: I **keep fit** by walking the dog for one hour a day.

Fill in the blanks

_____ _____ isn't easy when you don't have much free time. (Keeping)

242 keep healthy

Meaning: To maintain a healthy body.

Example: I **keep healthy** by eating fruits that are high in vitamin C.

Fill in the blanks

You need to _____ _____ this year so that you can work harder. (keep)

243 keep in touch (with)

Meaning: To continue to be in contact with someone.

Example: Make sure you **keep in touch** while you're traveling.

Fill in the blanks

I've _____ _____ _____ with my childhood friend for seventy years. (kept)

244 keep off

Meaning: To avoid or remain away from something.

Example: You must **keep off** the soccer field before the game starts.

Fill in the blanks

Mom said to _____ the dog _____ the carpet. (keep)

245 keep on + verb+ing

Meaning: To continue doing something.

Example: The baby **kept on** sleeping despite the noise outside.

Fill in the blanks

I _____ _____ eating the pizza even though I was already full. (kept)

246 keep one's balance

Meaning: To maintain stability to avoid falling over.

Example: He has trouble **keeping** his **balance** on the skateboard.

Fill in the blanks

The children learned how to _____ their _____ in class today. (keep)

247 keep silent (about)

Meaning: To deliberately not talk about something.

Example: Please **keep silent** about the surprise party for my wife.

Fill in the blanks

I _____ _____ about being sick because I didn't want to worry you. (kept)

248 keep up (with)

Meaning: To progress at the same rate as someone else.

Example: Try to **keep up** with the rest of the swimmers.

Fill in the blanks

My son is struggling to _____ _____ with the workload at school. (keep)

249 knock down

Meaning: To bring something to the ground by a forceful action.

Example: I was **knocked down** by a child running in the park today.

Fill in the blanks

You'll sometimes be _____ _____ when you play a football game. (knocked)

250 know each other

Meaning: To have two people that are aware of one another.

Example: My wife and I didn't actually **know each other** at school.

Fill in the blanks

We've _____ _____ _____ since elementary school. (known)

251 laugh at

Meaning: To react at something or someone funny with laughter.

Example: All the children **laughed at** the teacher when he dropped the chalk.

Fill in the blanks

He is _____ _____ the pictures in the comic book. (laughing)

252 lead the way

Meaning: To show others a direction of a route or a way of doing something.

Example: You know this walking track well, so you can **lead the way**.

Fill in the blanks

Tesla _____ _____ _____ in electric vehicle technology. (leads)

Test 14 Write the answer next to the letter "A"

A: ___ **1.** I always try to keep my ___ to my friends and family.

a. trust   b. promise   c. agreement

A: ___ **2.** The secretary keeps a ___ of everyone who visits the office.

a. data   b. document   c. record

A: ___ **3.** You might want to consider reducing the sales price to keep the deal ___.

a. safe   b. open   c. alive

A: ___ **4.** You can play in the yard, but keep away ___ the vegetable garden.

a. to   b. from   c. off

A: ___ **5.** Grandpa has been ___ busy by working in the garage.

a. keeping   b. keeps   c. keep

A: ___ **6.** If there's a fire, keep ___ and find the nearest exit.

a. relaxed   b. calm   c. composure

A: ___ **7.** I've been keeping ___ by riding my bike to work instead of driving.

a. strong   b. health   c. fit

A: ___ **8.** My grandmother ___ healthy by walking to the shops.

a. keep   b. keeps   c. keeping

A: ___ **9.** We didn't keep ___ touch after she moved overseas.

a. at   b. on   c. in

- 424 -

A: ___ **10.** Please keep ___ the carpet when you're wearing shoes.

a. out   b. away   c. off

A: ___ **11.** It was getting dark, but the children kept ___ playing in the swimming pool.

a. to   b. on   c. by

A: ___ **12.** It gets harder to keep your ___ as the footpath gets steeper.

a. balance   b. steady   c. stability

A: ___ **13.** Make sure to keep ___ about my poor grades.

a. quietly   b. silence   c. silent

A: ___ **14.** Cathy wasn't able to keep ___ with the other runners.

a. up   b. on   c. for

A: ___ **15.** They're going to knock ___ the old shed today.

a. off   b. flat   c. down

A: ___ **16.** The young kids didn't know ___ other, but happily played together.

a. every   b. each   c. an

A: ___ **17.** Everyone in the audience was laughing ___ me for making a mistake.

a. to   b. with   c. at

A: ___ **18.** Whoever has the flashlight, should lead the ___.

a. direction   b. path   c. way

253 lead to

Meaning: To result to something.

Example: Extra training in the off season will surely **lead to** better results.

Fill in the blanks

I hope all this advertising will _____ _____ more sales. (lead)

254 learn by heart

Meaning: To memorize something.

Example: I've already **learned** how to spell the vocabulary words **by heart**.

Fill in the blanks

Please _____ the game plan _____ _____ for Sunday's competition. (learn)

255 learn from

Meaning: To gain knowledge from someone or something.

Example: I **learned** a lot of Spanish words **from** summer camp in Mexico.

Fill in the blanks

Tina has been _____ how to cook _____ her grandmother. (learning)

256 leave a message

Meaning: To record a written or spoken note to someone.

Example: Someone **left a message** on my answering machine.

Fill in the blanks

I _____ _____ _____ on your phone regarding the meeting. (left)

257 leave out

Meaning: To not include someone or something from something else.

Example: Janet felt **left out** when the others didn't invite her to play.

Fill in the blanks

Please _____ _____ the nuts in the salad because I'm allergic. (leave)

258 let in

Meaning: To allow someone to enter a room or be involved with something.

Example: My older brother never **lets** me **in** his bedroom.

Fill in the blanks

You should _____ the dog _____ the house before it starts raining. (let)

259 listen to

Meaning: To give attention to something by listening.

Example: I'm **listening to** a podcast about investing.

Fill in the blanks

I like to _____ _____ audiobooks while driving to work. (listen)

260 live by

Meaning: To follow a particular belief, idea or set of principles.

Example: My father **lives by** always being honest with everyone.

Fill in the blanks

Most people in this town _____ _____ their religious beliefs. (live)

261 live on

Meaning: To survive by using or consuming something.

Example: Some dinosaurs **lived on** plants only.

Fill in the blanks

Snakes in this area mostly _____ _____ frogs and other small animals. (live)

262 look after

Meaning: To care for someone or something.

Example: Are you able to **look after** my dog while I'm away?

Fill in the blanks

My parents agreed to _____ _____ the kids this evening. (look)

263 look around

Meaning: To see or explore what's around a place.

Example: We can **look around** the town for a new house this weekend.

Fill in the blanks

The children had fun _____ _____ the beach for shells. (looking)

264 look at

Meaning: To think about a subject carefully.

Example: My father is **looking at** putting solar panels on the house.

Fill in the blanks

You should _____ _____ which university you'd like to study at. (look)

265 look back on

Meaning: To think about a past experience.

Example: I **look back on** my time at school fondly.

Fill in the blanks

I was _____ _____ _____ all the different jobs I had. (looking)

266 look for

Meaning: To search for something.

Example: Jane's been **looking for** her watch all morning.

Fill in the blanks

I _____ _____ a local Thai restaurant, but I couldn't find one. (looked)

267 look forward to

Meaning: To eagerly wait for something to happen.

Example: I **look forward to** watching the game with you.

Fill in the blanks

The kids are _____ _____ _____ the summer holidays. (looking)

268 look like

Meaning: To appear similar to someone or something else.

Example: It doesn't **look like** it's going to rain this afternoon.

Fill in the blanks

Your friend _____ _____ a famous actor. (looks)

269 look out for

Meaning: To watch over someone to ensure their wellbeing.

Example: My aunt always **looked out for** me when I was a child.

Fill in the blanks

Thank you for _____ _____ _____ Peter while he was sick. (looking)

270 look over

Meaning: To inspect some information.

Example: I need to **look over** these documents before I make a decision.

Fill in the blanks

The manager will _____ _____ the proposal tomorrow. (look)

Test 15 Write the answer next to the letter "A"

A: ___ **1.** Investing in more advertising should lead ___ an increase in sales.

a. for   b. on   c. to

A: ___ **2.** Paula has learned the whole song by ___.

a. heart   b. mind   c. memory

A: ___ **3.** Jerry's been learning how to play guitar ___ videos on the internet.

a. of   b. for   c. from

A: ___ **4.** He ___ a message on the refrigerator door reminding Mom to buy some milk.

a. leave   b. left   c. leaving

A: ___ **5.** The new basketball coach is fair and doesn't ___ anyone out of the game.

a. put   b. stay   c. leave

A: ___ **6.** The manager doesn't let anyone ___ his office without him being there.

a. in   b. to   c. at

A: ___ **7.** Have you ___ to this audiobook yet?

a. listen   b. listened   c. listening

A: ___ **8.** My gym instructor lives ___ consuming a limited amount of sugar to stay healthy.

a. for   b. on   c. by

A: ___ **9.** The ducks in this area mostly live ___ the vegetation near the river.

a. by   b. for   c. on

- 432 -

A: ___ **10.** Gina can look ___ your daughter while you're away.

a. after　　　　　　　　　　b. for　　　　　　　　　　c. to

A: ___ **11.** I looked ___ the house for my keys, but I couldn't find them.

a. at　　　　　　　　　　b. around　　　　　　　　　　c. to

A: ___ **12.** We're ___ at this neighborhood because the streets are safe and quiet.

a. look　　　　　　　　　　b. looking　　　　　　　　　　c. looked

A: ___ **13.** Looking back ___ my childhood always makes me smile.

a. to　　　　　　　　　　b. at　　　　　　　　　　c. on

A: ___ **14.** Tom is looking online ___ a cheap hotel to stay at.

a. to　　　　　　　　　　b. around　　　　　　　　　　c. for

A: ___ **15.** The children are looking ___ to playing at the beach.

a. back　　　　　　　　　　b. forward　　　　　　　　　　c. around

A: ___ **16.** It looks ___ my team is going to win the tournament.

a. like　　　　　　　　　　b. as　　　　　　　　　　c. on

A: ___ **17.** My older brother looked out ___ me when I was having problems.

a. to　　　　　　　　　　b. for　　　　　　　　　　c. on

A: ___ **18.** Once we've finished looking ___ the documents, we will contact you.

a. around　　　　　　　　　　b. on　　　　　　　　　　c. over

271 look the same (as)

Meaning: To say something appears the same as something else.

Example: This painting **looks the same** as the one I have at home.

Fill in the blanks

The website from these two companies _____ _____ _____. (look)

272 look up

Meaning: To check some information.

Example: I spent the evening **looking up** some hotels to stay at.

Fill in the blanks

I _____ _____ which airlines offer the cheapest flights. (looked)

273 look up to

Meaning: To have a lot of respect for someone.

Example: I have always **looked up to** my father for being an honest person.

Fill in the blanks

She _____ _____ _____ her brother after he became a doctor. (looks)

274 lose heart

Meaning: To become discouraged about something.

Example: Don't **lose heart** even if you fail the first time.

Fill in the blanks

He's _____ _____ about finding work after going to four interviews. (losing)

275 lose one's balance

Meaning: To fail to keep one's weight spread evenly to stay upright.

Example: I kept **losing** my **balance** when I tried to skate.

Fill in the blanks

Don't _____ your _____ when you walk on the rocks. (lose)

276 lose one's life

Meaning: To cease to be alive.

Example: He sadly **lost** his **life** while riding a motorcycle.

Fill in the blanks

I don't know what I would do if you _____ your _____. (lost)

277 lose sight of

Meaning: To fail to remember or consider something.

Example: I think you've **lost sight of** why you are studying.

Fill in the blanks

Don't _____ _____ _____ why you want to start a business. (lose)

278 make a decision

Meaning: To decide something that typically has more than one choice.

Example: Let's **make a decision** at the meeting on Tuesday.

Fill in the blanks

I've _____ _____ _____ to study at a university overseas. (made)

279 make a fire

Meaning: To start burning something.

Example: Let's **make a fire** before the sun goes down.

Fill in the blanks

Dad is _____ _____ _____ so that we can cook the sausages. (making)

280 make a mistake

Meaning: To do something incorrectly or make the wrong decision.

Example: I think I **made a mistake** on the second question of the math test.

Fill in the blanks

Don't _____ _____ _____ and turn left onto the bridge. (make)

281 make a noise

Meaning: To speak or act in a way that attracts attention.

Example: He **made a noise** when he announced he's running for president.

Fill in the blanks

You _____ _____ _____ around town after cleaning the beach. (made)

282 make a plan

Meaning: To develop a set of steps to demonstrate how to do something.

Example: We should **make a plan** to meet for dinner soon.

Fill in the blanks

I _____ _____ _____ for the science project that's due next week. (made)

283 make a promise

Meaning: To tell someone you will do something without failing to fulfill it.

Example: You **made a promise** to travel overseas this year.

Fill in the blanks

I _____ _____ _____ to my daughter to get her ice cream. (made)

284 make a speech

Meaning: To give a talk on a particular topic to an audience.

Example: I'm going to **make a speech** in history class today.

Fill in the blanks

I've been asked to _____ _____ _____ at my sister's wedding. (make)

285 make an effort

Meaning: To attempt to do something with the intention to accomplish it.

Example: If you **make an effort**, I think your grades can improve.

Fill in the blanks

John always _____ _____ _____ to play with his kids. (makes)

286 make ends meet

Meaning: To earn enough money to live on.

Example: He's been finding it difficult to **make ends meet** this year.

Fill in the blanks

_____ _____ _____ is more difficult with the increasing prices. (Making)

287 make friends (with)

Meaning: To become a friend of someone.

Example: I'm so happy my son has finally **made friends** with the neighbor.

Fill in the blanks

Have you _____ any _____ at you new school? (made)

288 make progress

Meaning: To move forward towards accomplishing a goal.

Example: They are finally **making progress** on the new road.

Fill in the blanks

It's important to _____ some _____ every day. (make)

Test 16 Write the answer next to the letter "A"

A: ___ **1.** This sock ___ the same as that one.

a. look   b. looking   c. looks

A: ___ **2.** Did you look ___ any information about what symptoms the virus causes?

a. out   b. on   c. up

A: ___ **3.** Johnny will listen to my husband because he looks up ___ him.

a. to   b. for   c. of

A: ___ **4.** You shouldn't lose ___ and never give up on your dreams.

a. mind   b. heart   c. stomach

A: ___ **5.** Be careful not to ___ your balance when you cross the river.

a. less   b. fall   c. lose

A: ___ **6.** My uncle lost his ___ when I was a small child.

a. life   b. living   c. live

A: ___ **7.** Let's not lose ___ of what we are trying to achieve.

a. heart   b. mind   c. sight

A: ___ **8.** You need to ___ a decision about where you want to work.

a. give   b. make   c. find

A: ___ **9.** I taught my children how to make ___ during our camping trip.

a. fire   b. fires   c. a fire

- 440 -

A: ___ **10.** I made a ___ when I was baking today and had to throw away the cake.

a. wrong   b. error   c. mistake

A: ___ **11.** The professor made a ___ after he joined the protest with the students.

a. sound   b. noise   c. bang

A: ___ **12.** We ___ a plan to have a picnic, but it started to rain.

a. made   b. makes   c. make

A: ___ **13.** If you ___ a promise, you need to keep it.

a. tell   b. do   c. make

A: ___ **14.** The president ___ a speech about improving the economy.

a. said   b. told   c. made

A: ___ **15.** Sarah didn't ___ an effort and that's why she got fired from her job.

a. made   b. make   c. making

A: ___ **16.** I'm grateful that we are able to make ___ meet during this difficult time.

a. ends   b. sides   c. edges

A: ___ **17.** He hasn't made any new ___ since we moved here.

a. friend   b. friends   c. friendship

A: ___ **18.** The science lab has been making ___ on a vaccine.

a. movement   b. advance   c. progress

289 make sense (of)

Meaning: To gain an understanding of something.

Example: It's difficult to **make sense** of what's going on in this movie.

Fill in the blanks

Are you able to _____ _____ of what he is saying in German? (make)

290 make sure

Meaning: To confirm that something is correct or will happen.

Example: Make sure that the lights are turned off before you leave the office.

Fill in the blanks

Did you _____ _____ that there's enough fuel in the tank? (make)

291 make up

Meaning: To think of or create something that is imaginary.

Example: I need to **make up** an excuse of why I can't come to work.

Fill in the blanks

My five-year-old child _____ _____ the most amazing stories. (makes)

292 make up one's mind

Meaning: To make a decision, typically of importance.

Example: Make up your **mind** and tell me what you want for dinner.

Fill in the blanks

I still haven't _____ _____ my _____ about which dress to buy. (made)

293 make use of

Meaning: To use something for a purpose.

Example: Joe **made use of** the broken fence by building a tree house.

Fill in the blanks

It's great that you're _____ _____ _____ these old boxes. (making)

294 move away (from)

Meaning: To go to another area to live.

Example: I'll be **moving away** from this town as soon as I graduate.

Fill in the blanks

When do you plan to _____ _____? (move)

295 move in

Meaning: To take possession of a home to live in.

Example: I **moved in** with Daniel about five years ago.

Fill in the blanks

If you'd like to _____ _____, we have a spare room for you. (move)

296 move on (from)

Meaning: To progress by starting something new.

Example: It's time to **move on** and begin the next chapter of my life.

Fill in the blanks

I hope to _____ _____ from this job by the end of the year. (move)

297 move to

Meaning: To live in another area.

Example: It's a dream of mine to **move to** a place near the ocean.

Fill in the blanks

My wife _____ _____ this country when she was twenty years old. (moved)

298 open up (1)

Meaning: To share one's feelings or become more communicative.

Example: I wish my husband would **open up** more about his childhood.

Fill in the blanks

Thank you for _____ _____ to me about the situation. (opening)

299 open up (2)

Meaning: To become accessible to the public, typically a business.

Example: There's a new bakery that **opened up** nearby.

Fill in the blanks

The company plans to _____ another store _____ in the city. (open)

300 pass on

Meaning: To no longer be alive.

Example: My grandmother **passed on** before I was born.

Fill in the blanks

I will inherit my parent's house when they _____ _____. (pass)

301 pay a visit

Meaning: To visit someone or something, typically with a purpose.

Example: I will **pay a visit** to your teacher this afternoon.

Fill in the blanks

Can you _____ _____ _____ to the house and check on the pets? (pay)

302 pay attention (to)

Meaning: To focus or concentrate on someone or something.

Example: Jack wasn't **paying attention** to what the teacher was saying.

Fill in the blanks

Try to _____ _____ more in geography class. (pay)

303 pay back (1)

Meaning: To repay a loan.

Example: I can **pay** you **back** at the end of the month.

Fill in the blanks

Paul hasn't _____ me _____ for last month's rent yet. (paid)

304 pay back (2)

Meaning: To get revenge on someone.

Example: I want to **pay** her **back** for talking badly about me.

Fill in the blanks

It's about a man trying to _____ _____ someone for taking his gold. (pay)

305 pay for

Meaning: To make a payment to purchase something.

Example: My father always **pays for** dinner when we go out.

Fill in the blanks

I _____ _____ the movie tickets online. (paid)

306 pay off

Meaning: To pay the full amount of a loan.

Example: I finally was able to **pay off** my credit card after six months.

Fill in the blanks

It will take another ten years to _____ _____ this home loan. (pay)

Test 17 Write the answer next to the letter "A"

A: ___ 1. It isn't easy to make ___ of what's happening in this story.

a. sense　　　　　　　　　　b. mind　　　　　　　　　　c. understanding

A: ___ 2. You need to make ___ that there's enough cake for everyone.

a. sense　　　　　　　　　　b. sure　　　　　　　　　　c. up

A: ___ 3. The girls can make ___ amazing games with their dolls.

a. on　　　　　　　　　　　b. up　　　　　　　　　　　c. of

A: ___ 4. I can't make up my ___ about which meal I will order.

a. decision　　　　　　　　　b. sense　　　　　　　　　　c. mind

A: ___ 5. It's great that you can make ___ of these old toys.

a. use　　　　　　　　　　　b. do　　　　　　　　　　　c. play

A: ___ 6. Many families have moved ___ because there isn't much work around here.

a. far　　　　　　　　　　　b. off　　　　　　　　　　　c. away

A: ___ 7. I'll be ___ in with my best friend when I attend college.

a. move　　　　　　　　　　b. moved　　　　　　　　　　c. moving

A: ___ 8. It's important that the team moves ___ from last week's loss.

a. on　　　　　　　　　　　b. up　　　　　　　　　　　c. out

A: ___ 9. My grandparents will have ___ to a quieter place by the start of next year.

a. move　　　　　　　　　　b. moving　　　　　　　　　　c. moved

A: ___ **10.** This is the first time I've heard him ___ up about his divorce.

a. bring   b. speak   c. open

A: ___ **11.** The new swimming pool will have opened ___ by summer.

a. up   b. out   c. over

A: ___ **12.** We were all shocked when we heard the music teacher had ___ on.

a. passed   b. gone   c. died

A: ___ **13.** Andrew ___ me a visit when I was in hospital.

a. made   b. gave   c. paid

A: ___ **14.** I hope you were paying ___ in science class today.

a. attentive   b. attentively   c. attention

A: ___ **15.** Are you able to pay me ___ before the end of the week?

a. down   b. back   c. up

A: ___ **16.** The best way to ___ them back after they cheated is to win the next game.

a. give   b. hit   c. pay

A: ___ **17.** The tenant said he would pay ___ rent this Friday.

a. for   b. off   c. to

A: ___ **18.** It will take me six months to pay ___ this car loan.

a. over   b. out   c. off

307 persist in

Meaning: To continue in one course of action.

Example: My child **persisted in** asking me to buy her a new doll.

Fill in the blanks

The protestors will _____ _____ giving pressure to lawmakers. (persist)

308 pick out

Meaning: To choose one thing or person from a choice of others.

Example: You can **pick out** a new dress for this weekend's party.

Fill in the blanks

The boss _____ Greg _____ from all the others to help her. (picked)

309 pick up (1)

Meaning: To catch an illness or infection from something or someone else.

Example: Cody has **picked up** a cold from one of the children at playgroup.

Fill in the blanks

I hope I don't _____ _____ the same illness as what you've got. (pick)

310 pick up (2)

Meaning: To take hold of something and lift it.

Example: Could you help me **pick** the blocks **up** and put them in the box?

Fill in the blanks

This cupboard is too heavy to _____ _____ by myself. (pick)

311 play a part in

Meaning: To be a participant that influences something in some way.

Example: The lady also **played a part in** the bank robbery.

Fill in the blanks

Chris _____ _____ big _____ _____ the company's success. (plays)

312 play a role in

Meaning: To act as a particular participant that has an effect on something.

Example: He **plays an** important **role in** how the factory operates.

Fill in the blanks

Steven _____ _____ _____ _____ the team's success this season. (played)

313 play a trick on

Meaning: To have fun by deceiving someone.

Example: We **played a trick on** our father, but he didn't think it was funny.

Fill in the blanks

I want to pay him back for _____ _____ _____ _____ me. (playing)

314 play with

Meaning: To have fun with someone or something.

Example: I got some kites that the boys can **play with** at the park.

Fill in the blanks

You can invite Lucy to come over and _____ _____ you today. (play)

315 point out

Meaning: To direct someone's attention to something.

Example: You need to **point out** the factory's exits for the new workers.

Fill in the blanks

The guide _____ _____ which trees koalas like to climb up. (pointed)

316 poke fun at

Meaning: To tease someone.

Example: You shouldn't always **poke fun at** your younger brother.

Fill in the blanks

The kids were _____ _____ _____ their friend's new haircut. (poking)

317 prefer to

Meaning: To like something better than another thing.

Example: My father **prefers** drinking coffee **to** tea.

Fill in the blanks

I _____ the seafood pizza _____ the pepperoni one. (prefer)

318 prevent...from

Meaning: To keep or avoid something from happening.

Example: These pegs will **prevent** the tent **from** blowing away.

Fill in the blanks

Planting more trees in this area _____ the soil _____ eroding. (prevents)

319 promise to + verb

Meaning: To tell someone you will do something.

Example: You **promised to** take the kids to the beach this weekend.

Fill in the blanks

I _____ _____ cook dinner for everyone this evening. (promised)

320 pull off

Meaning: To accomplish something difficult.

Example: I can't believe you **pulled off** that skateboard trick.

Fill in the blanks

If we can _____ _____ this plan, revenue will increase significantly. (pull)

321 pull out of

Meaning: To cancel participation from something.

Example: I've decided to **pull out of** this building project.

Fill in the blanks

One of the musicians has _____ _____ _____ the concert. (pulled)

322 pull up (1)

Meaning: To stop a car at a particular place, typically for a short time.

Example: You can **pull up** here and I'll get out.

Fill in the blanks

There are a lot of taxis that _____ _____ in front of the train station. (pull)

323 pull up (2)

Meaning: To take a chair and sit on it.

Example: Pull up a chair and tell me what's on your mind.

Fill in the blanks

Joe suddenly _____ _____ a chair and joined the meeting. (pulled)

324 push over

Meaning: To push someone or something with force so that it falls over.

Example: I was deliberately **pushed over** during the soccer game.

Fill in the blanks

One boy always _____ my son _____ at school. (pushes)

Test 18 Write the answer next to the letter "A"

A: ___ **1.** If you ___ in studying the text book, you'll get better grades.

a. consist					b. persist					c. enlist

A: ___ **2.** Hansel ___ out a purple necktie to wear to work.

a. chose					b. found					c. picked

A: ___ **3.** Jacky picked ___ a skin infection after going to the swimming pool.

a. out						b. up						c. on

A: ___ **4.** Thank you for helping me ___ up Toby from school yesterday.

a. pick						b. picked					c. picks

A: ___ **5.** The teacher thinks violent video games play a ___ in an increase in fighting.

a. part						b. game						c. piece

A: ___ **6.** The students also play a role ___ keeping the schoolyard tidy.

a. for						b. of						c. in

A: ___ **7.** Fran was ___ with her two cousins last weekend.

a. playing					b. played					c. plays

A: ___ **8.** Could you please point ___ which person is your teacher?

a. on						b. out						c. at

A: ___ **9.** My friends like to ___ a trick on the teacher by pretending to sleep in class.

a. play						b. do						c. make

A: ___ **10.** Stop ___ fun at the photos of me when I was younger.

a. pushing   b. poking   c. pulling

A: ___ **11.** My teenage son prefers snowboarding ___ skiing.

a. for   b. to   c. from

A: ___ **12.** Exercising and eating well can prevent you ___ being overweight.

a. from   b. of   c. to

A: ___ **13.** I had ___ my mother to do more chores around the house.

a. promise   b. promised   c. promising

A: ___ **14.** Engineers have been trying to ___ off driverless cars for years.

a. push   b. pull   c. put

A: ___ **15.** Stephen had to ___ out of tomorrow's competition after he injured his hand.

a. come   b. pull   c. go

A: ___ **16.** There is a space you can pull ___ at next to the road.

a. off   b. out   c. up

A: ___ **17.** Let me pull ___ a chair for you to sit on.

a. down   b. up   c. out

A: ___ **18.** Which one of you ___ over the sandcastle?

a. pushed   b. pushing   c. No, she won't be.

325 put away

Meaning: To place something in its usual place.

Example: You must **put** all your toys **away** before watching TV.

Fill in the blanks

Thank you for _____ the dishes _____ for me. (putting)

326 put down

Meaning: To criticize something or someone.

Example: He **put** my essay **down** because there were too many mistakes.

Fill in the blanks

I noticed she often _____ her husband _____. (puts)

327 put in prison

Meaning: To confine someone to jail for a period of time.

Example: You can be **put in prison** for drink-driving in some countries.

Fill in the blanks

He was _____ _____ _____ for three years. (put)

- 458 -

328 put into

Meaning: To put energy or time into something.

Example: I've already **put** twelve months **into** fixing this house.

Fill in the blanks

I'll be _____ more energy _____ learning a new language this year. (putting)

329 put into practice

Meaning: To begin doing something that was previously discussed.

Example: Once you **put** this diet **into practice**, you'll start feeling better.

Fill in the blanks

I've started _____ your investment advice _____ _____. (putting)

330 put on

Meaning: To wear clothes.

Example: You should **put on** a raincoat before you go out.

Fill in the blanks

You have to _____ a helmet _____ before riding on the road. (put)

331 put out

Meaning: To put something out to use or consume.

Example: Please **put** the cheese and crackers **out** before the guests arrive.

Fill in the blanks

I _____ _____ some games for the children to play. (put)

332 put up

Meaning: To display something, typically on a wall or board.

Example: The teacher **put** all the student's grades **up** on the wall.

Fill in the blanks

Mom wants to _____ some paintings _____ in the living room. (put)

333 put up with

Meaning: To tolerate someone despite being annoyed or frustrated by them.

Example: We have to **put up with** the neighbor's dog coming into our yard.

Fill in the blanks

If you can _____ _____ _____ the cold weather, it's a nice home. (put)

334 refer to

Meaning: To talk about someone or something.

Example: He is **referring to** the broken garage door.

Fill in the blanks

I'm not sure what she was _____ _____ in the meeting. (referring)

335 remind one of

Meaning: To cause someone to remember something.

Example: This picture **reminds** me **of** where I grew up.

Fill in the blanks

The professor _____ her _____ her grandfather. (reminded)

336 result in

Meaning: To occur as a consequence of what happened.

Example: Failing to pay the loan will **result in** the bank taking the house.

Fill in the blanks

Doing regular exercise _____ _____ being able to sleep better. (resulted)

337 return to

Meaning: To come back to a place or put something back.

Example: One day, I will **return to** my homeland.

Fill in the blanks

Stacy and I _____ _____ the place where we first met. (returned)

338 ring back

Meaning: To return a phone call to someone who was previously unanswered.

Example: I will **ring** you **back** after dinner.

Fill in the blanks

He still hasn't _____ me _____. (rung)

339 ring up

Meaning: To make a phone call to someone.

Example: I **rang** Polly **up** this morning, but she didn't answer.

Fill in the blanks

You should _____ the bank _____ and cancel your credit card. (ring)

340 roll over

Meaning: To overturn someone or something.

Example: Help me **roll** this mattress **over**.

Fill in the blanks

The dog _____ _____ onto his side and went to sleep. (rolled)

341 round up

Meaning: To gather a group of people or things.

Example: Let's **round up** all the children before it starts raining.

Fill in the blanks

The library is about to close, so _____ _____ all your things. (round)

342 run away (from)

Meaning: To escape from someone or something by running.

Example: The cat was **running away** from the dog.

Fill in the blanks

Some of the soldiers _____ _____ when the tanks arrived. (ran)

Test 19 Write the answer next to the letter "A"

A: ___ 1. I've already put the dishes ___.

a. away   b. over   c. after

A: ___ 2. You need to stop putting your little brother ___ for getting poor grades.

a. under   b. down   c. below

A: ___ 3. A man who lives on my street was put ___ prison for twelve years.

a. in   b. at   c. to

A: ___ 4. I'm amazed about how much you ___ into this project.

a. putting   b. putted   c. put

A: ___ 5. It's important that you put what you're saying into ___.

a. practice   b. practices   c. practicing

A: ___ 6. Rising unemployment ___ a rise in crime.

a. referred to   b. resulted in   c. returned to

A: ___ 7. You can return the bowl ___ me when you've finished eating.

a. for   b. to   c. give

A: ___ 8. You need to ring your mother ___ today.

a. back   b. behind   c. return

A: ___ 9. I still haven't ___ Jessie up to invite her to the party.

a. ring   b. rang   c. rung

- 464 -

A: ___ **10.** How do you put up ___ the noise from the passing trains near your home?

a. which   b. when   c. with

A: ___ **11.** My grandmother put ___ new curtains in the bedroom.

a. up   b. on   c. out

A: ___ **12.** I'm going to put ___ the cheesecake when everyone arrives.

a. on   b. out   c. up

A: ___ **13.** The math teacher reminds me ___ my uncle.

a. of   b. to   c. as

A: ___ **14.** I forgot to put ___ a jacket and I caught a cold.

a. over   b. out   c. on

A: ___ **15.** The president was ___ to the situation in Europe.

a. refers   b. referring   c. referred

A: ___ **16.** Roll the tennis ball ___ to me.

a. give   b. bounce   c. over

A: ___ **17.** Once we've rounded ___ all the chickens, we can go inside.

a. out   b. up   c. around

A: ___ **18.** I tried to pick up the chicken, but it ___ away.

a. run   b. ran   c. running

343 run out of

Meaning: To no longer have enough of something.

Example: It looks like we've **run out of** milk.

Fill in the blanks

We better find a gas station before we _____ _____ _____ fuel. (run)

344 save one's life

Meaning: To stop someone from dying.

Example: Paramedics are trained to **save** people's **lives**.

Fill in the blanks

We _____ the kitten's _____ after it fell into the river. (saved)

345 say hello to...for

Meaning: To request someone to greet someone on their behalf.

Example: Please **say hello to** your mother **for** me.

Fill in the blanks

The teacher wanted me to _____ _____ _____ you _____ her. (say)

346 see a doctor

Meaning: To consult with a doctor at a clinic or hospital.

Example: You should **see a doctor** about that infection on your arm.

Fill in the blanks

I _____ _____ _____ and she gave me medicine for my headache. (saw)

347 see one off

Meaning: To accompany someone to a place where they will depart.

Example: My wife and I will **see** you **off** at the airport.

Fill in the blanks

Thank you for _____ me _____ at the train station. (seeing)

348 see to

Meaning: To handle a situation.

Example: Please **see to** why the shipment is delayed.

Fill in the blanks

I will _____ _____ it that the children go to bed earlier. (see)

349 sell out (of)

Meaning: To no longer have any more products left to sell.

Example: The fruit market had **sold out** of strawberries when we arrived.

Fill in the blanks

You should buy a ticket before they _____ _____. (sell)

350 send away

Meaning: To order someone to leave a place.

Example: The soldier was **sent away** after he failed the mission.

Fill in the blanks

I _____ the workers _____ because of the safety concerns. (sent)

351 send for

Meaning: To request for someone to come to one's location.

Example: You need to **send for** a doctor immediately.

Fill in the blanks

I have _____ _____ an electrician to fix the lighting. (sent)

352 send out

Meaning: To email or mail something to many different people.

Example: I **sent** an email **out** to the staff reminding them about the meeting.

Fill in the blanks

There will be a newsletter _____ _____ to everyone shortly. (sent)

353 sentence to

Meaning: To declare a punishment for someone.

Example: The criminal was **sentenced to** five years in prison.

Fill in the blanks

The judge didn't _____ him _____ prison as it's his first offence. (sentence)

354 separate into

Meaning: To split into smaller groups or parts.

Example: Help me **separate** the cards **into** three equal groups.

Fill in the blanks

We were _____ _____ five groups of four. (separated)

355 set free

Meaning: To let someone or something be released from captivity.

Example: I'm happy to hear that the orca was **set free** from the aquarium.

Fill in the blanks

The soldiers were _____ _____ when the war ended. (set)

356 set on fire

Meaning: To start burning something.

Example: Police believe that the house was deliberately **set on fire**.

Fill in the blanks

Firefighters _____ the fallen trees _____ _____ to clear the area. (set)

357 set an example

Meaning: To act in a way that demonstrates to people how to be.

Example: You should **set an example** for your children and stop smoking.

Fill in the blanks

The school _____ _____ _____ by using less paper. (sets)

358 set aside

Meaning: To put something away for later use.

Example: I **set aside** some money every month to save for a new car.

Fill in the blanks

Did you _____ some warmer clothes _____ for the evening? (set)

359 set out

Meaning: To begin a journey, adventure or plan.

Example: They **set out** early so that they can reach their destination on time.

Fill in the blanks

Rolf will _____ _____ on a voyage to Antarctica tomorrow. (set)

360 set sail

Meaning: To hoist the sails of a boat.

Example: Once we **set sail**, we should arrive at the port in about two hours.

Fill in the blanks

The wind isn't strong enough to _____ _____ today. (set)

Test 20 Write the answer next to the letter "A"

A: ___ 1. Please send ___ a doctor. My grandmother is feeling ill.

a. off   b. for   c. to

A: ___ 2. The man was ___ free after being falsely convicted of the crime.

a. setting   b. sets   c. set

A: ___ 3. I'm going to the market now because we've ___ out of eggs.

a. run   b. ran   c. running

A: ___ 4. I believe the teachers should ___ an example for the students.

a. get   b. set   c. make

A: ___ 5. Beeping my car horn saved that little boy's ___.

a. live   b. living   c. life

A: ___ 6. I still haven't ___ the wedding invitations out to my friends.

a. mail   b. sent   c. post

A: ___ 7. The child was sent ___ to his bedroom for not listening to his mother.

a. over   b. up   c. away

A: ___ 8. They separated the museum ___ four different areas.

a. out to   b. into   c. onto

A: ___ 9. My symptoms have gotten worse, so I'm going to ___ a doctor this afternoon.

a. meet   b. have   c. see

A: ___ **10.** The adventurers set ___ and waved goodbye to their friends and family.

a. sails   b. sail   c. sailing

A: ___ **11.** We have to ___ early if we want to arrive on time.

a. set on   b. set to   c. set out

A: ___ **12.** I appreciate you ___ me off at the bus stop.

a. sending   b. seeing   c. taking

A: ___ **13.** The firefighters were able to save the house after it was ___ on fire.

a. put   b. let   c. set

A: ___ **14.** Austin is ___ to how we can get from the airport to the meeting on time.

a. checking   b. seeing   c. learning

A: ___ **15.** Dad set ___ some food for when you come home.

a. abide   b. beside   c. aside

A: ___ **16.** Jake asked me to say hello to you ___ him and hopes you're feeling better.

a. for   b. from   c. of

A: ___ **17.** The defendant was ___ to four weeks of community service.

a. sentencing   b. sentenced   c. sentence

A: ___ **18.** The toy store has sold ___ of the doll that she wants.

a. off   b. out   c. over

361 set up

Meaning: To organize something in a specific way.

Example: I love the way you've **set up** your living room.

Fill in the blanks

Where will you be _____ _____ the campfire? (setting)

362 shout at

Meaning: To raise your voice loudly at someone, typically with emotion.

Example: The teacher was **shouting at** a student when we arrived.

Fill in the blanks

My father has never _____ _____ me before. (shouted)

363 show off

Meaning: To attract attention to oneself or a thing.

Example: The boy was **showing off** in front of his classmates.

Fill in the blanks

You should stop _____ _____ so much! (showing)

364 show one around

Meaning: To introduce a place to someone by leading them through it.

Example: Let me **show** you **around** our new home.

Fill in the blanks

A lady _____ us _____ the university campus on the first day. (showed)

365 sit down

Meaning: To go from a standing position to a sitting one.

Example: The children **sat down** on the floor to listen to a story.

Fill in the blanks

Susan is the girl _____ _____ by the slide. (sitting)

366 slow down

Meaning: To reduce the speed of doing something.

Example: Try to **slow down** when you're making the speech.

Fill in the blanks

Make sure to _____ _____ when you drive by the school. (slow)

367 speak about

Meaning: To talk about a particular topic.

Example: The professor will be **speaking about** the exam in class today.

Fill in the blanks

We didn't _____ _____ wages during the interview. (speak)

368 speak to

Meaning: To have a conversation with someone.

Example: Could you please **speak to** Janet about the wedding cake for me?

Fill in the blanks

I hadn't _____ _____ him for over five years. (spoken)

369 speak up

Meaning: To speak louder or to express an opinion.

Example: You'll need to **speak up** if you want me to hear you from here.

Fill in the blanks

I'm proud of you for _____ _____ about the bullying at school. (speaking)

- 476 -

370 speed up

Meaning: To accelerate or make something go faster.

Example: The car behind us is suddenly **speeding up**.

Fill in the blanks

If you _____ _____, we might be able to get there on time. (speed)

371 spend on

Meaning: To give money or use time for something.

Example: My grandfather **spent** two months **on** his boat.

Fill in the blanks

I've been _____ too much money _____ makeup. (spending)

372 stand for

Meaning: To be an abbreviation or symbol for something.

Example: I don't know what the letters in her message **stands for**.

Fill in the blanks

The "A" in NATO _____ _____ "Atlantic". (stands)

373 stand up

Meaning: To go from a sitting or lying position to a standing one.

Example: The man **stood up** and made a speech.

Fill in the blanks

Why are you _____ _____? (standing)

374 stand up for

Meaning: To speak or act in support of someone or something.

Example: It's important that the community **stands up for** minority groups.

Fill in the blanks

You need to _____ _____ _____ yourself if someone bullies you. (stand)

375 stare at

Meaning: To focus on something by looking at it.

Example: The person in the blue hat is **staring at** us.

Fill in the blanks

My daughter can't stop _____ _____ her smartphone. (staring)

376 start + verb+ing

Meaning: To begin doing something.

Example: I've **started** going for a run in the evening.

Fill in the blanks

I want to _____ eating more fruit and vegetables. (start)

377 stay up

Meaning: To not go to sleep at one's usual time.

Example: The kids **stay up** until midnight on New Year's Eve.

Fill in the blanks

I _____ _____ late last night and now I don't have any energy. (stayed)

378 stop one from + verb+ing

Meaning: To prevent someone from doing something.

Example: The goalkeeper **stopped** the player **from** scoring two goals.

Fill in the blanks

I tried my best to _____ her _____ driving the car. (stop)

Test 21 Write the answer next to the letter "A"

A: ___ **1.** The teacher has ___ about this historical event before.

a. speak   b. speaking   c. spoken

A: ___ **2.** I've asked Joe to show you ___ town.

a. about   b. around   c. to

A: ___ **3.** Ken and I spent three hours ___ putting this table together.

a. for   b. in   c. on

A: ___ **4.** We should start ___ badminton once a week.

a. played   b. playing   c. play

A: ___ **5.** Please don't hesitate to ___ up if you have any concerns.

a. talk   b. shout   c. speak

A: ___ **6.** The lady at the store helped me set ___ my new smartphone.

a. up   b. down   c. to

A: ___ **7.** Chris wasn't able to stop me ___ winning the game.

a. for   b. to   c. from

A: ___ **8.** The morning traffic will slow us ___, so we might be a little late.

a. over   b. down   c. up

A: ___ **9.** Does anyone know what these letters ___ for?

a. stand   b. mean   c. are

A: ___ **10.** My older brother used to stand ___ me against bullies at school.

a. up   b. up for   c. up to

A: ___ **11.** The geography teacher shouts ___ Bradley whenever he doesn't concentrate.

a. at   b. to   c. for

A: ___ **12.** You can ___ up once you get to the top of the hill.

a. quicken   b. fasten   c. speed

A: ___ **13.** We ___ up late to watch the comet passing by.

a. stood   b. kept   c. stayed

A: ___ **14.** Let's sit ___ under the tree where there's some shade.

a. up   b. down   c. by

A: ___ **15.** I haven't ___ to my friends from school in years.

a. speaking   b. spoke   c. spoken

A: ___ **16.** The children were all staring ___ the snake in the tree.

a. at   b. to   c. on

A: ___ **17.** You don't have to ___ up when you speak.

a. stood   b. stand   c. standing

A: ___ **18.** Stephen was showing ___ his ball skills during the game.

a. over   b. up   c. off

379 stop + verb+ing

Meaning: To finish doing something.

Example: Please **stop** forgetting to bring your text book for class.

Fill in the blanks

You need to _____ working on the weekend. (stop)

380 stop + verb+ing + to + verb

Meaning: To stop doing something to do something else.

Example: My brother has **stopped** surfing **to** concentrate on his studies.

Fill in the blanks

I've _____ eating junk food _____ be healthier. (stopped)

381 struggle with

Meaning: To have a lot of difficulty with something.

Example: She'd been **struggling with** the baby until her husband came home.

Fill in the blanks

I'm _____ _____ this math homework. (struggling)

382 succeed in

Meaning: To accomplish something successfully.

Example: He **succeeded in** convincing his wife to buy a bigger car.

Fill in the blanks

I'm sure she will _____ _____ whatever she decides to do. (succeed)

383 suffer from

Meaning: To be afflicted by an illness or endure something unpleasant.

Example: My mother occasionally **suffers from** insomnia.

Fill in the blanks

I hope you're not _____ too much _____ this hot weather. (suffering)

384 switch off

Meaning: To turn off something so it no longer has power to work.

Example: Please **switch off** the lights before you leave the house.

Fill in the blanks

I forgot to _____ _____ the computer in the office. (switch)

385 take a look at

Meaning: To deliberately view something with attention.

Example: You should **take a look at** the electricity bill this month.

Fill in the blanks

I haven't _____ _____ _____ _____ your article yet. (taken)

386 take a photo of

Meaning: To capture a moment with an image using a camera.

Example: I **took a photo of** a snake lying on the road.

Fill in the blanks

Could you help me _____ _____ _____ _____ the family? (take)

387 take a rest

Meaning: To stop what one is doing momentarily to relax.

Example: You should **take a rest** on your day off.

Fill in the blanks

She's been feeling unwell so she's _____ _____ _____ today. (taking)

388 take a walk

Meaning: To walk for exercise or relaxation for a period of time.

Example: I'm about to **take** the dog for **a walk**.

Fill in the blanks

I've been _____ _____ _____ around the lake. (taking)

389 take action

Meaning: To do something to achieve a goal.

Example: If you want to be successful, you first have to **take action**.

Fill in the blanks

Have you decided to _____ any _____ yet? (take)

390 take along (with)

Meaning: To bring something to a particular place.

Example: You should **take** a water bottle **along** with you.

Fill in the blanks

I regret not _____ _____ my umbrella. (taking)

391 take an interest in

Meaning: To be curious about something.

Example: Max has **taken an interest in** playing table tennis.

Fill in the blanks

I hope he can _____ _____ _____ _____ an outdoor activity. (take)

392 take away

Meaning: To remove something or someone from a place.

Example: Please **take** that ugly armchair **away**.

Fill in the blanks

I'm going to _____ the tools _____ before the kids arrive. (take)

393 take one by surprise

Meaning: To be astonished by something.

Example: It **took** me **by surprise** when the hero died at the end of the movie.

Fill in the blanks

James _____ her _____ _____ when he asked her to marry him. (took)

- 486 -

394 take care of

Meaning: To keep safe and provide for someone or something.

Example: Thank you for **taking care of** the dog for the day.

Fill in the blanks

Have you been _____ _____ _____ the bicycle we got for you? (taking)

395 take notice of

Meaning: To give attention to something.

Example: I don't think he **took** any **notice of** anything I was saying.

Fill in the blanks

Have you been _____ _____ _____ what's happening in Europe? (taking)

396 take charge of

Meaning: To accept responsibility and take control over something.

Example: I want you to **take charge of** the manufacturing department.

Fill in the blanks

Susan has _____ _____ _____ organizing the party food. (taken)

Test 22 Write the answer next to the letter "A"

A: ___ 1. My son ___ with the weather for a few years before he got used to it.

a. survived   b. suffered   c. struggled

A: ___ 2. When do you expect we can ___ action on this plan?

a. make   b. take   c. do

A: ___ 3. I forgot to switch ___ the air conditioner.

a. over   b. of   c. off

A: ___ 4. You ___ us all by surprise when you told us you're leaving the company.

a. got   b. took   c. gave

A: ___ 5. Frank succeeded ___ designing a house that is more energy efficient.

a. to   b. on   c. in

A: ___ 6. Sherry will be taking charge ___ decorating the room.

a. of   b. for   c. on

A: ___ 7. Did you ___ a photo of the hotel that you stayed at?

a. make   b. take   c. do

A: ___ 8. The company had to stop manufacturing goods ___ reduce costs.

a. so that   b. to   c. because of

A: ___ 9. Could you please take Larry ___ with you to the supermarket?

a. along   b. over   c. across

A: ___ **10.** I've decided to take this old painting ___.

a. away						b. way						c. a way

A: ___ **11.** It's important to take notice ___ what the swim instructor is teaching you.

a. for						b. of						c. to

A: ___ **12.** You must stop ___ on the bed.

a. to jump					b. jumping					c. jumps

A: ___ **13.** I took ___ of mowing the lawn while you were gone.

a. careful					b. caring					c. care

A: ___ **14.** Drink plenty of water so that you don't ___ from heatstroke.

a. suffer					b. survive					c. struggle

A: ___ **15.** We both like to ___ a walk along the beach.

a. go						b. take						c. make

A: ___ **16.** I've decided to take ___ this weekend.

a. a rest					b. resting					c. to rest

A: ___ **17.** My parents have never taken an ___ my job.

a. interest to					b. interesting					c. interest in

A: ___ **18.** Could you ___ a look at the water pressure in the shower for me?

a. take						b. make						c. get

397 take down

Meaning: To write something on paper.

Example: Take down my number just in case you need to contact me.

Fill in the blanks

I _____ _____ the name of the product so that I don't forget it. (took)

398 take heart from

Meaning: To feel comfortable or courage because of something.

Example: You can **take heart from** knowing that your parents support you.

Fill in the blanks

I _____ _____ _____ the fact that I tried my best and learned a lot. (took)

399 take hold of

Meaning: To grasp or grip something securely.

Example: Take hold of Dad's hand when we cross the road.

Fill in the blanks

You _____ _____ _____ this side of the sofa and I'll take the other. (take)

400 take it easy

Meaning: To act in a calm and relaxed way.

Example: If you're feeling unwell, you should **take it easy** today.

Fill in the blanks

We'll be _____ _____ _____ on our holiday this time. (taking)

401 take medicine

Meaning: To consume some medicine.

Example: The doctor told me to **take medicine** three times a day.

Fill in the blanks

Don't forget to _____ _____ after you finish eating lunch. (take)

402 take off

Meaning: To remove a piece of clothing.

Example: If you're too hot, you can **take off** your jacket.

Fill in the blanks

I wish I hadn't _____ _____ my coat because it's about to rain. (taken)

403 take on

Meaning: To undertake a task, typically a challenging one.

Example: I've decided to **take on** a coaching role at the soccer team.

Fill in the blanks

My boss asked me to _____ _____ more responsibility. (take)

404 take one's time

Meaning: To do something slowly.

Example: Please **take** your **time** when riding your bike here.

Fill in the blanks

Jimmy is _____ his _____ with the puzzle. (taking)

405 take one out for

Meaning: To bring someone on a date, typically for a meal.

Example: The manager **took** me **out for** lunch to discuss my promotion.

Fill in the blanks

I'm going to _____ my wife _____ _____ our wedding anniversary. (take)

406 take...out (of)

Meaning: To remove someone or something from a place.

Example: I think you should **take** the children **out** of the room.

Fill in the blanks

I still haven't _____ the trash _____ the pizza. (taken)

407 take part in

Meaning: To participate in something.

Example: We **took part in** cleaning up the local beach.

Fill in the blanks

He'll be _____ _____ _____ the golf tournament. (taking)

408 take place

Meaning: To occur at a particular time or location.

Example: Have you decided where the wedding will **take place** yet?

Fill in the blanks

The crime _____ _____ in the middle of the night. (took)

409   take possession (of)

Meaning: To own something, typically by purchasing it.

Example: The bank **took possession** of the neighbor's house yesterday.

Fill in the blanks

I'll be _____ _____ of my father's company when he retires. (taking)

410   take pride in

Meaning: To be proud of how one does something.

Example: He **takes pride in** his job and that's why everyone likes him.

Fill in the blanks

You should _____ _____ _____ what you did for the school. (take)

411   take sides

Meaning: To support a person, group or team against an opposing side.

Example: I haven't **taken** any **sides** in this debate.

Fill in the blanks

My parents never _____ _____ when my brother and I would argue. (took)

412 take turns

Meaning: To do something one after another in regular succession.

Example: The sign says that children must **take turns** on the swings.

Fill in the blanks

We _____ _____ playing the new video game. (took)

413 take the place of

Meaning: To replace or be a substitute for someone or something.

Example: The smartphone had quickly **taken the place of** telephones.

Fill in the blanks

Nobody knows who will _____ _____ _____ _____ the manager. (take)

414 take up

Meaning: To begin doing something regularly, typically a hobby or sport.

Example: My parents want to **take up** golf once they're both retired.

Fill in the blanks

I've recently _____ _____ cooking classes with an Italian chef. (taken)

Test 23 Write the answer next to the letter "A"

A: ___ **1.** You two need to take ___ when you play with this toy.

a. turningb. turnc. turns

A: ___ **2.** You should take ___ from knowing you can retire earlier than most people.

a. mindb. heartc. heat

A: ___ **3.** Greg has taken ___ a management position at a tech company.

a. holdb. afterc. on

A: ___ **4.** Try to take it ___ this weekend so that you can recover from your cold.

a. easyb. relaxc. rest

A: ___ **5.** Make sure to ___ your medicine after lunch.

a. takenb. takingc. take

A: ___ **6.** The graduation ceremony will ___ place on Friday.

a. happenb. takec. have

A: ___ **7.** Take ___ of the fishing rod when you see it move.

a. grabb. handc. hold

A: ___ **8.** The students all took ___ in decorating the wall.

a. timeb. heartc. part

A: ___ **9.** The electric car will eventually take the ___ of cars with combustion engines.

a. replacementb. placec. role

A: ___ **10.** This evening, I plan to take out my daughter ___ her birthday.

a. to   b. for   c. at

A: ___ **11.** I'm going to take ___ of my uncle's fishing boat tomorrow.

a. position   b. procession   c. possession

A: ___ **12.** The teacher never takes ___ when there's an issue in the classroom.

a. groups   b. sides   c. teams

A: ___ **13.** I suggest you take ___ as much information as you can.

a. on   b. down   c. up

A: ___ **14.** Sally ___ off her shoes when she got to the beach.

a. took   b. got   c. brought

A: ___ **15.** Could you help me ___ the garbage out before you leave?

a. bring   b. take   c. move

A: ___ **16.** I would like to take ___ surfing one day.

a. on   b. thinks   c. up

A: ___ **17.** It ___ a lot of time to get here this morning because of the traffic.

a. spent   b. took   c. had

A: ___ **18.** My grandmother takes pride ___ growing fruit and vegetables in her garden.

a. over   b. on   c. in

415 take up arms

Meaning: To pick up weapons and begin to fight.

Example: Men of all ages **took up arms** to defend their country.

Fill in the blanks

The rebels have _____ _____ _____ against their own government. (taken)

416 talk about

Meaning: To discuss a particular topic.

Example: We were just **talking about** you when you called.

Fill in the blanks

What would you like to _____ _____ in English class today? (talk)

417 talk to

Meaning: To have a conversation with someone.

Example: I need to **talk to** my teacher about the physics test.

Fill in the blanks

I was _____ _____ your sister yesterday at the supermarket. (talking)

418 teach oneself

Meaning: To learn something without the help of others.

Example: I **taught** myself how to play guitar when I was a teenager.

Fill in the blanks

He tried to _____ himself to speak Japanese, but eventually gave up. (teach)

419 tear down

Meaning: To demolish something, typically a building.

Example: They're going to **tear down** the old library to build a new one.

Fill in the blanks

Uncle Rick and Dad are _____ _____ the garage. (tearing)

420 tear off

Meaning: To leave quickly.

Example: The bus **tore off** as I arrived at the bus stop.

Fill in the blanks

The kids _____ _____ down the street to play at the park. (tore)

421 tell a lie

Meaning: To not tell the truth about something.

Example: You shouldn't **tell a lie** to your parents.

Fill in the blanks

I can't remember the last time that I _____ _____ _____ to anyone. (told)

422 tell apart

Meaning: To see the difference between two things.

Example: I'm having trouble **telling apart** the twins.

Fill in the blanks

It's difficult to _____ the two goldfish _____. (tell)

423 tell one about

Meaning: To inform someone about something.

Example: Fran **told** me **about** this cookbook.

Fill in the blanks

I was _____ Russell _____ the great Indian restaurant we went to. (telling)

424 tell the truth

Meaning: To be frank and say what you really think.

Example: I suggest you **tell** the teacher **the truth** about cheating on the test.

Fill in the blanks

Were you _____ _____ _____ when you said you might retire? (telling)

425 think about

Meaning: To consider something before making a decision.

Example: I've been **thinking about** buying a new car.

Fill in the blanks

Have you _____ _____ which university you'd like to attend? (thought)

426 think of

Meaning: To consider, imagine or remember something.

Example: I can't **think of** what his name is.

Fill in the blanks

I _____ _____ an idea we can try for the comedy act. (thought)

427 think over

Meaning: To consider something carefully before making a decision.

Example: I need to **think over** how we can overcome this challenge.

Fill in the blanks

I've _____ _____ what you said and I think you're right. (thought)

428 throw...at

Meaning: To toss something towards a target.

Example: You have to **throw** the ball **at** the board.

Fill in the blanks

We used to _____ rocks _____ at the tree. (throw)

429 throw away

Meaning: To dispose of something, typically rubbish.

Example: I'm probably going to **throw** these old clothes **away**.

Fill in the blanks

You need to _____ this frypan _____ because it's too old. (throw)

430 translate...into

Meaning: To convert one language into another.

Example: This book has been **translated into** twenty different languages.

Fill in the blanks

You can ask Marcello to _____ this article _____ Italian. (translate)

431 try on

Meaning: To wear an item to see if it fits or is desirable.

Example: Monica has already **tried on** five different dresses.

Fill in the blanks

You should _____ the pants _____ before you buy them. (try)

432 try one's best

Meaning: To make the most effort or do everything one can to succeed.

Example: Polly **tried** her **best** not to laugh when her father fell over.

Fill in the blanks

I think Harry _____ his _____, but he just wasn't good enough to win. (tried)

Test 24 Write the answer next to the letter "A"

A: ___ **1.** Kevin is ___ himself how to cook Italian food.

a. teaches   b. taught   c. teaching

A: ___ **2.** I was shocked to hear my brother ___ a lie to his teacher.

a. said   b. spoke   c. told

A: ___ **3.** What do you think ___ the new chemistry teacher?

a. over   b. around   c. about

A: ___ **4.** Mom needs to ___ to my teacher about the physics test.

a. talk   b. talks   c. talked

A: ___ **5.** Your brother was excited when I ___ him about the new tennis courts.

a. told   b. tell   c. telling

A: ___ **6.** I'm trying my ___ to learn the song, but it's not easy.

a. hard   b. most   c. best

A: ___ **7.** The children had fun throwing water balloons ___ each other.

a. at   b. on   c. for

A: ___ **8.** Did you think ___ any ideas about how we can reduce expenses?

a. about   b. of   c. on

A: ___ **9.** It's difficult to ___ apart the two paintings, but only one of them is genuine.

a. know   b. tell   c. set

A: ___ **10.** I'd like to try ___ these shoes to see how comfortable they are to walk in.

a. up					b. off					c. on

A: ___ **11.** The kids like to play with boxes so don't throw them ___.

a. back					b. away					c. off

A: ___ **12.** Were you telling the ___ about what happened in class today?

a. truth				b. true					c. truthful

A: ___ **13.** Give me one day to think ___ what we can do with all the leftover food.

a. on					b. over					c. under

A: ___ **14.** I was shocked to hear that my favorite skateboard ramp was ___ down.

a. tearing				b. tore					c. torn

A: ___ **15.** What were you ___ about with Dorothy?

a. talk					b. talking				c. talked

A: ___ **16.** I wish this Japanese cartoon was translated ___ English.

a. to					b. in					c. into

A: ___ **17.** The mouse tore ___ when I entered the room.

a. away					b. off					c. over

A: ___ **18.** The president had called for men to take up ___ to defend against the attack.

a. guns					b. army					c. arms

433 try out

Meaning: To test something new to see if it is suitable or satisfactory.

Example: Have you **tried out** the kite yet?

Fill in the blanks

Jason _____ _____ this pillow, but found it too soft. (tried)

434 try to + verb

Meaning: To make an attempt to do something.

Example: I **tried to** warn you, but you didn't listen to me.

Fill in the blanks

Luke was _____ _____ change a lightbulb when he fell off the chair. (trying)

435 turn away (from)

Meaning: To face a different direction to someone or something.

Example: Dave missed the ball because he **turned away** from it.

Fill in the blanks

Why do you keep _____ _____ from me when I'm speaking? (turning)

436 turn down

Meaning: To decrease the volume of something.

Example: Please **turn down** the music while I'm talking on the phone.

Fill in the blanks

You'll need to _____ _____ the TV when the baby goes to sleep. (turn)

437 turn into

Meaning: To become something new or different.

Example: The movie is about a man who **turns into** a wolf at night.

Fill in the blanks

I'd like to _____ this garage _____ an extra bedroom. (turn)

438 turn off

Meaning: To stop the function or power of something.

Example: Make sure to **turn off** the air conditioner when you leave the house.

Fill in the blanks

I have no idea how to _____ the sound _____ on this toy. (turn)

439 turn on

Meaning: To start the function or power of something.

Example: Sorry I didn't answer your call, but I forgot to **turn** my phone **on**.

Fill in the blanks

Did you _____ the fan _____ in the bathroom? (turn)

440 turn over

Meaning: To invert something so that the bottom is now facing the top.

Example: You should **turn over** the hamburger patties before they burn.

Fill in the blanks

The baby has _____ _____ onto his back. (turned)

441 turn to

Meaning: To consult someone for advice, support or help.

Example: When I have a problem, I **turn to** my older sister for help.

Fill in the blanks

I don't who I should _____ _____ about this issue. (turn)

442 turn up

Meaning: To increase the volume of something.

Example: You need to **turn** your speaker **up** so that you can hear me clearly.

Fill in the blanks

_____ the music _____, so everyone can listen to it. (Turn)

443 use one's head

Meaning: To think intelligently before doing something.

Example: He wasn't **using** his **head** when he drove without a seatbelt.

Fill in the blanks

As long as you _____ your _____, you should be safe. (use)

444 used to + verb

Meaning: To be familiar with something so that it's normal.

Example: Your uncle and I **used to** fly kites when we were kids.

Fill in the blanks

My grandmother _____ _____ bake delicious cookies for us. (used)

445 use up

Meaning: To no longer have any supply of something.

Example: We've **used up** all the straws.

Fill in the blanks

The children are _____ _____ all the glue to make their pictures. (using)

446 vamp up

Meaning: To repair or improve something so that it's better.

Example: You can **vamp up** your dress with a pink jacket.

Fill in the blanks

Melody _____ her workbook _____ with stickers. (vamped)

447 vary from

Meaning: To differ from something else.

Example: How quickly you can learn a language **varies from** person to person.

Fill in the blanks

These dumplings _____ _____ the ones we ate in Shanghai. (vary)

448 vow to

Meaning: To make a solemn promise to do something.

Example: Luke **vowed to** never drink alcohol again.

Fill in the blanks

I _____ _____ to keep studying until I graduate. (vow)

449 wait for

Meaning: To expect something in anticipation.

Example: I'll **wait for** you in front of the train station.

Fill in the blanks

I'm still _____ _____ the package to arrive. (waiting)

450 wait on

Meaning: To serve people at a restaurant.

Example: The gentleman **waiting on** us was very polite.

Fill in the blanks

There aren't enough people _____ _____ tables at this restaurant. (waiting)

Test 25 Write the answer next to the letter "A"

A: ___ **1.** He had nobody to turn ___ when he needed help.

a. to   b. up   c. on

A: ___ **2.** I've been ___ to eat healthier food this year.

a. tried   b. trying   c. try

A: ___ **3.** The paper cups were all used ___ when we went camping.

a. over   b. up   c. for

A: ___ **4.** My family ___ to go on a trip to the beach during the summer holidays.

a. use   b. uses   c. used

A: ___ **5.** There's a new pizza flavor at my favorite restaurant that I want to try ___.

a. to   b. on   c. out

A: ___ **6.** Vegetation varies ___ place to place depending on the climate and type of soil.

a. between   b. from   c. for

A: ___ **7.** You can turn ___ the headlights once you drive out of the tunnel.

a. over   b. down   c. off

A: ___ **8.** He has a lot of skill, but needs to use his ___ if he wants to be a champion.

a. head   b. brain   c. knowledge

A: ___ **9.** It's a good idea to turn ___ the oven first so that it heats up.

a. on   b. off   c. down

- 512 -

A: ___ **10.** The teacher ___ up the CD player so that all the students could hear it.

a. turned	b. turn	c. turns

A: ___ **11.** My husband ___ to me that he would never work on Sundays.

a. vamped	b. vowed	c. viewed

A: ___ **12.** After two minutes, turn ___ the pancakes.

a. around	b. up	c. over

A: ___ **13.** You could use background music to ___ up the video.

a. turn	b. vamp	c. vow

A: ___ **14.** The sun was so bright that I had to turn ___ from it.

a. from	b. off	c. away

A: ___ **15.** Let's wait ___ Dad to come home before we have dinner.

a. for	b. on	c. until

A: ___ **16.** You need to ___ down the ringtone on your phone.

a. turn	b. turned	c. turning

A: ___ **17.** My name is Ruby and I'll be waiting ___ your table this evening.

a. for	b. to	c. on

A: ___ **18.** They're going to turn the house ___ a small hotel.

a. onto	b. into	c. out of

451 wait out

Meaning: To stay until the end of something.

Example: We may have to **wait out** until the rain stops before we walk home.

Fill in the blanks

I want to _____ the surgery _____ to see if Mom is okay. (wait)

452 wake up

Meaning: To no longer be sleeping.

Example: We should go to bed because we have to **wake up** early tomorrow.

Fill in the blanks

I keep _____ _____ in the middle of the night. (waking)

453 walk along

Meaning: To follow a path or route by foot.

Example: It was nice **walking along** the beach this morning.

Fill in the blanks

If you _____ _____ this path, you might come across a squirrel. (walk)

454 walk away (from)

Meaning: To leave someone or something by foot.

Example: The dog **walked away** from us when it saw we had no food.

Fill in the blanks

Don't _____ _____ from me when I'm talking to you! (walk)

455 walk away with

Meaning: To win first prize in a competition.

Example: The best actor **walked away with** three awards tonight.

Fill in the blanks

We were all shocked when the team _____ _____ _____ the win. (walked)

456 walk in on

Meaning: To unexpectedly enter a room while someone is inside.

Example: Please don't **walk in on** me when I'm doing my makeup.

Fill in the blanks

The boss _____ _____ _____ the meeting and sat down. (walked)

457 walk off

Meaning: To try to reduce the pain of an injury by walking.

Example: I'm going to get some fresh air and **walk off** this headache.

Fill in the blanks

The player was able to _____ _____ his injury during the game. (walk)

458 walk on by

Meaning: To continue walking after seeing something.

Example: Gretel **walked on by** without stopping to say hello to us.

Fill in the blanks

There were too many people, so we decided to _____ _____ _____. (walk)

459 walk out

Meaning: To leave a room, typically as an emotional response.

Example: Some politicians **walked out** during the president's speech.

Fill in the blanks

We _____ _____ because the movie was too violent for kids. (walked)

460 walk out on

Meaning: To abandon someone whom you have responsibility to.

Example: His wife **walked out on** him a few years ago.

Fill in the blanks

I would never _____ _____ _____ my family. (walk)

461 walk up to

Meaning: To approach someone or something by foot.

Example: A man **walked up to** us and asked for some money.

Fill in the blanks

You should _____ _____ _____ the boss and ask for a job. (walk)

462 want out (of)

Meaning: To no longer want to be part of something.

Example: The model **wants out** of all forms of social media platforms.

Fill in the blanks

I _____ _____ after the coach told me to exercise more. (wanted)

463 warm up

Meaning: To prepare oneself for an activity.

Example: Once he **warms up**, he'll start scoring goals.

Fill in the blanks

I usually _____ _____ for ten minutes before going for a run. (warm)

464 wash away

Meaning: To carry away or remove something with the force of water.

Example: The heavy flood **washed** a lot of small trees **away**.

Fill in the blanks

I used the hose to _____ _____ the leaves off the driveway. (wash)

465 wash down...with

Meaning: To use a beverage to make it easier to swallow something.

Example: You can try **wash down** the bitter medicine **with** water.

Fill in the blanks

He _____ _____ the spicy food _____ lemon soda. (washed)

- 518 -

466 wash out

Meaning: To clean the inside of something with water.

Example: You should **wash out** the bucket before putting it away.

Fill in the blanks

You'll need to _____ the boat _____ after you finish fishing. (wash)

467 wash up

Meaning: To remove dirt, food or stain from something by cleaning it.

Example: Everyone needs to **wash up** their own dirty dishes.

Fill in the blanks

I need to go home and _____ _____ before we go out for dinner. (wash)

468 watch out for

Meaning: To be aware, careful or watchful of something or someone.

Example: We should **watch out for** bears when we go hiking.

Fill in the blanks

You have to _____ _____ _____ holes on this road. (watch)

Test 26 Write the answer next to the letter "A"

A: ___ 1. Sorry for walking in ___ you this morning. I thought you were awake.

a. of	b. on	c. to

A: ___ 2. What time should we ___ up in the morning?

a. woke	b. waking	c. wake

A: ___ 3. I usually like to ___ down pizza with soda.

a. clean	b. wash	c. drink

A: ___ 4. We saw a bear walking ___ the river on our hike yesterday.

a. among	b. above	c. along

A: ___ 5. The wave is washing ___ the sandcastles that we made.

a. along	b. away	c. among

A: ___ 6. My father wants ___ of the investments he made in the stock market.

a. out	b. away	c. off

A: ___ 7. One of the employees got angry and walked out ___ the company today.

a. on	b. over	c. along

A: ___ 8. You should watch out ___ sharks if you're going for a surf at that beach.

a. on	b. for	c. of

A: ___ 9. I tried to walk ___ the pain in my leg, but it still hurts.

a. along	b. away	c. off

- 520 -

A: ___ **10.** Make sure to warm ___ first before you start running.

a. down	b. up	c. over

A: ___ **11.** The lions walked ___ from the river when the elephants came.

a. around	b. off	c. away

A: ___ **12.** The police officer ___ up to the kids and told them to leave.

a. walk	b. walked	c. walks

A: ___ **13.** Once I've finished ___ up, we can watch a movie.

a. washing	b. washed	c. wash

A: ___ **14.** Why did you walk ___ of today's meeting?

a. off	b. away	c. out

A: ___ **15.** Robert thinks Brazil will walk ___ with the World Cup.

a. over	b. away	c. on

A: ___ **16.** We've decided to wait ___ inside the house for the hurricane to leave.

a. over	b. out	c. off

A: ___ **17.** By the time the restaurant closes, we'll have ___ out most of the ovens.

a. washing	b. wash	c. washed

A: ___ **18.** Everyone walked ___ by without picking up any rubbish.

a. away	b. off	c. on

469 watch over

Meaning: To guard, protect or take responsibility for someone or something.

Example: There's a lifeguard at the pool that **watches over** everyone.

Fill in the blanks

Someone needs to go to the park to _____ _____ the children. (watch)

470 water down

Meaning: To dilute the content of a liquid using water.

Example: My mother used to **water down** the fruit juice.

Fill in the blanks

Do you think they've _____ _____ the soda at this restaurant? (watered)

471 wear away

Meaning: To gradually erode, disappear or become damaged.

Example: The drawing on the footpath **wore away** in the rain.

Fill in the blanks

Some of the statues have _____ _____ over time. (worn)

472 wear one down

Meaning: To make someone so tired that they no longer can handle it.

Example: Working at the café on the weekend is **wearing** me **down**.

Fill in the blanks

Babysitting these two children will _____ you _____. (wear)

473 wear off

Meaning: To gradually lose effectiveness or intensity.

Example: The medicine is **wearing off** and my headache is back.

Fill in the blanks

The vaccine typically _____ _____ after twelve months. (wears)

474 wear out

Meaning: To use something until it is no longer in good condition.

Example: I will have **worn** this umbrella **out** by the end of winter.

Fill in the blanks

Your sneakers are completely _____ _____ from running every day. (worn)

475 weed out

Meaning: To remove an unwanted person or thing from a group.

Example: The HR department is **weeding out** anyone who is not working well.

Fill in the blanks

The coach _____ _____ the players that weren't making an effort. (weeded)

476 weigh up

Meaning: To consider all options before making a decision.

Example: I'm **weighing up** whether I should buy a house or rent one.

Fill in the blanks

Chad is still _____ _____ which universities to apply for. (weighing)

477 whip out

Meaning: To bring something out quickly.

Example: The magician **whipped out** some flowers from under his jacket.

Fill in the blanks

He _____ _____ his phone and called for an ambulance to come. (whipped)

478 whip up

Meaning: To make a meal quickly.

Example: I can **whip** a sandwich **up** for you to take with you.

Fill in the blanks

Mom _____ _____ soup for us because we hadn't eaten all day. (whipped)

479 whisk away

Meaning: To abruptly remove someone or something from a place.

Example: Two security guards **whisked** the intruder **away** from the property.

Fill in the blanks

The children were _____ _____ before they could see the gifts. (whisked)

480 wimp out

Meaning: To not be brave enough to do something.

Example: The boy **wimped out** halfway up the ladder and climbed down.

Fill in the blanks

Will Jack dive into the water or will he _____ _____? (wimp)

481 wind down

Meaning: To be in the process of being more relaxed.

Example: I like to **wind down** in the evening with a cup of hot chocolate.

Fill in the blanks

Sometimes, I play video games to _____ _____ after work. (wind)

482 wind up

Meaning: To irritate someone.

Example: You need to stop **winding up** your cousin about his haircut.

Fill in the blanks

This politician always _____ me _____ when he talks. (winds)

483 wipe out

Meaning: To eliminate something completely.

Example: The tornado **wiped out** two houses last year.

Fill in the blanks

This bomb can _____ _____ an entire town. (wipe)

484 wise up

Meaning: To become more aware of or sensible about something.

Example: You need to **wise up** if you want to avoid getting into trouble.

Fill in the blanks

The lady _____ _____ when she realized she was getting cheated. (wised)

485 work off

Meaning: To exercise to reduce stress or weight.

Example: I've been running every day to **work off** my waistline.

Fill in the blanks

Hiking has been helping me _____ _____ the pressure I'm under. (work)

486 work on

Meaning: To improve or develop something.

Example: The engineers have been **working on** a new electric car.

Fill in the blanks

I _____ _____ the new video for over three hours last night. (worked)

Test 27 Write the answer next to the letter "A"

A: ___ 1. The police officer ___ out the pepper spray when she was being attacked.

a. wimped   b. weeded   c. whipped

A: ___ 2. The doctor recommended me to work ___ some fat with regular exercise.

a. off   b. out   c. on

A: ___ 3. We should ___ out any problems that may arise.

a. wipe   b. wear   c. weed

A: ___ 4. The unruly person was ___ away by the police officers.

a. wiped   b. whisked   c. whipped

A: ___ 5. All the news about gun violence is ___ me down.

a. wear   b. worn   c. wearing

A: ___ 6. Sally wimped ___ and decided not to sing in front of the class.

a. out   b. off   c. away

A: ___ 7. The meal you ___ up for me was delicious.

a. whip   b. whipped   c. whips

A: ___ 8. I like to ___ down the apple juice a little so that it doesn't taste so sweet.

a. wind   b. weigh   c. water

A: ___ 9. The frogs at this pond were ___ out by the increase in bird population.

a. worn   b. whipped   c. wiped

A: ___ **10.** You need to weigh ___ the pros and cons of buying an electric car.

a. on	b. up	c. out

A: ___ **11.** I'm going away this weekend to ___ down after a busy month of work.

a. wind	b. wear	c. wise

A: ___ **12.** The cliff is starting to wear ___ due to the rising sea level.

a. off	b. away	c. over

A: ___ **13.** It's time you ___ and make better decisions in your life.

a. watch over	b. wise up	c. wind down

A: ___ **14.** Getting up early for my new job is starting to ___ me out.

a. wear	b. wind	c. work

A: ___ **15.** Have you started working ___ the new project yet?

a. off	b. on	c. away

A: ___ **16.** A teacher has a big responsibility to watch ___ the students in class.

a. on	b. out	c. over

A: ___ **17.** Who is the person that ___ you up the most?

a. winding	b. winds	c. wind

A: ___ **18.** The sunscreen will start to wear ___ after about three hours.

a. off	b. out	c. away

487 work out (1)

Meaning: To calculate or think about the result of something.

Example: The last question on the math test was difficult to **work out**.

Fill in the blanks

Have you _____ _____ how much food we need for the barbecue? (worked)

488 work out (2)

Meaning: To engage in exercise.

Example: I've started **working out** at the gym in the evening.

Fill in the blanks

Make sure to _____ _____ correctly so that you don't hurt yourself. (work)

489 wrap up

Meaning: To cover something completely with some paper or other material.

Example: I **wrapped** the birthday present **up** with pink wrapping paper.

Fill in the blanks

The shopkeeper will _____ _____ the fish and put it in a bag. (wrap)

490 write down

Meaning: To write notes on something, typically on paper.

Example: I **wrote** his phone number **down** on the back of a napkin.

Fill in the blanks

Did you _____ carrots _____ on the shopping list? (write)

491 write in

Meaning: To write to an organization, typically with a question or comment.

Example: Someone **wrote in** to tell us that they're happy with our products.

Fill in the blanks

Please _____ _____ with your questions and I'll do my best to reply. (write)

492 write off

Meaning: To cancel the use of something because it is too badly damaged.

Example: The car was **written off** after the accident.

Fill in the blanks

The engineer _____ _____ two of the machines in the factory. (wrote)

493 write out

Meaning: To complete something in writing.

Example: My grandma **wrote out** the recipe for the pasta sauce for me.

Fill in the blanks

Have you _____ _____ the email to the accountant yet? (written)

494 yell at

Meaning: To scold someone loudly.

Example: The coach was **yelling at** the players for not trying hard.

Fill in the blanks

I don't like when the teacher _____ _____ the students. (yells)

495 yield to

Meaning: To submit to, be persuaded by or give victory to someone.

Example: The tennis player had to **yield to** his opponent after getting injured.

Fill in the blanks

I don't think we should _____ _____ the customer's demands. (yield)

496 zero in on

Meaning: To direct all of one's attention to one thing.

Example: The police are **zeroing in on** the people near the crime scene.

Fill in the blanks

The mining company will _____ _____ _____ resources in Australia. (zero)

497 zero out

Meaning: To reduce the amount of something to zero.

Example: The goal is to **zero out** malaria cases in the region.

Fill in the blanks

Make sure to _____ _____ the bank account before closing it. (zero)

498 zip around

Meaning: To move quickly from one place to another.

Example: A smaller car is better to **zip around** the city with.

Fill in the blanks

It was fun to watch the kids _____ _____ the park on their scooters. (zip)

499 zip by

Meaning: To have something pass quickly.

Example: The English class always **zips by** because it's so much fun.

Fill in the blanks

I just saw Peter _____ _____ on his skateboard. (zip)

500 zip up

Meaning: To close something with a zipper.

Example: You forgot to **zip up** your backpack.

Fill in the blanks

I always have difficulty _____ _____ this jacket. (zipping)

501 zone in on

Meaning: To focus or concentrate on something.

Example: Try to **zone in on** information regarding the Vietnam War.

Fill in the blanks

I _____ _____ _____ city parks and found one with a tennis court. (zoned)

- 534 -

502 zone out

Meaning: To lose concentration and become inattentive.

Example: I **zoned out** while the history teacher was reading to us.

Fill in the blanks

Try not to _____ _____ during the meeting this time. (zone)

503 zoom in (on)

Meaning: To magnify the image of a distant object using a zoom lens.

Example: Could you please **zoom in** on the plate of food in this photo?

Fill in the blanks

If you _____ _____ on her arm, you can see a small tattoo. (zoom)

504 zoom out

Meaning: To decrease the size of an image using a zoom lens.

Example: If you **zoom out**, you should be able to see the whole room.

Fill in the blanks

You've _____ _____ too much and I can't see the faces clearly. (zoomed)

Test 28 Write the answer next to the letter "A"

A: ___ **1.** The goal of developing public transport is to zero ___ traffic jams in the area.

a. off   b. out   c. over

A: ___ **2.** We watched the fighter jets zip ___ the mountaintop.

a. by   b. pass   c. up

A: ___ **3.** The old train was finally ___ off after being used for over fifty years.

a. writing   b. written   c. wrote

A: ___ **4.** Make sure to zip ___ the tent so that bugs don't get in.

a. of   b. over   c. up

A: ___ **5.** Did you write the teacher's homework ___ in your notebook?

a. up   b. down   c. on

A: ___ **6.** The surgeon has zeroed in ___ what is causing the headaches.

a. on   b. at   c. over

A: ___ **7.** The manager shouldn't yell ___ everyone all the time.

a. to   b. at   c. by

A: ___ **8.** I cannot ___ out why the air conditioner isn't working properly.

a. work   b. understand   c. think

A: ___ **9.** Sorry, but I didn't have time to ___ your gift up.

a. wrap   b. put   c. roll

- 536 -

A: ___ **10.** The teacher will be ___ this week's spelling words out on the blackboard.

a. written   b. writing   c. write

A: ___ **11.** The scientists are trying to zone ___ where the virus first starting spreading.

a. in on   b. on in   c. into

A: ___ **12.** If you ___ in on the left of the photo, you'll see me in the crowd.

a. zone   b. zoom   c. yield

A: ___ **13.** You can write ___ to the company through the website.

a. over   b. on   c. in

A: ___ **14.** The criminal refused to yield ___ the police officer and got arrested.

a. on   b. for   c. to

A: ___ **15.** I think Ben was ___ out when I was teaching him chemistry today.

a. zeroing   b. zoning   c. zooming

A: ___ **16.** There's a gym at my workplace where I can ___ out in the evenings.

a. exercise   b. work   c. play

A: ___ **17.** It's more convenient to zip ___ on a bike in this town.

a. by   b. up   c. around

A: ___ **18.** Are you able to ___ out so that we can see the whole family?

a. zoom   b. zone   c. zero

Answers

Test 1-14	Test 1	Test 2	Test 3	Test 4	Test 5	Test 6	Test 7	Test 8	Test 9	Test 10	Test 11	Test 12	Test 13	Test 14
Question 1	b	c	c	b	c	c	c	a	a	b	a	a	c	b
Question 2	a	b	a	a	b	b	a	b	b	c	c	c	b	c
Question 3	b	b	b	c	a	b	b	b	c	a	c	a	b	c
Question 4	c	a	b	b	a	a	a	c	b	b	a	c	a	b
Question 5	b	c	c	b	b	c	c	a	a	c	b	c	c	a
Question 6	c	b	b	c	c	b	b	b	c	b	b	b	c	b
Question 7	a	c	c	c	b	a	b	c	b	b	c	c	a	c
Question 8	c	a	a	a	a	b	a	b	a	c	a	a	b	b
Question 9	b	a	c	b	b	a	c	c	c	a	b	c	a	c
Question 10	b	b	c	a	c	c	b	a	a	c	b	a	a	c
Question 11	a	c	b	b	c	a	c	c	c	b	a	b	c	b
Question 12	b	b	a	b	a	a	b	b	b	b	b	c	c	a
Question 13	a	b	b	a	a	b	b	b	b	a	c	a	b	c
Question 14	c	a	c	c	a	b	a	c	c	b	c	b	b	a
Question 15	c	a	b	b	c	a	b	a	a	c	b	c	a	c
Question 16	a	c	a	c	b	c	c	b	c	a	c	a	c	b
Question 17	b	b	b	c	b	b	b	c	a	c	b	a	b	c
Question 18	c	c	c	b	a	b	a	a	b	a	c	c	c	c

Test 15-28	Test 15	Test 16	Test 17	Test 18	Test 19	Test 20	Test 21	Test 22	Test 23	Test 24	Test 25	Test 26	Test 27	Test 28
Question 1	c	c	a	b	a	b	c	c	c	c	a	b	c	b
Question 2	a	c	b	c	b	c	b	b	b	c	b	c	a	a
Question 3	c	a	b	b	a	a	c	c	c	c	b	b	c	b
Question 4	b	b	c	a	c	b	b	b	a	a	c	c	b	c
Question 5	c	c	a	a	a	c	c	c	c	a	c	b	c	b
Question 6	a	a	c	c	b	b	a	a	b	c	b	a	a	a
Question 7	b	c	c	a	b	c	c	b	c	a	c	a	b	b
Question 8	c	b	a	b	a	b	b	b	c	b	a	b	c	a
Question 9	c	c	c	a	c	c	a	a	b	b	a	c	c	a
Question 10	a	c	c	b	c	b	b	a	b	c	a	b	b	b
Question 11	b	b	a	b	a	c	a	b	c	b	b	c	a	a
Question 12	b	a	a	a	b	b	c	b	b	a	c	b	b	b
Question 13	c	c	c	b	a	c	c	c	b	b	b	a	b	c
Question 14	c	c	c	b	c	b	b	a	a	c	c	c	a	c
Question 15	b	b	b	b	b	c	c	b	b	b	a	b	b	b
Question 16	a	a	c	c	c	a	a	a	c	c	a	b	c	b
Question 17	b	b	a	b	b	b	b	c	b	b	c	c	b	c
Question 18	c	c	c	a	b	b	c	a	c	c	b	c	a	a

Printed in Great Britain
by Amazon